SERVICE WITH A SMILE

Jobs of Bygone Days

Ann Roberts

Published by the Author

Copyright © 2005 Ann Roberts

Published in 2005 by
Ann Roberts
Tŷ Clyd, Benson Street
Penclawdd, Swansea SA4 3XY
Telephone: (01792) 850501

The right of Ann Roberts to be identified as the Author of the Work
has been asserted by her in accordance with the Copyright,
Designs and Patents Act 1988.

*All rights reserved. No part of this publication may be reproduced, stored
in a retrieval system or transmitted, in any form or by any means
without the prior permission of the publisher, nor be otherwise
circulated in any form of binding or cover other than that in which
it is published and without similar condition being
imposed on the subsequent purchaser.*

A CIP catalogue record for this book is
available from the British Library.

ISBN 0-9540836-1-X
9 780954 083618

Printed and bound in Wales by
Dinefwr Press Ltd.
Rawlings Road, Llandybie
Carmarthenshire, SA18 3YD

For
Geoffrey

Acknowledgements

I wish to thank Freda Arnould, Ann Beck, Gwen Beynon, Mair Bowen, Josephine Budge, Lucinda Methuen-Campbell, the late Gwyneth Crowley, Alice Draper, Betty Doherty, the late Gwyneth Ellis, Bessie Evans, Dora Evans, Dorothy Evans, Lovaine Fisher, Eileen Foote, Kathleen Guy, Olive Hackford, Margaret Harvey, Win Henry, May Hughes, Edna Jenkins, Kath Jones, Anne Karim, Joan Lewis, Miriam Lewis, Rosie Lloyd, Sonia Machell, Ann McDonnell, the late Phyllis Morgan, Joan Pye, Mary Richards, Ruby Skinner, Marian Slade, Tina Tomkins, Catherine Wort, Jenny Wren, Gillian Yates, Rose Young, George Bean, Alan Brown, the late Gilbert Davies, Gwilym Davies, Frank Firth, Ivor Lloyd, the late John Morgan, Fred Neal, Vincent Rees, Ray Stock, Ron Tooney and Jim Treharne for their stories and my friends for their contacts. It was with great sadness that I heard of the passing away of friends who gave me their stories.

I am indebted to Alan Jones and Ray Stock for their invaluable old postcards.

I especially thank Anne Karim for her proof-reading and Emyr Nicholas, Eddie John and the staff of Dinefwr Press for their co-operation and work in producing this book.

Mostly, I thank my husband, Geoffrey, for his help, patience and encouragement in my work.

Contents

Introduction 9

1. Life at Penrice Castle 11
2. Maids and Mistresses 36
3. Going to the Flicks 78
4. Working at Bens 124
5. All with Good Grace 171
6. Determined to Volunteer 212

Bibliography 263

Introduction

While researching *Service with a Smile* over the past three years, I have thoroughly enjoyed the company of many as I listened, with fascination, to their stories. All were so kind in giving me their time and co-operation.

The characters' written words are their own, which I have endeavoured to place in historical context.

All mentioned monies are pre-decimalization, and measurements, imperial.

That Golden Time

When will it come, that golden time,
When every man is free?
Men who have power to choose their tasks
Have all their liberty.

They'll sweat and toil who love to feel
Their muscles swell and move;
While men whose minds are more to them,
Create the dreams we love.

When will it come, that golden time,
When every heart must sing?
The power to choose the work we love
Makes every man a king.

W. H. Davies

1.

Life at Penrice Castle

Penrice Castle is situated in Oxwich, in South Gower. A beautiful Georgian mansion with stunning views over the bay and Bristol Channel, it is the only Gower country estate to have been retained as a private dwelling. Thomas Mansel Talbot inherited the Penrice and Margam estates in 1758, when ten years old, through his grandmother, Mary, daughter of the 1st Lord Mansel of Margam. Later, having spent many years travelling the Continent, mainly in Italy, he had by 1772 returned to Britain and in 1774 started building the present Penrice Castle. In 1794, he married Lady Mary Lucy Fox Strangways, second daughter of the 2nd Earl of Ilchester, who bore him eight children: Mary Theresa, Jane Harriot, Christiana Barbara, Charlotte Louisa, Ellinor Sybella, Christopher Rice Mansel, Isabella Catherine and Emma Thomasina. Penrice Castle was not large by country house standards – just adequate for the family and staff. A walled kitchen garden was built in the grounds. All Thomas Mansel's children were interested in gardening and each had their own patch to tend. Their mother encouraged them to use their hands and to love botany and horticulture.

The estates were inherited by Thomas Mansel's only son, Christopher Rice Mansel. During the early 1830s, at a cost in excess of fifty thousand pounds, Christopher built Margam Castle in the Tudor/Gothic style – a great contrast to the elegant Georgian mansion at Penrice. He married Lady Charlotte Jane Butler in 1835 and the couple had four children – Theodore, Emily Charlotte, Olivia, and Isabella. His only son died before him and so, on his death in 1890, his eldest daughter, Emily, inherited the Penrice and Margam estates and consequently became extremely wealthy, worth an estimated thirteen million pounds.

In the 1890s, Emily completely rebuilt the central portion of Penrice Castle mainly to provide additional accommodation for visitors and servants. A deeply religious woman, she closed most of the Gower pubs. She was a very forceful character: she was six feet tall; always dressed entirely in black; and smoked a pipe. She never married. Having no issue, on her death in 1918 she left Penrice to her favourite niece, Evelyn, third daughter of her sister Isabella, and John Fletcher of Salthoun Hall, East Lothian, Scotland, who inherited it in 1920. Penrice and Margam estates were separated for the first time since the mid-sixteenth

Penrice Castle with added Victorian Wing, 1915.

Entrance Hall, Penrice Castle.

The young Evelyn.

The young Olive.

Fishing party. Olive on left, Lady Blythswood 3rd from left.

ENGAGED TO THE HON. LAURENCE METHUEN (INSET): THE HON. OLIVE CAMPBELL.

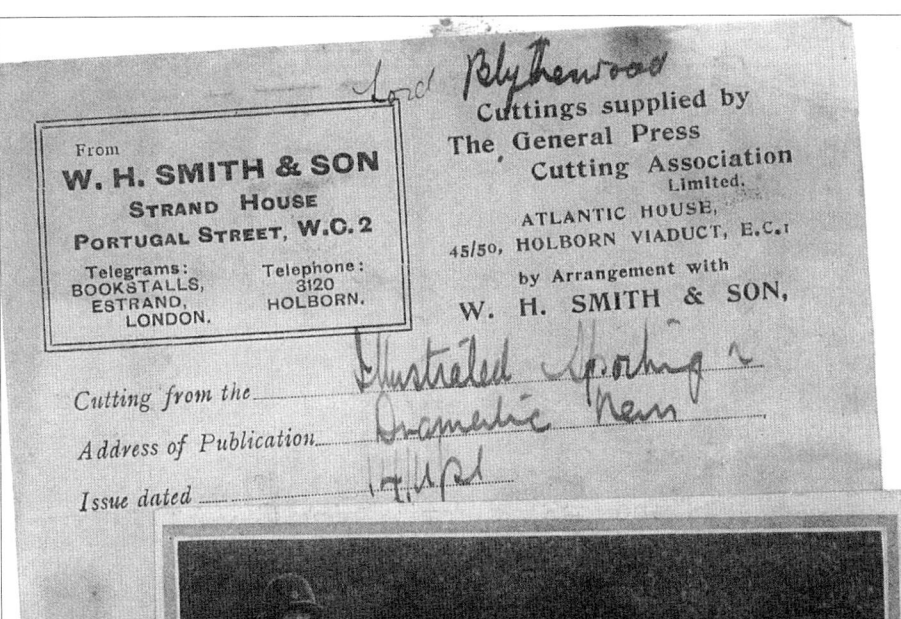

A SOCIETY ENGAGEMENT: THE HON. LAURENCE METHUEN AND THE HON. OLIVE CAMPBELL AT BLYTHSWOOD HOUSE.

An engagement is announced between the Hon. Laurence Methuen, the youngest son of Field-Marshal Lord Methuen, G.C.B., G.C.M.G., G.C.V.O., and Lady Methuen, and the Hon. Olive Campbell, the only daughter of Lord and Lady Blythswood. The engaged couple are here seen at Blythswood House, Renfrew, the residence of the bride's father.

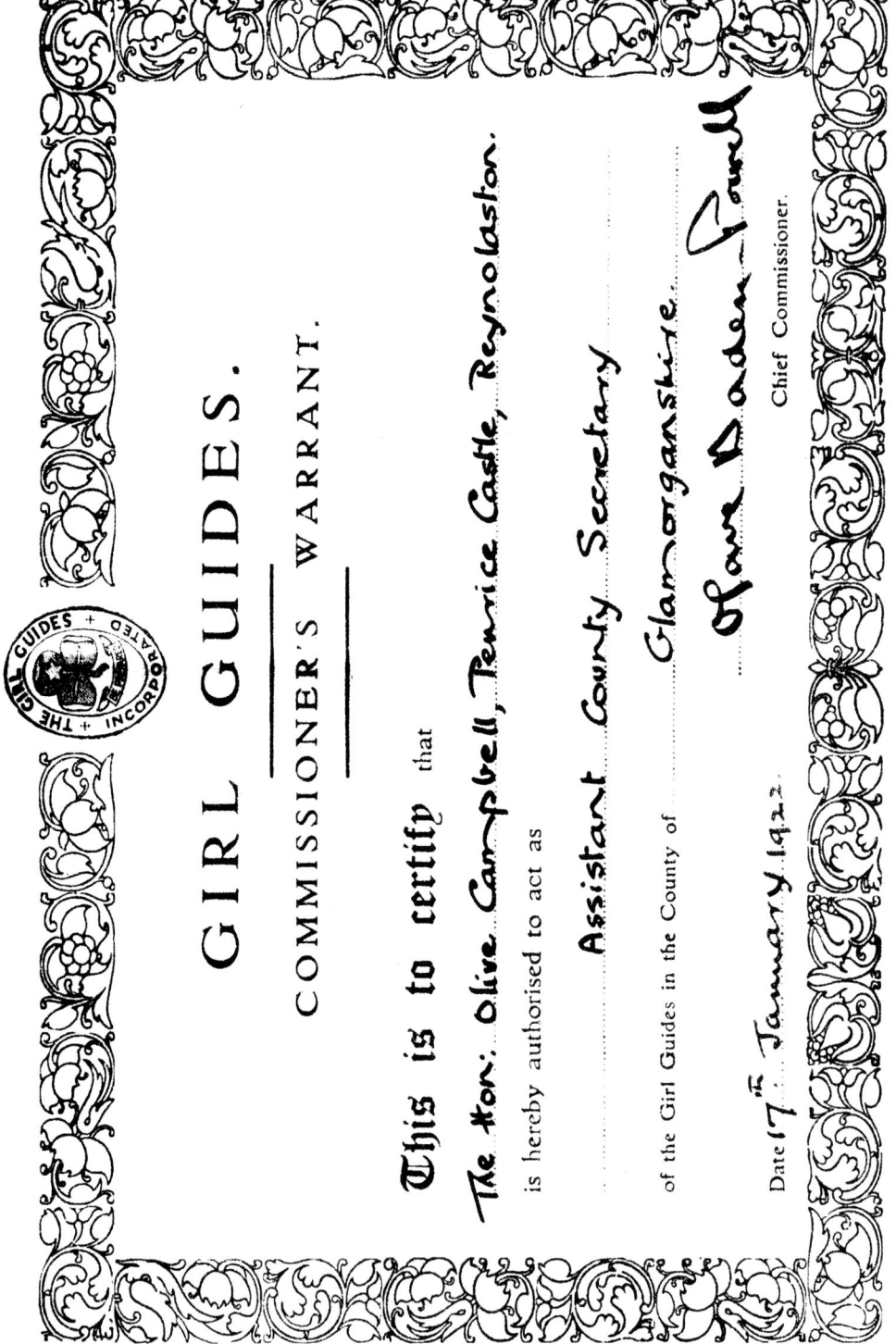

Lady Blythswood, 5 November 1927.

Lady Blythswood, centre, 5 November 1927.

Lady Blythswood.

55, Montagu Square, W.

Penrice

~~Blythswood.~~

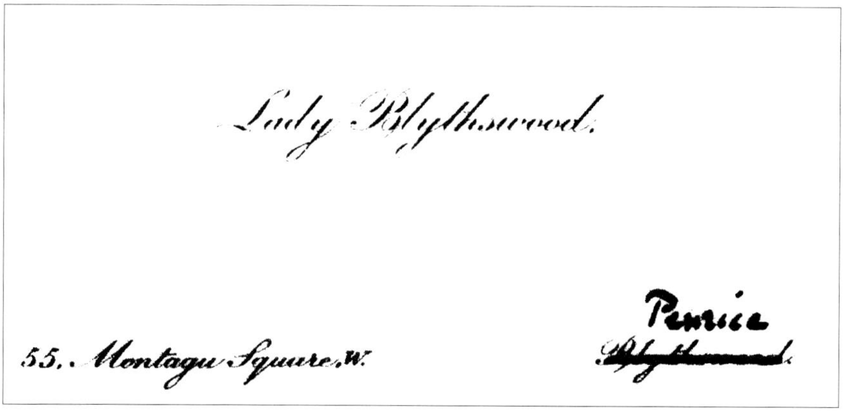

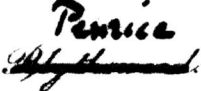

Lady Blythswood's calling card.

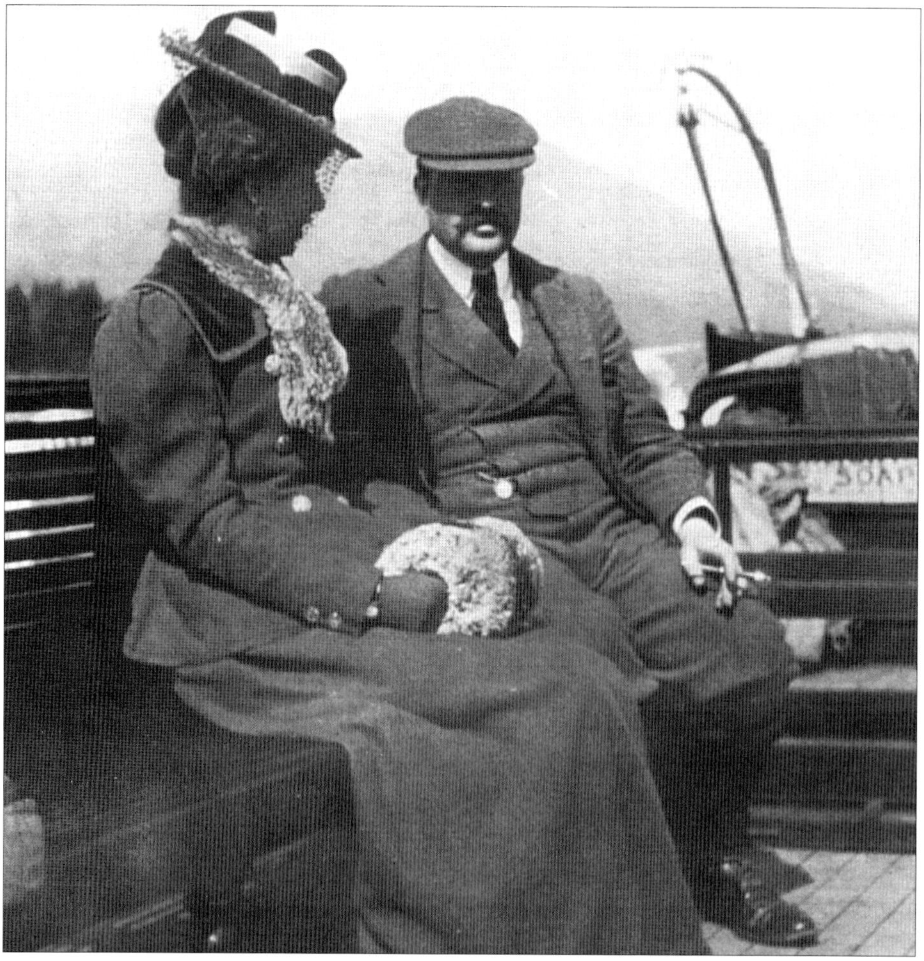

Lord Blythswood.

century, the latter going to Evelyn's brother, Captain Andrew Mansel Talbot Fletcher.

In 1895, Evelyn had married Archibald Douglas-Campbell, 4th Baron Blythswood, owner of estates in Scotland. Lord and Lady Blythswood shared their time between Penrice and Scotland. In February 1927, their only child Olive married Laurence Paul Methuen-Campbell, youngest son of Field Marshal Lord Methuen of Corsham Court, Wiltshire. The couple were to have four children, Christopher Paul Mansel, David Archibald James, Diana Evelyn Kitty (Wendy) and Daphne Mary Jean. Lord Blythswood died suddenly at his home, Blythswood House, Renfrewshire, Scotland on 14 November 1929 at the age of fifty-nine years. After his passing, Lady Blythswood made Penrice Castle her primary residence.

Bessie Evans – Housemaid

In the mid-1930s, Bessie Evans, née Andrews, was employed at Penrice Castle as a housemaid.

"I can't remember how Lady Blythswood got to know of me, but, after I had come home from working in London,[1] she came to our house to ask if I would work for her at Penrice Castle. A date was arranged and she came to pick me up in her little car – a two-seater with a little dicky seat.[2] My mother and I met her by Blackpill Post Office. She took my case, put it on the dicky seat and strapped it in. She let me get in the car with her and put a rug over my legs. It must have been winter I suppose.

The Castle was a lovely old place but much larger that it is now: they've taken a lot of it down. We were a biggish staff and had a wing of our own. Among the staff were two boys starting on their career as butler/footman/chauffeur, a few housemaids like myself, quite a few gardeners, and of course, the kitchen staff. I shared a bedroom with another girl. The food was good, which we ate in the servants' hall.

There were no electric lights, only lamps. I got up early, lit the paraffin lamp and carried it around with me as I did my housework. I swept the floors with big heavy brushes: there weren't any hoovers then. I cleaned the bedrooms, stairs, hallway, the downstairs rooms and the bathroom. I lit the fires and the brass bars of the grate had to be polished everyday with chains. It was really hard work but you didn't notice it in those days because that was how it was. A nice old man used to saw the logs and chop the sticks, and bring them in early in the morning with the coal. The family had dinner every evening and I used to give a hand in the kitchen and wash up. I finished work about seven o'clock.

---

1. See Chapter 2, pp. 71-74.
2. A folding outside seat at the rear of some early cars.

All housemaids seemed to dress the same then: blue frock in the morning and a black one with a pretty white apron after lunch. I earned the same salary in all my employment: ten shillings a week; two pounds a month.

A girl I befriended – her surname was Evans – who worked in the kitchen, lived with her sister and parents in the round building – like a lodge – at the big gates of the Castle, at the top of the hill leading down to Oxwich Bay. The building (The Towers) looks like a ruin, now, and even looked like a ruin then.[3]

I had one afternoon a week off and every other Sunday. I always had to be back at the Castle by ten o'clock. It wasn't much time to go home to Blackpill, especially as there weren't many buses then, but I did have a few hours off every afternoon when I used to go to Oxwich Bay and paddle, in the summer. I loved going to the little church by the beach at Oxwich when I had a Sunday off.

The Methuen-Campbells – Lady Blythswood's daughter, and family – stayed with her sometimes. Christopher was about five or six, and then there were David, Diana (Wendy), and Jean. The nursery had beautiful views over Oxwich Bay. The family owned houses in Scotland where they also lived, but I never went to them. Lady Blythswood was a very nice person. She was tiny but her husband was a big man. He had passed away by the time I worked there, but I saw pictures of him. I don't remember a lot of entertaining at the Castle, but they did used to go pheasant shooting in the winter.

I only worked there for a short time, but I loved it."

Lady Blythswood had given over the estate to her only child, Olive, to avoid death duties, and to make sure of continuity. However, Olive's death preceded her mother's and so the object was defeated, incurring double death duties on Lady Blythswood's death in 1958. Having inherited the Penrice estate from his mother, a short time before his coming of age at twenty-one years, and Penrice Castle on the death of his grandmother, Christopher was left to cope with the huge financial problem. At the time, he was farming and living in Broncroft Castle in Shropshire. When, it seems, he was asked what was to be the fate of the Castles, he was reported to have replied, 'I have no intention of selling either of them. But they are not nearly so grand as they sound – Penrice is a Georgian house below a ruined castle, and Broncroft is a farmhouse built on the remains of an old castle.'[4] He later moved to Penrice, with his wife, Oona, and children Joanna, James, and Lucinda. Their third daughter, Catherine, was born a few years later.

---

3. When Thomas Mansel Talbot built Penrice Castle, by way of a gatehouse he erected the sham ruin or folly now generally called The Towers.
4. *The Sunday Express*, London, 14 September 1958.

Penrice Castle staff with children. Christopher Methuen-Campbell standing on left.

Christopher and Oona Methuen-Campbell.

George Brown – Butler

George Brown, a native of Suffolk, was Lady Blythswood's butler. On 30 April 1934, he married Irene Callaghan, of Irish extraction, who was living in Oxwich where her father was a coastguard. They were given a Westminster Chiming Clock as a wedding present from Lady Blythswood's staff. The couple set up home in Marsh View, a tithe cottage on the estate in Penrice village. A year later their daughter, Marjory, was born and Alan, twelve years later.

Alan relates his family's story. "I vaguely remember Lady Blythswood. She used to drive to St Andrew's Church, Penrice in her car, but she was so short that you could barely see her – just a car coming up the hill with hands on the top of the steering wheel, and the top of a hat.

During the war, my father was in the RAF, and when he was demobbed, he returned to his job as butler. He asked Lady Blythswood for a pay rise; he was reluctant to do so as it was unheard of, but she doubled his salary! My father liked his job. He wore a suit and waistcoat. At first he was a butler in the true sense of the word: he waited table and was in charge of staff – footmen, etc. There were dozens and dozens of staff then. In time, they dwindled and my father undertook more and more jobs such as answering the door and tending the fires.

After Lady Blythswood's time, her grandson, Christopher Methuen-Campbell and his family came to live at the Castle. Some said the family was snobby but that was not true; David, Christopher's brother was very chatty, and Christopher less, but they were all very friendly and as good as gold. David had a little 50cc motor bike. I can remember someone relating how they watched him weaving to get up Stembridge Hill: the bike had such a small engine and the hill is very steep. I used to play with the children now and then; Joanna and James were more my age and Lucinda was some years younger. We'd play in the grounds and sometimes wander around the Castle. The winters of 1962 and '63 were very cold with lots of snow. Mr. Campbell drove Joanna, James, Lucinda and me in his Mark 10 Jaguar to Broad Pool, at the foot of Cefn Bryn, to play on the ice. The pool was quite safe, as it is only two feet deep – unless you fell through it head first.

I used to walk to school – Oxwich Junior School – and later went to Dumbarton Private School in Uplands, Swansea, by bus. During my teens, on Saturdays and in the school holidays I used to help in the gardens of the estate and earned a bit of pocket money. When I was about sixteen, I had a pay rise of a few pennies.

The young George Brown.

George and Irene Brown's Wedding Day, 30 April 1934.

George Brown in RAF uniform.

Left to right: Irene Brown with sisters Winnie and Phyllis, father and daughter, Marjory.

My father went back and forth to his work by bike. In 1960, we were invited to live in a flat in the Castle – in the old servants' quarters in the Victorian part. It was very nice with a large sitting room, three bedrooms, kitchen and bathroom, overlooking the terrace and Oxwich Bay. Our bulldog and the Castle's Old English mastiffs didn't get on so we had a bolted door to the flat so our dog couldn't get out on his own. It was so much easier for my father living there, and my mother was offered the job of cook at the Castle – for six guineas a week. They had a half-day on Thursday, and after serving breakfast, went out for the day – usually to Swansea.

Amy at the rear of Penrice Castle – Winter 1962/63.

Mr. Campbell had brought Amy and her two pups – part of a big litter – Chinxy who was male, and Measles a bitch, with him from Broncroft, in Shropshire. Amy was very nervous at first and used to sit under the table in the hall; she could only just fit under it, nearly lifting it. I often used to take Measles out for a walk; when she was fully-grown I went wherever she took me! She had an embarrassing name but apparently she had spots on her nose when a puppy. Chinxy went to live in a cottage in Norton, in Oxwich Green. He liked sitting in front of the fire and completely hid it so nobody in the room could either see it or feel it.

Many of the staff lived in tithe cottages on the estate. Edgar and Irene Pierce lived in Underhill Cottage. Christopher brought Frank and Ann

Bennett, and their four children – they had another one later – down from Broncroft. They lived in Marsh View after we left. He was the odd-job man, and undertook any maintenance work on the estate. They were both very nice people. Laundry Cottage was originally the old laundry house, and later converted into a habitable bungalow, but with no electricity. Gibb, the chauffeur, and his wife lived there, and when he retired, Ray Davies the gardener occupied it and electricity was installed. Ray left, and when the Victorian wing was demolished, we moved to Laundry Cottage in about 1967. Mr Kerr who came from Cumbria, was also a gardener, and lived in the bottom house by the marsh – Garden House. He used to say, 'I don't care if you call me Ker or Kar.'

My mother died in 1968, and my father in 1973 when he was in semi-retirement – working in the mornings only. I was not pressurized into leaving the cottage, but did so in my own time – about two years. I would have liked to buy the cottage, but that was not possible."

Betty Doherty

Betty Doherty, née Roberts, a native of Horton, joined the staff of the Penrice estate in 1945.

"I left Gregg's Commercial School, (The Gregg School Secretarial Training College with Secondary Education Department) in Swansea, at the age of fifteen. One of the girls from the school had started working at Penrice, but her mother fell and broke her leg, so she had to stay home to look after her. As I was local, I was lucky enough to replace her as secretary; it was a case of being in the right place at the right time. I was to work there for forty-two years – the only job I ever had.

When I started in January 1945, there was a large staff. They consisted of:

>The agent – Arthur Anthony
>The clerk
>The clerk of works
>Myself
>
>*Masons*
>Harry Bevan
>Cyril Grove
>Alf Daniels
>Leonard Bidder

Carpenters
Jim Evans
D. J. Jenkins

Men in charge of the woods
The foreman – Parry Jenkins
Edgar Johnson
Stanley Grove
Melbourne Jenkins
Levi Grove

Game keepers
Thomas Woodward
Bert Jones

Beaters
Ron Gibson
Edgar Pierce
David Jones – son of Bert Jones.

Gardeners
Arthur Clement
Alf Knudsen
Leonard Grove

Office cleaners

Groundsmen
Arthur Clark
Andrew Clement – also looked after the children's ponies.

In the house
The butler – George Brown.
The chauffeur – Gibbs.
The cook – Kate Gibbs – then Irene Brown and later Irene Pierce, née Evans.
A maid – Iris Grove
Two odd-job men

Cleaners
M. Jones
M. Kent

There were quite a few romances amongst the staff. Kate, the cook married Gibbs the chauffeur and one of the maids, Iris, married the mason, Cyril Grove. Some travelled with the family between their estates in Gower and Scotland. Edgar Pierce was originally Lady Blythswood's butler in Scotland. While at Penrice, he met Irene Evans who worked in the kitchen, and lived in The Towers. They married and Edgar settled in Gower, being employed as a gamekeeper, and later, in the 1960s, Irene became cook.

At first, I used to cycle from home, but when the evenings darkened, it was rather a long, lonely run on my own, so I caught the bus. Some of the men from Horton worked in the woods, but if they were working near Horton, they would have gone home before me.

Lady Blythswood was in residence then. She used to drive a Riley car. She was so short she couldn't see over the steering wheel, but she used to go like a dart; she was a villain in the Gower lanes. Her daughter, Olive, and family lived in Scotland. Edgar Pierce used to bring me game, shot on the estate, to send to the family. They spent time at the Castle but I did not see much of her as she suffered from poor health, and died on 8th March 1949.

I enjoyed working there very much. A Victorian wing – the Italian wing we used to call it – had been added to the Castle in the 1890s. I used to go through the back door, walk upstairs, and down a corridor with rooms on either side. One of these was the office where I worked. Mr. Methuen-Campbell took over Home Farm and the estate office was relocated there. It also had living quarters – a kitchen, a bathroom, two bedrooms and a nice big lounge. When I married in 1951, my husband and I lived with my in-laws in Reynoldston. Alterations were carried out to the estate office and when completed, we moved there. The building had very high ceilings, but it was very cosy, as every Christmas we were given a load of wood for our open log fires and Rayburn stove in the kitchen; there was plenty of wood on the estate. In 1956, when my son was born, a room was added onto the building for him. He was to live there until he was thirty-one.

The building had a strongroom in the middle with big bars – not where I would have liked to have been shut in! All the estate documents – the copies of the tenancies, the ledgers, etc. – were kept there. There were shelves all around the room piled high with them. We had a break-in at one time but they failed to get into the strongroom. The thieves were caught near London, but had only pinched stamps and petty cash from the outer room. I worked office hours – nine to five – with an hour for lunch when I often used to visit the old lady who cleaned – she lived in a cottage nearby. I had an annual fortnight's holiday and other days off during the year.

At first, the agent, Mr. Anthony, did all the accounts, and I assisted him. He worked in one room, and I worked in the outer office. A native of Llanelli, he had come to the estate in 1900 after being agent to the Benson estate in Penclawdd. He was a pioneer of the Gower Show, which was held on the estate. He was one of the founders of the Gower Agricultural Society and its honorary secretary for forty-five years. He and his wife lived in Hayes Cottage in Reynoldston. After his death in 1951, Mrs. Anthony continued living there until March 1967, when it was bought by Gwen Beynon – by then widowed. Gwen had been house parlour-maid in Oxwich Rectory and Fairy Hill.[5] On Mr. Anthony's death, an agent of the London firm John D. Wood Co. London came down, and I helped him. He returned to London and I carried on.

I used to go down to the Castle once a week and sort out Mr. Methuen-Campbell's accounts – pay his bills for him, etc. He used to dictate to me and I took it down in shorthand and typed it out. I was also involved in organizing the Gower Show.

I remember Mr. Methuen-Campbell's first wife living there. She was a lovely woman, she really was; she was a tiny, sweet little lady. I got to know the family well and the children were always around and about.

I saw Princess Anne and Pat Smythe when they came to the Gower Show and many of the show-jumping personalities. I knew Mr. Patrick McNair Wilson the Conservative MP, married to Wendy (Diana), sister of Mr. Methuen-Campbell.

We were often invited to parties at the Castle, particularly after Mr. Methuen-Campbell's second marriage. We – the staff – had excellent nights on 5th November when they organized fireworks and Irene Brown used to do the cooking – she made lovely flapjacks. A family from Shropshire, called the Bennetts, who had four children, used to come to the Guy Fawkes' nights. Later, after Mr. Methuen-Campbell passed away, we were taken out for meals about a fortnight before Christmas. We went to several venues, one being Swn-y-Môr, in Penclawdd.

As the staff died, they were not replaced. I finished working there in 1987 and we moved, with my son and family, to a small-holding in Llanrhidian."

Christopher and Oona Methuen-Campbell's daughter, Lucinda, relates her happy memories of living at Penrice.

---

5. See Gwen's story – Chapter 2.

"My family has lived at Penrice since the Norman Conquest. It is called a castle but is really an eighteenth century house built in the grounds of a Norman castle, the ruins of which stand on a hill overlooking the house as if regarding it with the protective eyes of a great-great-grandmother.

My father and his siblings must have had a magical childhood in Scotland: rowing to the island Innischonain, in Loch Awe, which was part of the estate in Argyllshire in Scotland. The family, with their staff from Penrice, spent about six months of the year there. When my grandmother, Olive, died in 1949, my father inherited the estate. His father, however, had sold the island, much to the sorrow of his children.

My mother, when engaged to my father, spent a lot of time at Penrice. They were young, and married when she was twenty, and he, twenty-one. My sister, Joanna, was born a year after my parents married and my brother, James, a year later. There was a six-year gap before I was born.

When my great-grandmother, Lady Blythswood, died in 1958, she was eighty-eight. I was born six months later. At the time, we were living in Shropshire, and although visited Penrice, we were not to move there until I was two and a half years old. Lady Blythswood left the property in a complete state of disrepair: there were mice living in the furniture and mice's nests amongst her clothes in the drawers. She was quite eccentric: she used to put saucers of milk on top of her four-poster bed for the bats; if any of the family left a garment – cardigan, etc. – while visiting her, on their next visit, she would be wearing it – with no comment.

As a child, one does not appreciate one's privileges, but just takes them for granted. I realize now that mine was an idyllic, if unconventional childhood in a house with half of its rooms out of action. A lot of the Castle hadn't been used for years: there were flats that had belonged to cooks, no longer needed and so shut up. It was really weird wandering around there: I used to peep under the dustsheets and find their belongings – glass cases of frightened stuffed animals or other peculiar items from a bygone era. It was almost like living in a dream world.

During the Second World War, the Victorian wing was used as a hospital for American soldiers. As a child, I can remember being intrigued by the carvings and names on the trees in the grounds. I didn't realize until I was older that they had been carved and inscribed by the soldiers – some carvings are still there.

Lucinda Methuen-Campbell.

The house is hung with ancestral portraits with whom, as a child I used to have intimate conversations while their eyes regarded me long and hard as I skipped around the huge rooms and twisted to the Beatles on my sister's Dancette record player.

In the grounds there were walled gardens and long greenhouses of grapes and the most wonderful peaches. Most days we'd all troop to the garden, accompanied by the dogs, carrying plaited-palm baskets to pick fruit – strawberries, etc. – and vegetables. I spent most of my time gardening with my father – his great love, which I have inherited, walking with my mother, riding with my sister, and playing ping-pong with my brother. We swam in the muddy fish pond, rode our donkeys in the park, and cycled down to the sea. We watched a little television, but mostly played in the extensive grounds. The Norman castle is dangerous now, but we used to clamber all over it, playing in the battlements. There was an old dump. My brother used to pretend to be an archaeologist and we spent hours digging in it, finding bits of china, etc. There was living history all around us; it was quite unique. We were quite isolated and seldom went elsewhere.

I can remember going to the food hall in David Evans in Swansea, with my mother; it was the only posh food store then. However, most

The old Norman castle.

things were ordered over the telephone: bread, milk and meat, from Lyndon Lee, the butcher in Reynoldston, and groceries from Shepherds in Parkmill, were delivered to the Castle. We went to Shepherds every day, and when I was older I'd buy bottles of wine there and say, 'Put it on the Castle's account.'

My father would occasionally look at the bill and be furious saying, 'Oh my God! What's all this?'

I had a nanny and lived in the nursery, which was completely separate from the main part of the house. I only saw my parents after meals and this was in the 1960s! There was an old nanny there as well, known as Nanna; she had been my father's nanny, never married, and had carried on living with the family – so there were two nannies. Nanna loved watching wrestling on television on Saturday afternoons, so we'd have to draw the curtains to darken the room. There were still a lot of mice around so every now and then she'd try and hit them with her walking stick.

By then, the early 1960s, the house had been modernized – made liveable in? However, later, in 1967, the Castle was made more manageable by the deteriorating Victorian extension being demolished, reverting the building to its original size – as it still stands today. In a sense, it is in layers: on the bottom, the cellars – a cooling room, laundry room, boiler room and safe; on the ground floor – the drawing room, sitting room, and dining room; on the first floor – the adults' bedrooms; on the top floor – the servants' quarters, now the attic. I used to imagine all the servants – the housemaids, etc. – living there. It must have been freezing cold, but quite small and cosy, and so I feel that they must have had a lot of fun up there together.

The members of staff that my parents inherited were quite old; well they seemed old to me – but probably not all that old. There were two housemaids, a butler, a cook and a chauffeur. I was driven to Oakleigh House School, in Swansea, by this eighty-year-old chauffeur in a car that had to be started with a starting handle; it was like the last episodes of the television series, *Upstairs Downstairs*. Quite a few people worked on the estate as well as the house staff: men looked after the car parks at Horton and Oxwich beaches; and there were quite a few gardeners – one was a woman.

When my parents went away, I stayed with various people on the estate. I used to stay with Mrs. Evans who lived in The Towers – by the gates – with her husband, who had been a gamekeeper, and two daughters, Irene and Joan. Their home was just a one up and one down round stone building, with few amenities in those days. Mrs. Evans came from Suffolk. I remember her telling me that her home there was very rural – they put straw on the floor and brushed it out every day – so compared with that, she didn't find The Towers too spartan. I can remember going to the loo – in the other tower – which was just a bucket and a wooden seat. Mrs. Evans had a little garden in Perriswood where she grew vegetables; she was a keen gardener. Her daughter, Irene, was married to Edgar, then the footman. She became our cook in the 1960s and also worked for our family in our estate in Scotland. Irene told me that her mother used to collect all the water that came down the drainpipes to wash their hair: she thought it pure water. They had no hot water and flush loo until the early 1970s when my father built them a bathroom in a building attached to the original. The Towers used to be covered in ivy and within five years of it being removed, the building started to leak like a sieve and became unliveable, so Mrs. Evans had to move. The staff were like part of my family: it was an us and them situation in so much as they were employed by my parents, but as a child, I could go in-between the two.

The butler, Mr. Brown, and his wife lived in Laundry Cottage – a little cottage within the estate. They had a son, Alan, who grew up on the estate, and before living in the cottage had lived in a flat in the Castle. I stayed with them quite often.

The Browns had a huge black bird; I think Alan must have found it as a fledgling and reared it. It used to try and land on my head; I suppose it was trying to be friendly, but it frightened me, and for years I had nightmares about it. My father used to breed budgies, and had parrots and a cockatoo; he always had birds in cages. At first, the cockatoo lived in the house, continually shouting obscenities. He used to imitate me calling, 'Mummy, Mummy' and everyone used to tell me to shut up not realizing it was the bird. He became such a nuisance that he was put in an outhouse. He was so strong that he used to rip his cage and get out. He would sit on a windowsill trying to rip at the window frame to get in at us: he was sexually imprinted and loved males but hated females – loved my father but hated my mother. He hovered around the house and we couldn't go out for fear of being attacked. My father used to send my mother outside with an umbrella and as the cockatoo flew down at her, she put up the umbrella and the bird would slide down it to the ground, to be caught by my father.

We were in an unique situation, as, by then, Penrice was the only inhabited country estate in Gower. In a way, my parents put pressure on me to meet, and perhaps marry, the same kind of people – of similar social standing – but there weren't any. All my friends were local children who went to school locally. I wanted to do the same but, unfortunately, I was packed off to boarding school at the age of ten. This is why I choose to live here in Gower and near my friends: it gives me a sense of normality.

My childhood came to an abrupt end, however, when I was fourteen: my mother announced in a matter of fact way that she was leaving. I was given the option of going with her to Suffolk or staying on at the Castle; I opted for the latter: I loved Gower so much. During the next four years the upheavals affected me dreadfully. With my mother and younger sister gone, and my older siblings only visiting intermittently, the house became a quiet and lonely place. I had chosen to stay with my father to whom I had always been close, and during this period we became closer.

I felt hugely betrayed when he suddenly married, telling us two weeks before what he intended to do. My new stepmother was the woman I blamed for my mother's departure, and she and her three children took over as my new family, moving into my own brother and sisters' bedrooms and trampling all over my life, which I then realized would never be the same. I was not happy.

Every year on the first Thursday of August, part of the estate was given over to the Gower Show – an agricultural show of the traditional kind; I loved it. Half the goldfish in our pond had been won on the coconut shy and darts, and grotty painted plaster cast trophies littered my bedroom. My father as president, presided over the occasion adorned with a large badge made of cardboard and ribbon. He found it stressful but enjoyable. Every one drank masses of sherry and beer, and a lunch was held for the Show's elite in one of the large white tents. My mother, grandmother, and great-grandmother before her, had, over the years, presented a cup to the best bull or turnip, etc. in the Show wearing a new hat bought for the occasion. It was the summer of 1978 and I was nineteen. This year it would be my stepmother's turn to show off her new-found status.

I am not sure if it was a conscious design of mine to try and steal the limelight, but a vague idea seemed to form in my mind during the days leading up to the event. At the side of the main show-jumping ring we had a family caravan stocked with booze and food. Every one was busy during lunchtime and nobody noticed as I sat there and got solemnly and extremely drunk. In the afternoon, the main show-jumping events were watched by thousands as every one gathered around the ring. In-between these events in the privacy of the caravan, I totteringly removed all my clothes and stepped out, unannounced by the Tannoy. I felt a huge surge of exhilaration and freedom as I ran around the ring stark naked waving to the crowd who cheered, shouted, and waved back. I'm not sure how long I was out there, as time seemed telescoped, but it was long enough for every one to see me, and even take photographs. My father and stepmother were furious – especially when they saw the front page of the local paper the next day, which had the headline, 'Female Streaker Best in Show'. I later found out that there had been a major local disaster on that day, and luckily for me, they had not had the room to print my photograph!

The double death duties of Lady Blythswood, and her daughter Olive, destroyed the wealth of Penrice estate. Many farm estates – occupied by tenant farmers – were sold. My father always used to say, 'I have no money.' I didn't know how true it was, but as children, we had few things and my father was always selling possessions from the Castle. He passed away on 8th January 1998."

2.

Maids and Mistresses

By 1900, except for agriculture, domestic service was the country's largest employer with a workforce of nearly a million and a half. In the depressed years of the 1920/30s, many parents were not in a financial position to allow their children to further their education beyond the permitted school-leaving age of fourteen. School fees, books, uniform, transport, etc. were expensive; moreover, children's working wage was needed – small though it was – to supplement the family income. Domestic service was hard and the hours long, but food and lodgings were provided free of charge. It was often a relief for parents to have their children *off their hands*; and many children were pleased to be, to a certain extent, financially independent, and no longer a burden to their parents.

In no other situation were the classes – employer and employee – in more intimate and daily contact: in a sense, they were at each other's mercy.

> 'It is said that good masters and mistresses make good servants and this to a great extent is true. There are certainly some men and women whom it would be impossible to train into good servants, but the conduct of both master and mistress is seldom without its effect upon these dependents. The sensible master and the kind mistress know, that if servants depend on them for their means of living, in their turn, they are dependent on their servants for very many of the comforts of life; and that, using a proper amount of care in choosing servants, treating them like reasonable beings, and making slight excuses for the shortcomings of human nature, they will be tolerably well served, and surround themselves with attached domestics. Women servants are especially likely to be influenced by their mistresses' treatment of them.'[1]

---

1. Isabella Beeton. *Mrs. Beeton's Book of Household Management* (London and Melbourne), p. 1761.

Gwen Beynon – House Parlour-Maid

Mary Lloyd, a native of Hereford, came to work as housekeeper to the rector in Llanddewi rectory. It was through her that her cousin, Edith Lloyd, also from Hereford, came to work as a maid in Reynoldston rectory. Some time later, Edith was employed by Elsie, Emma and Maud Simmons, of Robins Rest, Horton. She met George Tucker, tenant farmer of Waterside Farm, Horton, and married him from the Misses Simmons.

Their oldest child, Gwen was born on 20 November 1912. Waterside Farm was part of the thirty thousand acre Penrice estate, then owned by Miss Emily Talbot. Gwen, however, was too young to remember her, but she does remember Hopkin Ll. Pritchard, the estate agent. "Mr. Pritchard used to ride to our farm on a beautiful white pony to collect the rent. I knew him by sight but he never spoke to me, mind. I knew Mr. Arthur Anthony – clerk of works – through the Gower Show. My father was on the committee just after it started. Books were issued to collect money for the event. Father had one, and I did the collecting – from the residents and visitors – for years around Horton. Mr. Anthony was always so pleased that I had collected so much money.

Mr. and Mrs. Evans, who lived in The Towers, were in charge of opening and closing the estate gates; in a sense, their house was a lodge. When the family was away in Scotland – and they went away a lot – the gates were left open and our family and all the tenants were allowed to drive through the park as opposed to up the steep hill. Of course it was pony and trap then – no cars."

On 12 August 1924, a *Pageant of Historical and Traditional Gower Episodes* was enacted in the grounds of Penrice estate in aid of the West Glamorgan Nurses' Association, Lady Blythswood being its president. Its author and director was Colonel Ernest Helme, owner of Hill End, a secluded house with beautiful views over Worms Head to the west of Llangennith Bay, and Burry Holmes to its east. He had inherited the house from his father – a city bank director – who, in the mid-nineteenth century, had discovered North Gower through a love of shooting game. Colonel Helme was much loved and respected in Llangennith. He said of the villagers, 'They treat you exactly as if you were royalty.'[2] His sister, Dorothy Anson said of him, 'My brother used to do a lot of singing in the villages. He used to sing in the choir at Winchester when he had a very good soprano voice. But it was forced for too long, and it never reformed – so he started whistling his songs. He had a very keen ear, you see. All those soprano songs with a lot of coloratura in them, he

---

2. J. Mansel Thomas, *Yesterday's Gower* (Llandysul, Dyfed, 1982), p. 226.

The Towers, Penrice Castle.

Gwen and sister Mary.

GOWER PAGEANT
—AT—
PENRICE CASTLE, GOWER

(By kind permission of Lord and Lady Blythswood), on

Thursday, August 14th, 1924,

In aid of the Gower Nursing Association.

PATRONS—

HIS GRACE THE DUKE OF BEAUFORT (Baron of the Seignory of Gower).
HER GRACE THE DUCHESS OF BEAUFORT.
THE RT. HONOURABLE THE MARQUESS AND MARCHIONESS OF WORCESTER.
MAJOR THE RT. HONOURABLE THE LORD BLYTHSWOOD, K.C.V.O.
THE RT. HONOURABLE THE LADY BLYTHSWOOD.

Historical and Traditional Gower Episodes
WILL BE ENACTED.

1. **Reynoldston :** Bestowal of Gower by King Arthur on Rheged ap Urien at Arthur Stone. 6th Century.
2. **Penmaen and Nicholaston :** The taking of the Veil by Nest at the Court of her father Cadwen, King in Gower. 7th Century.
3. **Llangenydd :** Attack on St. Cenydd's Priory by the Danes under Sweyn. 9th Century.
4. **Pennard :** Return of Crusaders to Pennard Castle. 13th Century.
5. **Porteynon and Horton :** Bidding Wedding. 14th Century.
6. **Llanrhidian :** Flight of Lady Katherine Gordon into Gower. 15th Century.
7. **Ilston :** Arbitration at Llythrid in the presence of St. Cenydd's relics. 16th Century.
8. **Oxwich and Penrice :** The Ann Mansel Episode. 16th Century.
9. **Llanmadoc and Cheriton :** St. Madoc's Mapsant. 17th Century.
10. **Llanddewi and Knelston :** Escape of Edward Mansel. 18th Century.
11. **Rhossili :** Smuggling Episode. 18th Century.
12. **GRAND FINALE :** Rendering of the Seigneural Tribute to Her Grace The Duchess of Beaufort by the Mansels.

With the valuable co-operation of THE GWENT GLEE SINGERS,
Conductor—J. W. JONES.

General and Musical Director—Lt.-Col. E. HELME, D.S.O.

Marshall of Episodes—ASHTON BOSTOCK.

No. 5—Port Eynon and Horton.

COMMITTEE—
Chairman—Rev. F. ATTERBURY THOMAS.
Secretary—Miss M. DUNCAN.
Director and Treasurer—Miss M. E. MORGAN.
Costumiers—Miss M. E. MORGAN, Mrs. J. B. JONES, Mrs. GEORGE TAYLOR, Mrs. GEORGE JENKINS, Mrs. THOS. GORDON, Mrs. TOM HUNT, Mrs. PHILLIP HARRIS, Mrs. DAVID ROBERTS, Mrs. WILLIAM ACE, Miss N. ROBERTS, Mrs. JOHN ACE, Miss ELIZABETH ACE, Miss HARIETTE PHILLIPS, Miss MAY EYNON, Miss FLORENCE HUGHES.

CAST—
At the Well—Mrs. Mansel Bevan, Haydn W. Jones, Marcus Lord, Frank Bevan, J. Eldridge Gordon, Fred Nuttall and Mansel Bevan.
The Bidder—Rowland Morgan.
Bride's Father—Wm. Grove.
Bride's Mother—Mrs. Frank Phillips.
Book Man—W. Grove.
Waiting Maids—Mrs. Bevan, Mrs. Albert Taylor, Mrs. George Jenkins, Mrs. M. A. Lord, Miss Gwladys M. Morgan.
The Fiddler—Albert Taylor.
Bride—Miss Edith S. Phillips.
Bridegroom—Arthur Jenkins.
Best Man—Herbert Bevan.
Bridesmaids—Miss Nellie Roberts, Miss Haritte Phillips, Miss May Eynon, Miss Minnie Grove, Miss Irene Stevens, Miss Vera Rowlands.
Bride's Sisters—Miss Dorothy Jenkins, Miss Violet Grove.
Bride's Brother—Fred J. Taylor.
Holders of rope—George Taylor, Phillip Harris.
Guests—Mrs. William Howell, Harry Phillips, Mrs. Thos. W. Gordon, Mrs. Wm. Ace, Tom Taylor, Mrs. George Howell, Ernest Stevens, Miss Elizabeth Ace, Mrs. William Jones, George Jenkins, Miss Ruth Phillips, Mrs. G. Tucker,[3] Mrs. Wm. Clement, Mrs. Leonard Jones, Miss Adeline Grove, Mrs. Phillip Hopkins, William Howell, George Howell, William Jones and Philip Hopkins.
Children—Mina Chamberlain, May Grove, Albert Nuttall, Mary Tucker, Wyndham Taylor, Lucy Morgan, Gwen Tucker, Mary Grove, Avis Gordon, Joyce Taylor, Gladys Johnson and Gladys Morgan.
Priest—Thos. W. Gordon.
Banner Bearer—Trevor Jenkins.
Cross Bearer—Wilfred Howell.
Acolytes—Frank Lord, Edgar Johnson.

3. Should read Mr. G. Tucker.

A "BIDDING" WEDDING.

Glee "Oh, by Rivers" *Sir H. Bishop.*
Scene—Early Morning, Midsummer Day.   ::   A.D. 1375.

Half-a-dozen villagers and later a few children. Enter Tim Hughes the bidder, who proclaims the "Bidding" preliminary address. All exit and there is an imaginary interval, after which there is the return procession from the Church headed by the musician, followed by the bride and bridegroom and their friends of all ages two by two (to the number of 30 or more). The procession is momentarily held up by a rope across the way and the bride's mother receives the guests at the entrance, where there are two long tables with plates to collect the money.

All join together and dance "Lumbers," and dance off to a merry roundel.

The Bidding Rhyme to be said by the Bidder—

I'm a messenger to you and to the whole house in general,
To invite you to the wedding of Morgan Eynon and Nancy Hopkins,
The wedding, which will be next Thursday fortnight
The wedding house will be the Ship Inn, Port Eynon,
Where the †brides will take breakfast on plenty of good bread, butter
   and cheese:
Walk to Port Eynon Church to get married, back and take dinner,
And then I'll see if I can get you some good tin meat and some good
   attendance.
And whatever you wish to give at the dinner table, the †brides will be
   thankful for.
There will be a fiddle in attendance, for there'll be plenty of
Music there and dancing, if you'll come and dance,
There'll be fiddlers, fifers, drummers, and the devil don't know what beside,
I don't know what.
There'll be plenty of drinkables there, so they tell me, but that
I haven't tasted.
And if you'll come to the wedding,
I'll do all that lie in my power that evening if required,
To get you a sweetheart apiece, if I don't get drunk,
But the †brides is wishful you should come or send."

The Bidder to have a stick with red, white and blue ribands.

Nowadays much firing of guns occurs, and the Bidder concludes his address by singing "Hurrah for the red, white and blue."

PROCEDURE AT A BIDDING WEDDING.

The bride and bridegroom sit together at top of table, and next them the man with the wedding book. The bidder goes round with two plates, into one of which the men guests place contributions. The Bidder calls out the name and the amount given, and then puts the sum into the second plate. The book keeper shouts out "Aye," should a guest give a big contribution he may say "Heave," which the bidder repeats, and which signifies that that same amount will be in turn given by the bridegroom and bride when the donor in his turn gets married.

As soon as all the money is collected, it is handed over in the one dish to the bride.

---

† *Bride and Bridegroom were alike called "Brides."*

whistled them all, very, very good he was. Until the war (First World War), that is, then he got a piece of shrapnel in his lungs, so that he couldn't take a deep breath, and he gradually had to give up the whistling. Such a pity. To hear him whistle *La Bohème* or *Lo Hear the Gentle Lark* was really something. Everywhere he went he kept people going as far as music was concerned. In 1924 he put together a Gower Pageant in Penrice Park that was a really memorable event in the lives of the people, and it's been talked about ever since.'[4] It seems the event was a financial success as the *Daily Post* reported, 'The gross receipts for Thursday's performance, which took place in dismal weather, amounted to £800' – a substantial amount in 1924.

Although only twelve years of age at the time, Gwen vividly remembers the occasion. "I knew Colonel Ernest Helme. I used to visit my cousin who lived near his house, Hill End, in Llangennith. He was such a gentleman, but he never married. Horton and Port Eynon enacted a bidding wedding; my father was a wedding guest, and my sister, Mary and I were flower girls. We so enjoyed the rehearsals at Miss Morgan's house, and in the estate grounds where we went to by horse and trap. It rained on the day, but that didn't stop it being a success."

When old enough, Gwen and her siblings were expected to help on the family farm, as were many farmers' children. "Before school, I fed the chickens and milked Daisy the cow. I remember visiting the Misses Simmons and taking them butter. Miss Elsie and Miss Emma kept lots of poultry – Light Sussex – which of course I had to go and see, as I loved chickens. They also kept rabbits in cages, which they had killed, and then skinned them and nailed the skins to the doors of the house; they made fur-backed gloves out of them, which they sold in the church bazaars, the proceeds going to the church. They had a maid, but did the gardening themselves; they were very hard workers. They started the WI in Port Eynon. I used to go to their house on a Saturday for rug-making lessons; they made beautiful rugs.

I delivered butter and milk to the Misses Duncans, who lived in The Retreat, in Horton. I always delivered to the back door. I couldn't reach the knocker, and so they tied a string to it with corks on the end so that I could knock the door. They had a nephew, Alan Duncan, who visited them occasionally and played golf on the burrows. When coming home from school, we'd go out of our way to see him, as he'd give us a penny. We'd then go to the shop in Horton and buy a packet of sweets for a halfpenny.

---

4. Ibid., pp. 226-227.

It was through supplying milk and butter to the Misses Duncans, that I later delivered to Borfa School. On my way to school, I delivered butter, and milk in cans, to Borfa House; I left the cans there, and on the way home, filled them with water from Old Well for our family's use."

In about 1914, Miss Gertrude Hocking established Borfa House Girls' Private School in Port Eynon.[5] By 1926, Miss Margaret Mitchell, a native of Scotland, had taken over.

Gwen has clear memories of the school. "The daughters of Mr. A. O. Thomas of Kilvrough Manor attended Borfa House School – situated on the green behind the Ship Inn. It was a boarding school and – apart from the Kilvrough girls – all its pupils were from outside the area. I remember them coming to St. Cattwg's Church in Port Eynon, in their uniforms; they occupied two pews. Miss Mitchell was assisted by Miss M. Emson, who was teacher and housekeeper. Miss Mitchell was friendly with Misses Bertha and Muriel Duncan, who were Sunday School teachers in St. Cattwg's Church; Miss Muriel Duncan was also church organist. I had piano lessons with Miss Muriel Duncan and played the piano in Sunday School; she also taught me to play the organ and was hoping that I would take over from her when she retired as church organist. They thought our family would always live in Horton; it was a big shock to the Misses Duncans when our family moved to Knelston, later in 1931. I went to the Girls' Friendly Society in the dining room of the Misses Duncans' house; Miss Duncan taught us to sew while her mother read to us.

I walked to Port Eynon School – a Church School – every day. Miss Hicks was its headmistress and Miss Phillips the infant teacher. Miss Phillips lived in a thatched cottage near the Ship Inn. Her mother gave the pupils a lovely party every Christmas in her home. There was a green shed in the garden where Mrs. Phillips made teas for visitors to the village – people who came in a charabanc.

Soldiers were convalescing in a large house in Horton, called The Hollies, which was converted into a hospital during the First World War. We were warned not to speak to them, as they were strangers."

Gwen's education was governed, not by her academic worth, but by her parents' financial position. This unfair situation was later accentuated when her two younger sisters were allowed to further their education due to the improved state of their parents' finances. "I was the oldest of seven: six girls and one boy. I had worked hard in school, and was also

---

5. The house continues in educational use to this day, owned and run by the City and County of Swansea.

coached in the evenings by Miss Bertha Duncan. I passed the scholarship examination to go to Gowerton County School but was kept at home to work. I was a bit disappointed, as I had wanted to attend Pencoed College – the agricultural college, near Bridgend – to take a course on poultry keeping. I had my own poultry shed where I kept Rhode Island Reds. I loved my chickens and used to let them out every morning; there were no foxes then. Mary, my sister next in age to me, didn't pass, and so the two of us were working at home. It was a small farm of only forty-three acres, and not enough work there for both of us, so I went into service. Later, my two younger sisters passed and went to Gowerton County School.

My first employers were Mr. Roberts, an estate agent, and his wife who lived in Burry Cottage in Burry Green. The house was later bought and enlarged by Sydney Heath; it is still known as Sydney Heath's house. I was nanny to their little daughter, Pat, and lived in. I had my own bedroom and the nursery was upstairs. I loved working there and used to walk as far as Old Walls, in Llanrhidian, with Pat in the pram. She was a lovely little girl. Jim was the gardener. His wife was cook, but had been nanny before my time there. It seems that she had preferred looking after Pat to cooking, and became jealous of me; she started interfering and making my situation difficult, so I left. I had been working there for a year.

In 1931, my father bought Knelston Hall Farm from the Dunraven estate. Waterside Farm was too small for our family by then, as we were seven children. Soon after we moved, he was asked if he would like to sell our field next to the school to extend the school premises. We were sorry to lose the field as it was near the house, and handy to fetch the cows in for milking when we grazed them there on spring nights. On the other hand, father had borrowed a lot of money to buy the farm, and there were no subsidies in those days. The sale of the land *put him on his feet* and he was able to pay off the money he had borrowed."

The establishment of the school for the parishes of Reynoldston, Knelston and Llanddewi had caused bitter argument between the Church of England and the big landowners, and the nonconformists. In 1870, the government accepted the problem of universal primary education and passed the Elementary Education Act. The whole country was divided into School Board areas, in each of which the School Boards were made the authorities of elementary education. The ratepayers of the district elected the members of the School Board who were employed

Mr. and Mrs. Roberts, 1929.

Pat in pram with her cousin at Burry Cottage.

Mrs. Roberts, centre, with friends and gardener Jim on her left at Burry Cottage.

to levy an education rate of up to three pence in the pound. This was an alternative to the old system of voluntary schools paid for by local people. However, the Church of England and the landowners strongly resisted this reform locally, wishing a voluntary National (Church) School to be built on the site of the existing Nation Church of England Day School at Gorse Green, Reynoldston. Eventually, compromises were reached, and on 14 March 1874, the United District Board School, a voluntary non-sectarian school, was opened in Knelston, and named Reynoldston School. In 1944, it became known as Knelston Primary School. The extension was eventually completed in 1968, and the old school premises closed. It has now been converted into private dwellings.

Having left her situation at Burry Cottage, Gwen was soon re-employed. "Thanks to my Aunty Mary, my mother's cousin, who worked at Oxwich Rectory – now the Oxwich Bay Hotel – I quickly obtained a position there."

The Oxwich Bay Hotel nestles under the wooded headland of Oxwich Point, on the west of Oxwich Bay. It is an extremely popular residential hotel, open to non-residents for bar and restaurant meals. On 20 March 1997, a licence was obtained to hold wedding ceremonies on the premises, so in a sense, the building has come full circle: now a venue for marriage services, it was originally the home of a marriage officiator, John Collins, rector of Oxwich and Llwchwr.

When Collins – then a bachelor – came to Oxwich as rector in 1772, he occupied the original rectory, which stood on a low narrow shelf of land between church and sea on Oxwich Point. It was in a bad state of repair, and some years after he married Ann, daughter of Robert Wells, rector of the neighbouring parishes of Ilston and Penmaen, it had become too small for their rapidly growing family. The new rectory – completed in 1789 – was built by Collins' good friend, Thomas Mansel Talbot, of the nearby Georgian mansion, Penrice Castle.

By 1925, the new rectory was occupied by Canon Basil Chastel and Mrs. de Boinville. In 1930, the couple employed Gwen Beynon as house parlour-maid.

"Canon and Mrs. de Boinville had no children and treated me as their own. I was house parlour-maid and Aunty was cook. We both had our own rooms at the rectory. My job was to wait table. In the mornings I wore a blue cotton frock; a big white apron with straps crossed at the back; and black shoes and stockings. I changed in the afternoons into a black dress; a little white apron; and I wore a little white cap on my head. There was a boy, Peter, who tidied up outside and tended the

Gwen in afternoon uniform at Oxwich Rectory, 1930.

Gwen – time off. Oxwich Rectory, 1930

Left to right: Kath (Gwen's cousin), Leslie (milkman), Gwen, Mary Lloyd, Car park attendant at Oxwich Rectory, 1930.

lamps: the house had no electricity. A gardener came from Penclawdd on his bicycle every Friday. Milk was delivered by Leslie, who lived with his sister on a farm in Penmaen. We had a nice bathroom at the rectory, which was unusual in those days. Leslie used to pump the water from the engine house in the back yard to the big tank in the loft. It was one of my jobs to make sure the tank was kept full of water.

Canon and Mrs. de Boinville – she was a very large lady – lived well. They had a Trojan car.[6] There was always wine on the sideboard, but I wasn't involved in that as they helped themselves. They had two lovely little dogs called Maisie and Jane.

During the summer months they took in paying guests: Mrs. de Boinville was a very sociable lady and loved company. Lilian Baylis, the famous founder of the first Old Vic Theatre, in London, spent many holidays at the rectory."

> 'Lilian Baylis was born in London in 1874. After being trained as a musician, she appeared in London concerts as a child prodigy, toured England and South Africa as a violinist and music teacher, and returned to London in 1898 to take up the post of assistant manager (under her aunt, Emma Cons) of the Royal Victoria Theatre, a music and lecture hall for workers founded on the principle of temperance. After her aunt's death in 1912, she became manager of the theatre, which was popularly known as the Old Vic, transforming it into a venue for opera and, only incidentally, drama.
>
> After Shakespearean drama became established as the Old Vic's main repertoire between 1912 and 1923, Lilian Baylis purchased the derelict Sadler's Wells Theatre in London and by 1931, had turned it into a celebrated showcase for opera and ballet productions. She hired Ninette de Valois, who developed the Sadler's Wells ballet company (later the Royal Ballet) into one of the world's leading dance ensembles. Baylis, who was renowned for her tireless promotion of all forms of theatrical entertainment, died in London in 1937.'[7]

Gwen enjoyed Baylis' visits to the rectory. "Dame Lilian did a lot of work for Oxwich Church: in 1931 she financed a ceiling decoration in

---

6. The Trojan car found considerable favour among the clergy and is probably the only make to have advertised in the *Church Times*. It could also climb virtually any gradient – a good choice for the Canon and his wife living in Oxwich, at the bottom of a hill with a 20% gradient.
7. *The Penguin Biographical Dictionary of Women* (Market House Books Ltd., 1998).

Left to right: Mr. Richardson (friend), Canon de Boinville, Mrs. Richardson (friend), Mrs. de Boinville, at Oxwich Rectory, 1930/32.

Left to right: Canon de Boinville, Mrs. de Boinville, Miss Lilian Baylis, Malcolm Hayes, Malcolm's mother, at Oxwich Rectory, 1930/32, in front of Trojan car.

Miss Lilian Baylis with her dogs, Oxwich Beach, 1930.

Miss Bell with Malcolm Hayes, Oxwich Beach, 1930.

the chancel painted by Leslie Young, the scenic artist of Sadler's Wells. Miss Baylis was accompanied on holiday by her dogs, and her companion, Miss Bell. Miss Bell was a lovely lady and befriended me. Miss Bell and Miss Baylis were very kind to me and invited me for a week's holiday in London to stay with friends of Miss Baylis. After their stay at the rectory, Miss Baylis went home in her car with her dogs, and Miss Bell and I went by train. They treated me to the Old Vic and Sadler's Wells Theatres every night of the week – such a great thrill!

Malcolm Hayes used to come to stay at the rectory with his family. He loved riding the horses, which were kept in the field in-between the house, and the church. I had to catch the horses for him: I was used to handling them as I had ridden them when at home on the farm.

I used to go to Oxwich Farm, on Oxwich Green, near the castle, and buy a jug of cream for the weekend guests. I'd put it in a bowl of cold water on the slab in the pantry; there were no fridges then; it would keep fresh Saturday and Sunday.

Through the winter, when Mrs. de Boinville didn't have paying guests, she organized bridge parties at the rectory in the afternoons when I used to serve tea. Lady Blythswood used to attend. I'd look out for her walking across the burrows from Penrice Castle in her black coat; she always walked, never drove. I'd answer the door to her and show her into the dining room. Mrs. de Boinville also held whist drives, dances and Christmas parties at the old village hall. We had such lovely times there.

When the Canon and Mrs. de Boinville were out, I used to enjoy playing their piano. In the summer, when I finished my work after the evening meal, I would go for a swim, play tennis, or take Maisie and Jane for a walk. The tennis court was up a lane near the village hall. I had a wonderful time. I always went to Oxwich Church on Sunday mornings. I used to see Lady Blythswood's daughter – Olive, Mrs Methuen-Campbell – there. She was such a smart, nice-looking lady. She was tall like her father – not a bit like her mother who was tiny.

Mrs. de Boinville died suddenly. One day I took their coffee in after lunch – they came into the library for coffee – and we were having our lunch. My aunt was Miss Lloyd: I never called her aunty when at work of course. Canon de Boinville came out and said, 'Oh Lloydy! Lloydy! The mistress has fallen!' She was on the floor in front of the fire. She was taken to hospital and died there. It was awful sad.

The two Miss Sainsburys lived in Oxwich School House: one sister was the schoolteacher and the other kept house. My aunt and I were friendly with both of them; they were also friends of the Canon and his wife. However, after Mrs. de Boinville died, Miss Sainsbury, the housekeeper, spent more time at the rectory! Then Canon de Boinville decided to move away to Radnorshire, where he took a parish, and married Miss Sainsbury. He gave me a Bible as a farewell present. Inside he wrote:

'To Gwen Tucker, from her old friend,
B. Chastel de Boinville
10th September 1933'

I still use it and treasure it greatly.

Aunty went to housekeep in a house on the seafront in Port Eynon and Mrs. Martin, the rector of Reynoldston's wife, found me a position in Fairy Hill."

Fairy Hill is a splendid Georgian property, situated in the heart of the Gower Peninsula, near Reynoldston. It is set amidst beautiful grounds of about thirty acres, including a lake and a portion of the Burry Pill.

The exact origins of the house are uncertain. The Lucas family had come to Gower from Essex, and by the eighteenth century, owned considerable land and property in the peninsula. Jenkyn Phillips of the Great House, Cheriton, possibly built the house in around 1700. His daughter Jane married Henry Lucas of Stouthall, bringing the property into the Lucas family. In the 1720s, Richard Lucas, younger son of John Lucas of the Stouthall estate was residing there with his wife, Barbara and daughter, Anne. In a letter of 1726 it was called Feryill but later became known as Peartree. Richard Lucas died in 1765 and some time later, his great-nephew, John, moved there with his young bride of sixteen, Catherine Powell, and it was they who gave it the name of Fairy Hill.

By 1814, Lady Barham – famous for her building of six chapels of the Calvinistic Methodist faith in the locality – was residing at Fairy Hill.

On her death in 1823, the Lucas family took up residence again. Henry, the second son of John and Catherine, had inherited the estate in 1818 from his father, and came from Carmarthen to live there with his wife and family. Unfortunately, Henry's passion for horse racing, with its ensuing debts, forced him to sell the estate.

The Reverend Samuel Phillips, and his bride, Anne Shaftesbury Horsley were to enjoy only one year together at Fairy Hill. Anne died in 1833 and a year later Phillips married Juliana Noel, daughter of Lady Barham. Both Phillips and his second wife passed away in 1855 leaving great debts.

Rhoda Bynon (probably back row 5th from left), Cheriton Hill School, c.1890.

In 1858, Fairy Hill was bought by Starling Benson. A one-time owner of the copper works in Penclawdd, his activities in Swansea and area were many and varied. On his death in 1879, his half-brother, General Henry Roxby Benson inherited the estate. As did Starling Benson, his half-brother and family greatly involved themselves in local philanthropy. Win Walters remembers her mother, Rhoda Eaton, née Bynon, who lived her formative years in Cwm Ivy, Llanmadoc, talking of the Bensons' patronage of Cheriton Hill School (Cheriton and Llanmadoc National School) where she was a pupil. "My mother often used to talk of Mrs. Benson and how she visited the school and arranged Christmas parties for them. When my mother was in the top class, she used to teach the younger pupils. Her teacher's husband was a ship's captain. Every time he came on leave, another baby was on the way. She used to bring them to school with her."

In 1921, Margaret Benson, daughter of General Benson, and the last of the Benson family, left Fairy Hill.

Gwen remembers Percy Stanley Rowland, a stevedore by trade, living there in the 1920s, with his widowed sister, Mary Anne Daniels, who was "such a nice lady." A sociable, generous, and convivial man, Rowland continued in the philanthropist trait of the Benson Family. He attended Sunday School, where he donated prizes to the pupils and organized parties to celebrate Empire Day. His sister taught at the school. Building of the new church hall in Reynoldston commenced in

1922, made possible by the land and much of the material being provided by Rowland. It was to replace the old vestry hall – situated opposite the church – which, by then, was being used as a reading room. The latter was demolished and a group of fir trees was donated and planted on the site by Rowland. In June of that year, he made available the grounds of Fairy Hill for a grand bazaar and fête, followed by an evening of dancing – a great financial and social success. The Lord Bishop of Swansea and Brecon opened the church hall on 12 November 1923. Rowland received a great ovation at the ceremony. The Gower Pageant again gave Rowland the opportunity to demonstrate his generosity. He provided a horse and trap for the inhabitants of Llanrhidian to travel to Penrice and also gave horses for the enacting of the pageant. It seems one of his last benevolent gifts was on the retirement of the Reverend R. W. Lockyer, rector of Reynoldston, when he paid off the entire remaining church hall debt of one hundred and seventy-two pounds. By 1929, Rowland himself was in financial difficulties, and Fairy Hill was put on the market.

In 1933, Gwen Beynon was employed as house parlour-maid by Tom Richard and Grace Harris, the new owners of Fairy Hill.

"I liked working at Fairy Hill very much. It was a lovely house and Mr. and Mrs. Harris, and their son Rhidian, were such nice people. Having been brought up on the farm I loved all animals, and so grew very fond of their little spaniel.

Mr. Harris – he was always known as Major T. R. Harris – was a Swansea solicitor; his brother Edward, was also a solicitor living in Langland, Swansea; the Harrises were Swansea people."

In 1933, Alderman Edward (Ted) Harris was mayor of Swansea. He was of a sturdy stature and possessed a mercurial temperament. An able lawyer and a first class administrator, he had served the council ably from 1924 on Parliamentary, Highways and Education Committees. However, it was as chairman of the Mains Drainage Committee that he is mostly associated with, having been the major force in producing the huge main drainage scheme in the town, which commenced operation in 1936.

He was the last mayor to officiate at the old Guildhall, Somerset Row (Place)[8] and when the new Civic Centre was opened by HRH Prince

---

8. Built in 1825, and altered in 1848, it fell into disrepair when discarded for the new Guildhall, built in Victoria Park, in 1934. It was sympathetically restored to become the home of the city's new National Literature Centre for the Year of Literature in 1995. Named Tŷ Llên, it is now referred to as the Dylan Thomas Centre.

George, the Duke of Kent, in October 1934, was the first to officiate in the new premises. He wrote a charming little book on the history of Swansea, which was published in the same year.[9] In its foreword he states, 'At my Mayoral Luncheon in November 1933, attention was forcibly called to the need for a brief, clear and readable, but inexpensive history of Swansea. The erection of the New Civil Buildings (Guildhall) and the visit of His Royal Highness Prince George to open them

Old Guildhall, Somerset Place.

9. Alderman Edward Harris, *Swansea its Port and Trade and their Development* (Cardiff, Western Mail & Echo, 1934).

have emphasized the position, and hence my humble attempt to meet what is an acknowledged demand.'

Alderman Harris' year as mayor was an interesting time for Gwen. "Although Mr. Edward Harris and his wife had a very nice house in Langland, Fairy Hill had larger rooms and spacious grounds, and was therefore more suitable for entertaining; so every weekend of his year in office, he and his wife brought their guests to Fairy Hill. The French doors of the drawing room were opened, and I served tea to the guests on the lawn. Mr. Tom Harris seemed pleased to entertain all those people in his home. We (the staff) had a very busy year.

The property had thirty-three rooms in all. There were three big rooms in the attic: the sewing room; a room for the ladies' maid; and I've forgotten the use of the third. Downstairs were the billiard room, dining room, drawing room, library, and a very large kitchen and scullery behind. There was a big black range in the kitchen with two ovens, and a big oil stove; it was always warm and cosy there. The scullery had a big slab where the men used to put the vegetables from the garden every morning. The milk pans were kept on the slabs against the walls either side of the dairy. We used to skim the milk before we had a separator. I had my own china pantry where I cleaned the silver. The gun room, which used to be the lamp room, was near the kitchen. Mr. Harris' guests used the back door into the gun room after they had been shooting in the grounds, and there was a little room where they washed and put themselves tidy before coming into the house. Fairy Hill had its own electricity generator housed in an outside building, and water was laid on from Cefn Bryn. The workmen brought their own breakfast and lunch, which they ate in the bothy;[10] it was situated in the garden and was very cosy with a fire in winter.

The staff included three gardeners: Albert Beynon who lived down the lane in Stackpool Cottage; Arven Jones from Landimore; and Trevor Beynon from Tankeylake, Llangennith. Willie, Arven's brother was working there, but he was called up and killed in action, and so Arven came to work there in his stead. The gardens were beautiful with three greenhouses and a peach house. Albert's father worked at Fairy Hill during the time of the Bensons. There was a bell on the wall in the back yard near the kitchen. It was his job to ring it at half-past seven in the morning to summons the men to work, and at half-past five in the evening for them to finish. He died about the same time as Albert left school and so Albert replaced him. Albert's mother also worked at Fairy Hill: I suppose she needed the money. Her job was to make butter, and

---

10. A hut, a cottage, a one-roomed building in which labourers are lodged.

possibly, milk the Jersey cows. There were two cooks: Edith Shepherd from Leason and Winnie Williams from Llanrhidian.

Mr. and Mrs. Harris had a car each but no chauffeur. Mrs. Harris' car was very large. Albert used to see to the cars every morning: take them out of the large garage and make sure they had petrol, etc.

I was house parlour-maid and lived in. I had my own bedroom with a very nice view over the garden to the lake. We had our own bathroom, which was wonderful. My job was waiting table. I cleaned the bedrooms and a woman came in twice a week to clean downstairs. During spring-cleaning time, she came in nearly every day. I was up at half-past six as I had the fires to do. Every morning in the winter, I lit a fire in the dining room. Later in the day, I lit a fire in the library, where Mr. and Mrs. Harris went every evening: it was smaller and so warmer than the drawing room. On Sundays, they used the drawing room to entertain friends. It was a beautiful room with three French windows overlooking the lawn. Mrs Harris talked of having a fire in her bedroom and I thought, 'Oh no! I don't fancy that,' but she didn't. Trevor brought in the coal and sticks and left them in the passage for me. I tended the fires all day. There was plenty of wood on the estate and always baskets of logs in the dining room, library and drawing room. Trevor was the middleman: he milked the cows in the morning; and worked in the garden for the rest of the day. Everything was very organized.

Our uniforms were not provided by our employers. I wore the same as I had at Oxwich Rectory. We had to launder them ourselves in the big black boiler – which I lit sometimes – in the corner of the scullery. I earned two pounds and ten shillings a month. I had every Thursday afternoon off. One Sunday I finished work after lunch at two o'clock, and the next Sunday I finished after tea at five o'clock. I always had to be back by ten o'clock. On my time off, I'd cycle through Burry, along the Horton road, and then the Penrice road, leave my bike inside a gate and go through a couple of fields to my aunt and uncle's house: there was never any fear of my bike being stolen. I didn't have much chance to make many friends, but I did know the girls in service in Penrice Castle and Mr. Pritchard's house in Penmaen – Penmaen House. It didn't worry me because I didn't know any different, although I'd had more freedom at Oxwich Rectory. However, I did form an attachment to Albert. It was quite difficult for us to spend time together: only Sunday afternoons and evenings and Thursday evenings; but when Mrs. Harris was out in her car, I used to sneak down the garden to pick blackcurrants and gooseberries and have a chat with him. He was ten years older than me but he didn't look it: I had grey hairs at forty, but he didn't, even when he died at sixty-seven.

Mr. Harris had met his wife during the First World War when he was stationed in Cambridgeshire. Mrs. Harris' family were landed gentry and had an estate in St. Neots. She was an only child and so quite wealthy. Her parents suffered from poor health and she spent much time with them. While she was away, I used to look after Mr. Harris. It was such a big house. In the week, he was not at home for lunch. He would have his evening meal in the kitchen after he came home from his office in Swansea: it saved me carrying it all the way to the dining room. Mr. Harris was quite ordinary really. She was a little bit uppish but she was alright mind; I got on alright with her. She was very reserved and didn't get involved locally as had Mrs. Benson. Mr. and Mrs. Harris went to Reynoldston Church and sat in the front seat up the steps where the choir sits now.

When Mrs. Harris' parents passed away, she sold the estate. Three lorry-loads of furniture came to Fairy Hill from St. Neots. Oh! It was lovely furniture; Fairy Hill was really well furnished then.

Their son, Rhidian, went away to school in Swansea and then to college. He didn't follow in his father's footsteps. He married and went to live abroad. He passed away a few years ago.

One summer, Mr. Harris' sister's son, Fred Arnold, came to stay in Fairy Hill in the school holidays, to study. He was such a nice boy. He took over the family business and is now practising in Gorseinon. He never married.

Albert and I were married in Llanddewi Church on November 18th, 1941. It was wartime and we were only ten at the ceremony. We had our wedding breakfast at the King Arthur Hotel, in Reynoldson, and went to Aberystwyth on honeymoon.

We lived in rooms in Dunraven Farm, on the Llangennith road, for two years and then moved to a cottage above the chapel (Bethesda) in Burry Green. A replacement for me could not be found at Fairy Hill and so Mrs. Harris asked if I would help them out a couple of days a week. It was unusual for married women to work then but I didn't mind, and it was conveniently near home. By then, Mr. Roberts had sold his house – Burry Cottage – to Sydney Heath. Mr. Heath had a gardener, Mr. Treble, coming from Swansea, Monday to Saturday, who lived in a nice flat above the garage. As it was wartime, everything was on ration. Mr. Treble used to go around Burry Green on a Friday night, before going home to Swansea, to see if he could get a few eggs or a bit of butter. We kept a few chickens and I used to save him half-a-dozen eggs. When Mr. and Mrs. Heath went on holiday, Mrs. Treble used to come down, and

Gwen and Albert Beynon. Wedding Day, 18 November 1941.

she and her husband lived in the house. On Saturday nights, they would invite Albert and me there to play cards with them; we enjoyed that. They were such nice people. Mrs. Harris died and I stayed on at Fairy Hill to look after Mr. Harris. I left in 1947 when Albert and I moved to Cilibion, Three Crosses to live. I had worked in Fairy Hill for fourteen years altogether.

Mr. Harris sold up and Mr. and Mrs. E. H. Philpotts – a market gardener and his wife – came to live there."

Fairy Hill was bought by John and Midge Frayne on 1 May 1983. 'Thirty-five years of vandalism by neglect had strangled the once magnificent gardens and left the house in a state of near collapse and complete loss of dignity.'[11] After the couple's intensive physical work on the property and gardens, Fairy Hill returned to its former glory. For the first time in its history, it opened as an hotel, in 1985. The Fraynes entertained artists of the highest calibre – Dame Joan Sutherland, Bryn Terfel, Leo Nucci, Francesco Ellera D'Artagnan, Cleopatra Ciurca, Michel Senechal – when Decca Recording Company recorded the opera *Adriana Lecouvreur* in the Brangwyn Hall, in Swansea, and on another recording session, the Russian pianist and conductor Vladimir Ashkenazy. John and Midge retired in 1993, having enjoyed a successful business for eight extremely hardworking, but exhilarating, years.

By October 1993, Paul Davies, Andrew Hetherington and Peter and Jane Camm were the new owners. Again, diligence resulted in success. Fairy Hill is now a five-star Country House Hotel, owned by Paul Davies and Andrew Hetherington. It has received many awards, the most prodigious being AA Hotel of the Year 1997. The rich and the famous are among its many visitors – Prime Minister Tony Blair, film stars, Paul Newman and his wife, Joanne Woodward, composers, Karl Jenkins and his wife Carol.

Lovaine Fisher – Housemaid

Stanley Llewellyn Grove was a thatcher on the Penrice estate. He lived in Shrubbery Cottage, Horton – a tithe cottage – with his wife Olive and children Lovaine, Llewellyn and Valerie. After Lovaine's time as a pupil of Port Eynon Elementary School, she went into service.

---

11. Midge Frayne, *A Gower Stripper* (The Forge, Fairy Hill, Reynoldston, Swansea, SA3 1BS, 1996), p.5.

Stanley Llewellyn and Olive Grove, 1917.

"I left school at fourteen and went to work for Elsie, Emma and Maud Simmons. They were three old maids who lived in a large house in Horton called Robins Rest. It had a beautiful garden with a big lawn, and apple trees down one side of it. The family was from Merthyr; they were gentry and upper class. The Misses Simmons were very educated ladies and often gave lectures in the village hall. They belonged to Port Eynon Church, the Womens' Institute; I don't know what they belonged to all together. They were comical, and as old-fashioned as could be. They were fussy and everything had to be just so in the house – everything in its right place.

I arrived for work at half-past seven in the morning and left at six o'clock. Once I was taught, I did everything. The kitchen had a great black stove. Every morning I riddled the fire, cleaned the stove, black-

Shrubbery Cottage, Horton. Peggy Grove with daughter, Heather.

Shrubbery Cottage, Horton.

leaded it and polished it until I could see my face in it. I prepared breakfast, which was toast and marmalade eaten with silver cutlery and the marmalade always had to be in a dish. Coffee was always drunk with breakfast. My work routine was rigid: Monday was washday – there was a laundry in the basement of the house; Tuesday I ironed; I had certain days for cleaning the brass and silver, etc.; Thursday afternoon I had off. When the Misses Simmons came home from church on a Sunday, dinner had to be on the table for them. After washing up, I went to Sunday School, and then back to Robins Rest to make tea. I can't remember my salary, but although meals were provided, it was precious little.

When I was going to get married I told the Misses Simmons. 'You'll have to leave, then,' they said.

'Thank God for that,' I thought. I married Tom Fisher from there when I was twenty.

Then the war (Second World War) broke out and Tom went away to the war. Three large houses in Horton were used as residential homes for old age pensioners evacuated from London: Talbot Lodge was for men; Springfield for ladies; and Lulsley was for both sexes who found difficulty in walking far. There was quite a crowd of them down here. I worked in Lulsley to begin with and then went to Talbot Lodge. Phyllis and I helped with the breakfast, made the beds, and cleaned, washed

Left to right: Peggy (wife of Llewellyn Grove), Lovaine, an evacuee, and sitting: Heather (Peggy's daughter), Celia (Lovaine's daughter). Photograph taken just after the war.

and fed those who couldn't help themselves. My meals were provided but their cost deducted from my wages; I took home about one pound a week. It was difficult to get staff then.

The resident cook had done a bunk: she couldn't stand it. Bill, one of the residents in Lulsley – he was ever such a nice chap – said that he could cook anything. He complained about the lumpy porridge. 'You don't get lumps in porridge girl,' he said to me.

Mrs. Maliphant who was in charge said, 'Well if he can cook, let him cook,' and he did. All the residents had to have the same amount of food otherwise they would quarrel. They loved pease-pudding and would say, 'This is dinner, but it's not half as nice as having a pint.'

Four of the men regularly picked winkles (periwinkles) on Horton beach. They collected them in a big tin bath given to them by Mrs. Maliphant. They washed them, and boiled them in a big boiler on a fire outside. They ate them, after their tea, with a big bowl in the middle of the table for the shells, and thoroughly enjoyed themselves.

Many of the old age pensioners died while in Horton. It was upsetting, as we became fond of them. I'd finished working before the end of the war. When they were leaving in their buses I went to see them and they said to me, 'We've had a lovely time.'

I said goodbye thinking, 'God help; half of you are going back, and the rest of you are buried here.'"

Rebecca Rees – Housemaid

John Thomas, a young student of Pontypool College, became minister of Trinity Baptist Chapel, Penclawdd, in 1874. The Reverend Thomas and his wife had three daughters, Lily, Laura and Vera.

Lily married Henry Folland and the couple set up home in the upper Swansea Valley, near Folland's employment in the steel/tin industry. By 1906, they were living in Llwynderw, a large, splendid house with magnificent views over Swansea Bay and Mumbles Head.

There, Rebecca Davies, a staunch member of Trinity Chapel, was employed by Lily as housemaid for a number of years until her marriage to William Rees in 1909. Their daughter, Gwyneth Evans, also a loyal member of the chapel, now lives in West End, Penclawdd.

In 1907, Folland was appointed a director, and the following year, managing director, of Grovesend Steelworks. In 1918, he filled the posts of both chairman and managing director. By 1923, Richard Thomas and Co. Ltd. had acquired what were originally Grovesend Steelworks, Gor-

On Tuesday, 29 June 2004 the stack of Bryngwyn Steelworks was demolished to make way for the new Bryngwyn Village housing development, to be built by Persimmon.

seinon Tin-plate Works, Grovesend Tin-plate Works, Bryngwyn Steelworks and the Mardy Tin-plate Works. Folland continued as chairman and director of the new firm until his death in 1927, at the age of fifty-eight. The previous year he had held the position of President of Swansea University.

Folland's widow held garden fêtes in the grounds of Llwynderw. Ruby Skinner née Davies recalls the occasions. "I can remember, when a child in the 1930s, being taken to the fêtes by my father. The lady members of Trinity Baptist Chapel, Penclawdd – my mother being one of them – and of Tirzah Baptist Chapel, Llanmorlais helped serve refreshments on a long table. The proceeds were donated to the old Swansea General and Eye Hospital."

The hospital was erected in 1869, at the corner of St. Helens Road and Bryn-y-Môr Road, at a cost of twenty-four thousand pounds, the architect being Alexander Graham, of London. The Richardson family involved in shipbuilding and the copper smelting industry in Swansea, contributed considerable sums to the building fund. At the hospital, a men's surgical ward was dedicated to Henry Folland – Folland's Ward. It was situated on the ground floor of the building, on St. Helens Road. On the opposite side of the corridor was a men's medical ward named after Graham Vivian, son of Henry Vivian, the industrialist who came from Cornwall to Penclawdd in the early 1800s to take over the copper works there. Both wards were damaged during the bombing of Swansea in the Second World War, but were later rebuilt, and the names retained.

Swansea General and Eye Hospital.

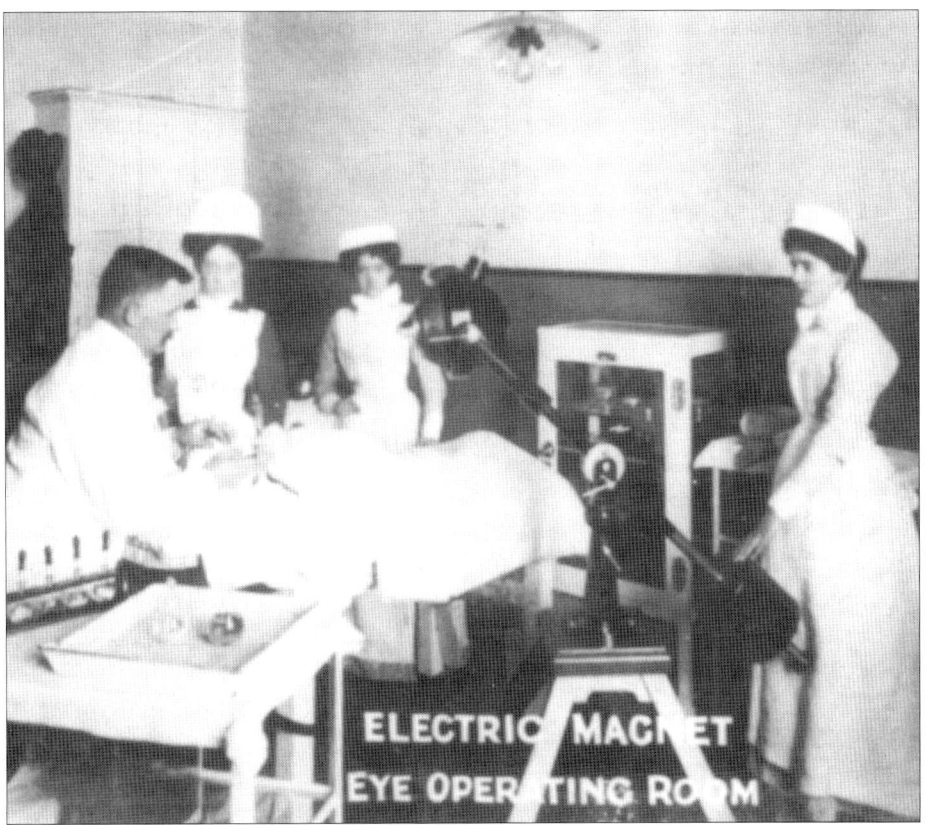
Circa 1900.

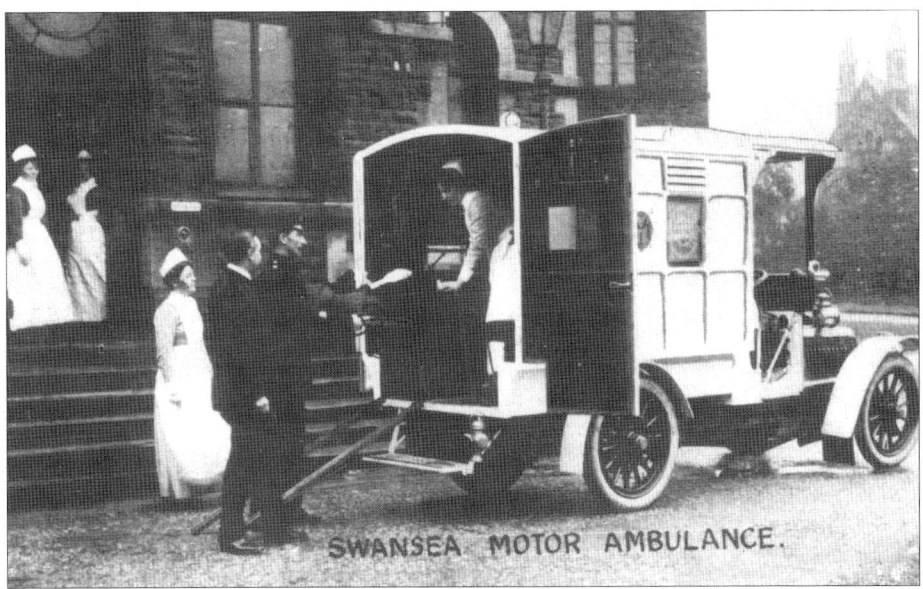

Dyer Ward. Sister Dyer with her little patients, Christmas 1910.

Swansea General Hospital. Pre-First World War.

*Swansea General Hospital. Nursing Training School.
Pre-First World War.*

Lily Folland vacated Llwynderw either before or during the war, and moved to The Lodge in the grounds by the main gates on the Mumbles Road. Her old home became an annexe of the General Hospital – a convalescent home. The latter was a precious commodity at the time: patients were kept in hospital longer then after operations; the two men's wards had been damaged; there was no room at the General Hospital to expand.

In 1954, Margaret Harvey, a native of Penclawdd, undertook part of her nurses' training there. "Mrs. Folland was still living at The Lodge when I was there but we never went near. Llwynderw seemed to have changed little since it had became a hospital. It was all very beautiful. The largest rooms and the conservatory were used for the beds. The floors were wooden and the walls clad with wooden panelling, and there was a large wooden staircase. The fireplaces were still in place but central heating had been installed – no open fires. We slept in, and my colleagues and I were in what had been the main bedroom. A lovely dressing table was still there, and the walls were covered with golden brown wooden cupboard doors, but one of them led to the bathroom. Any new arrivals would ask us where the bathroom was and we'd point at the cupboards; they'd have to open them one by one until they found

Margaret Harvey. Christmas 1953.

Llwynderw Annexe, Blackpill, Swansea – 'My board and lodge for a few weeks from end of March 1958. The very best of attention at all times' – Llewellyn Grove to his wife, Peggy.

the bathroom. It was all black marble that had come from Italy. The bath was semi-sunken, in an alcove, and there was also a shower. The toilet was in a separate room. The grounds were nice but we had snow in that January and so I saw little of them. It is so sad that it was all demolished for the building of houses and flats."

Bessie Evans – Housemaid

The Follands had a daughter, Martha Eugene and a son Dudley, who was, it seems, *a bit of a rake*. Martha Eugene married a Mr. Taylor, and the couple had one son when Bessie was in their employment.

Bessie, born in 1917, lived her formative years in Blackpill, Swansea. She relates her story. "My mother, Beatrix Andrews, was a native of Cheshire. She worked for her aunty in a biggish house in Ellesmere Port, but apparently was not treated very kindly. It was during the First World War, and her aunty had soldiers staying with her. One of the soldiers – Christopher (Chris) Adams – and my mother fell in love and were married in 1915. My father went away to war, and my mother travelled to Swansea by train – me a babe of six weeks in her arms – to meet her in-laws. At first, my mother and I lived in a house opposite the Woodmans pub, and later, near Blackpill School. By the time I was eight, my father had joined us and we were living in No. 10 Mill Lane – a seventeenth century cottage."

When at the age of fourteen, Bessie completed her education at Blackpill Elementary School, her parents could not afford the fifty pounds needed to buy her an apprenticeship, so, following in her mother's footsteps, Bessie went into service.

"After I left school, I went to work for Mrs. Taylor – known as Toots – in her house, Sŵn-y-Môr, in Langland. She was the daughter of Mrs. Folland, who lived in a beautiful, big, white, house – Llwynderw – on the Mumbles Road. Mrs. Folland had a big staff, and most came from the Brynamman area, I think, where Mr. Folland had had his tin-plate works. At first, I worked in Sŵn-y-Môr daily, travelling by bus from my home to Langland Corner; after a while, I occasionally stayed the night. It was not a large house: there were only the three of them – Mr. and Mrs. Taylor and their son. They had a cook called Gladys and I was the undermaid.

I liked the work so much that, when I had the chance to do the same work in London, I accepted it. I was told at home, in Blackpill, that they liked employing the Welsh girls in London. Admiral Algernon Heneage-

Walter-Vivian lived in Clyne Castle at the time. I don't know how it happened, but I was asked to go to work for his cousin, a single lady, who lived in Knightsbridge, just around the corner from Harrods.

My bedroom was on the top floor of the house. I was terribly homesick at first, and cried myself to sleep for many nights, but I stuck it out and soon got used to it. In time, I liked it so much that when I came home to Blackpill for a holiday I couldn't wait to get back to London: it was such a different life there than in Swansea.

I was only in the position for about nine months. I couldn't work my way up as the two sisters employed in the house were senior in position to me and had been there for years; one sister was a parlour-maid and the other was the housekeeper. The housekeeper was married to a butler who worked and lived in another house; sometimes she went to sleep where he worked, and sometimes he came to our house. There was also a cook and I was the one who did the dirty work – the skivvy. One of my jobs was to clean the marble steps outside the front door. There were terrible fogs in London in those days; I remember them well, as it was so cold. The sisters used to take me into London: I was too young – about fifteen – to go on my own. I had a nervous breakdown and came home to my parents.

I then worked for Lady Blythswood in Penrice Castle.[12] It was hard work but I loved it. However, at Penrice I only mixed with the staff, unlike London where I had made many friends. I was only at the Castle for a while as I think I was filling in for someone who had left. So, after my work there finished, I returned to London.

The two sisters, who worked for Admiral Heneage's cousin, helped me to join an agency for house staff. Short-term work was always plentiful in London and so I never worked anywhere for a long time. Through the agency, I was employed by the Marchioness of Dufferin and Ava."

Maureen Guinness was the beautiful middle daughter of Ernest Guinness and granddaughter of the First Earl of Iveagh. She captivated Twenties London as a fervent and witty socialite, partying with the likes of Cecil Beaton, Evelyn Waugh, John Betjeman and Diana Mitford.

In 1930, at the age of twenty-three, she fell in love with and married her handsome cousin, Basil Hamilton-Temple-Blackwood, Earl of Iveagh and heir to the Marquess title. Thousands lined the streets to see their lavish wedding – her hand-stitched gown and eleven bridesmaids.

---

12. See Chapter 1, pp. 19-20.

Three weeks later, while still on honeymoon, her father-in-law was killed in a plane crash and the couple returned to inherit the title. Their estate consisted of a house in Knightsbridge; a mansion in Kent; and Clandeboye, a three thousand-acre estate in County Down, Northern Ireland. It was a visit to the latter that instigated the Marchioness to employ Bessie: the need for a temporary supplement to her existing staff.

Bessie was well vetted before being employed. "I had to see two different secretaries and have three references before they took me on, and I hadn't worked in many places, but I dropped in lucky.

We sailed to Ireland but I can't remember from where: I only went there the once. The house was gorgeous. It was huge and every bedroom was done out in a certain country. The room called India had white walls and a white carpet. Everything was spick-and-span and the sheets were made of satin. The staff was big: there were two chauffeurs; two secretaries; and we were five housemaids. Their eldest daughter, Caroline, was three years old and their second daughter, Perdita, was born while I was there.

Their London house was in Hans Crescent, near Harrods.

They also had a beautiful house in Kent, which we drove to by car. When the family went away for weekends, a few of us staff – the butler, housekeeper and me – had a bit of fun: we used to play croquet on the lawn at the back of the house.

We very rarely saw the family as they used different staircases to ours. When the gong sounded for dinner, we would turn their beds down for the night, and then look over the balcony of their staircase to see them going into the dining room in their beautiful clothes. The men were in evening dress with tails, and the Marchioness always wore long gold evening gowns with trains, just like in the films.

I experienced the elegant life while I worked for the Marchioness. She was a great friend of the late Queen Elizabeth, the Queen Mother. The Marchioness and her husband were young, and in their heyday, and entertained on a grand scale. She was a very pretty girl and I have lovely memories of her. They were pleased with my work, and I learned a lot while I was there."

The Marquess was killed serving his country in the Second World War. Although before her death in May 1998, the Marchioness remarried twice, it is said that Ava, as she called him, was the love of her life.

Bessie left service and was employed as cleaner in a block of flats in Cromwell Road, Kensington. "I joined a team of seven girls. We lived in the employees' quarters of the building. There were seven floors: five flats to each. We were responsible for cleaning one floor each. On our afternoons off, we used to go to tea dances in Chelsea and Fulham Town

Hall. We were freer when working in the flats than in house service, as we had many evenings off; this meant that we were able to go to the evening dances as well. We girls wore dance dresses and the men were always smartly dressed in suits. It was at a dance on a Saturday night that I met my husband, David Evans. He was Welsh and from the Rhondda, where his father was a minister. He was working in Victoria.

We married in London in 1939. At the time, my brother was very ill – he died at the age of twenty-two – and so it was not suitable for us to be married in Swansea or for my parents to come to our wedding. My parents didn't meet my husband until after we were married. We rented a flat in Morden, in Surrey, but soon David was called up and joined the Army. He was not happy for me to stay in London on my own, and so I went back to Wales and lived between my parents and my parents-in-law.

My marriage was the end of my time in service, and the war was the end of my time in London."

May Hughes – Housemaid

May was born in 1911 to John and Catherine Harry, of Blue Anchor, Penclawdd. About three years after May had completed her education at the age of fourteen, John, a miner, fell victim to one of the many accidents that occurred in the local collieries: his leg was damaged beyond repair, necessitating amputation. Unable to continue working underground,[13] he established a barber/hairdressing and grocery business at Nurses Corner, to the east of the village, and May went into service.

"When I was about seventeen and a half, I went to work in Wimblewood Farm, near Three Crosses. I had to cross a big common to get to the farm. The first morning I went there, I saw cows in the field in front of the house; I was afraid so I climbed over a hedge to avoid passing them.

The farm had no running water, so I carried buckets of water from the well, which was quite a distance from the house. This was used for our drinking water and our washing water came from rainwater collected in an outside tank. We bathed in the little kitchen at the pine-end of the house. I used to wash the thick woollen blankets in a tin bath, and carry them in the bath to the orchard, and hang them there to dry on the long line; the orchard was far away from the house, and the tub of blankets was very heavy. I washed the rest of the clothes in a big tub with a dolly and turned the wheel for a quarter of an hour at a time. It was hard

---

13. Working underground – a term used locally for working in the collieries.

John Harry's shop at Nurses Corner, Penclawdd, c.1970.

work – enough to break your heart. I ironed the clothes with a box iron: it was a sort of steam iron. I also cleaned the house.

I milked every morning and evening, and separated the milk. In the evening I took the milk to the well to chill, and churned it the next day.

It was a nice farmhouse but not posh. Only a small little parlour she had, with a china cabinet. One day, I accidentally bumped against it and one of the cups inside fell and broke. Oh, she was very upset about that, but I couldn't do anything about it. I stayed in the farm during the week and went home every other weekend, usually with Joey Rees from Crofty. I went to Bethel Chapel, in Penclawdd, on Sunday evening and then back to the farm on Monday morning by half-past six. The farm was out in the wilds and I didn't see anybody from one weekend to the other.

I earned one pound and five shillings a month to start; the next year, one pound and ten shillings; and the third year, one pound and eighteen shilling: she won't give me the two pounds.

I left the farm after two and a half years, but she was not willing to have lost me.

I went to work for Mrs. Middleton in her house in Uplands in Swansea. I earned ten shilling a week – the going rate. I cleaned, washed and ironed there as well: I was their housemaid.

I arose about half-past seven. In the morning, I wore a long blue cotton frock with a long white pinafore. I lit the fires, including the one in the sitting room, every morning before they got up. I remember one night my clock had stopped and I had no idea of the time. I dressed and went downstairs only to find it was about three o'clock, so I went back to bed. I made breakfast and washed up. I cleaned the house, and washed the path from the gate to the front door on my hands and knees. After I cooked dinner and washed up, I changed into a black dress with a small frilly apron. Every Monday, I lit the fire in the wash house to boil water to wash the clothes. Mrs. Middleton cooked the dinner while I did the washing.

Mr. and Mrs. Middleton had a daughter; there's a pretty little girl she was. I fetched her from school every day at half-past three. She was very contrary and always wanted to go home a different way than me.

I lived in and had a nice bedroom. It was a treat to have a bathroom and water toilet: very few houses in Penclawdd had them then. I had Sunday afternoons off. The first time I went home, I didn't find out the time of the buses: I got off at Dunvant and walked through Three Crosses to Penclawdd; but afterwards, I learned the bus times and I caught the bus all the way to Penclawdd, which was one shilling and six pence return. I caught the two o'clock bus from Swansea and came back on the nine o'clock from Penclawdd. After I had worked there a while, I asked Mrs. Middleton if I could stay home on the Sunday night. She agreed, but when I returned on the Monday morning, the dirty supper dishes were waiting for me.

Mrs. Middleton's husband lost his job, so she was unable to keep me.

I then worked for Mrs. Hunt who also lived in Uplands. She was very fussy. There was an oilcloth on the floor, which I polished on my hands and knees until I could see my reflection in it. Oh! She was a tarter.

Mrs. Hunt had a lodger staying with her – a Scotch woman. You'd swear that she was the maid and not me: she wore a little dust cap on her head and used to spring-clean every room every week.

On Sunday morning, Mrs. Hunt made a big pan of dough and put it to rise when she was in chapel, and cooked it when she came home. I didn't have very good food there but what I did enjoy was my breakfast: she used to fry bacon and cook rounds of apple in the fat; she didn't like cream so I had it on my porridge. There was another lodger staying there in the front room – a retired bank clerk. On Sundays, Mrs. Hunt made a great big bakestone loaf cake with only one egg. The lodger's supper was a piece of this dry cake and a glass of water.

I had been working there for a year when I had a terrible pain in my side. My mother came to Mrs. Hunt's to explain that I was unwell, but Mrs. Hunt was annoyed that my mother had told her. My mother said to me, 'You are not to go back there again,' and so I left and found employment in Mrs. Samuel's home.

This was the last place I worked in. Mr. and Mrs. Wilfred Samuel were very nice people. He was an estate agent and often came home from work with muddy boots after being on the land.

There was lovely food there: Mrs. Samuel had been a cook before her marriage. I cooked the dinner and made Welsh cakes, but Mrs. Samuel did the rest of the cooking.

I wore the same uniform there as at my other employers' houses. Mrs. Samuel had a lovely big silver tray, which I used to carry the tea into them on. It was so heavy it was a wonder that I never dropped it! I was at it all day, but I could sit down after tea and was lucky to have every evening off; some girls in service only had an afternoon off. I had Wednesday afternoon off but I couldn't afford to go home. Mrs. Samuel encouraged me to go out on my time off. I had no company in the evenings but I used to visit some of my friends in the afternoons. Maggie – who later married Howard Evans – worked for Mrs. Crooks in a big house nearby. I also used to go and see Rosalind Guy, my friend from Penclawdd, who was in service in a house in Swansea.

Mr. and Mrs. Samuel had a daughter – Miss Nancy. She was going with a boy that her mother didn't like, but despite that, she married him later, after I'd left.

I married from there. Mrs Samuel gave me a dinner service as a wedding present, which she had bought in Cardiff while visiting her sister. Her sister gave me half a teaset. My husband, Philip John Hughes, was a butcher from Llanmorlais. We set up home there."

3.

Going to the Flicks

Music halls – and in a sense, public houses – were the closest thing Victorians had to public entertainment, but nearly all were built in towns or cities, even after their transformation into respectable variety theatre. The inhabitants of suburbia and rural areas therefore created their own entertainment. In 1908, a brief roller skating craze hit Britain from America, but this soon gave way to another American import, the moving pictures, nicknamed the movies or the flicks.

Initially, converted halls, etc. were used as makeshift cinemas, but the danger posed by highly combustible film in often inadequate buildings resulted in the passing of the Cinematography Act of 1909, which required local councils to license cinemas.

Many existing theatres and music halls were licensed. The first purpose-built cinema was possibly The Phoenix, built about 1910, in East Finchley, North London, followed by many more in cities, towns and now, suburbia. Atmosphere was created for the silent film by appropriate accompaniment, on the piano, or sometimes by quite large orchestras. Subtitles, and sound effects made by various means – some very primitive but effective – were also used. Legendary stars were born of the silver screen. At the start of his film career, in the early 1910s, Charlie Chaplin charmed the audiences with his endearing character dressed in a small bowler hat, slack trousers, long-toed boots, cane, and with a smudge moustache, flat-footed gait, and imperturbable impassivity. Greta Lovisa Gustafsson, a native of Stockholm, Sweden, starred in her first film, *Luffar Peter – Peter and the Tramp* – in July 1922. She was accepted as a student at the Royal Dramatic Theatre Academy and many films

Charlie Chaplin.

Greta Garbo.

followed. She stunned the film world with her beauty and on 9 November 1923, legally changed her name to Greta Garbo.

This entertainment was a new pleasure, but it wasn't always the films that attracted the young audience: a chance of a kiss and cuddle in the dark away from the watchful eye of parents was greatly appreciated. However, this in turn was frowned upon by the establishment and decency supervisors were sometimes appointed who, without warning, switched on the house lights to ensure rectitude.

In the late 1920s, synchronized sound-on-disk was invented to accompany films, and a little later, sound on film was perfected; the talkies had arrived heralding the golden age of cinema. Warner Brothers' *The Jazz Singer* opened in The Warner Theatre on Broadway on 6 October 1927. It was an all-singing film with no script, but the star, Al Jolson, sang new songs and old favourites and ad-libbed during the action of the story on the Vitaphone.[1] *Lights of New York* starring Helen Costello, again by Warner Brothers, was featured at The Strand Theatre, New York on 6 July 1928. It was the first one hundred percent all-talking film and was criticized by the *Variety* magazine as 'One hundred percent crude.' The world's centre of moving picture production evolved in Southern California. Los Angeles' climate of continuous sunshine and clear atmosphere made ideal conditions for perfect filming. Within a convenient distance lay ocean, mountains, desert and jungles of tropical swamp lands, and untouched forests, providing natural settings for a wealth of thrilling stories – cowboys and Indians, gangsters, musicals, period films, etc. Moreover, picturesque characters such as American Indians, Mexicans, and Orientals of the seaport towns were easily available for casting. The 1930s saw a dramatic growth of the film industry based in Hollywood, now a suburb of Los Angeles, and to a lesser degree in Elstree, Shepherd's Bush, and Pinewood Studios in Britain.

The talkies and Art Deco evolved almost simultaneously, and the latter's unashamedly modern style seemed suitably up-to-date for this new form of entertainment. Art Deco belonged to a world of luxury and decadence and the cinemas' chosen names – Plaza, Regal, Embassy – echoed the theme of wealth and grandeur. The Phoenix in East Finchley was modernized in 1938 and given an Art Deco makeover. Other more exotic themes were also used such as Egyptian, and Italian Renaissance. The populace was happy to escape from the stuffy mock-Tudor style previously favoured for houses, shops, pubs, etc. Large, plain façades were rendered in cream faïence-ware and Oscar Deutsch's Odeon chains usually had flat-topped towers, often floodlit at night, to attract attention. Oscar Deutsch was born at Balsall Heath, Birmingham, in 1893, to a Jewish scrap merchant, Leopold Deutsch, a Hungarian by birth, and Leah Cohen, a Jewish emigrant from Poland. In just ten years from 1930/31 to his death in 1941, he demonstrated breathtaking energy, opening two hundred and fifty-eight Odeons throughout Britain. The

---

1. Proprietary name for an early process of sound film recording in which the soundtrack is recorded on discs.

word Odeon probably came from odeum – a building for the performance of vocal and instrumental music especially among the ancient Greeks and Romans. Oscar Deutsch's name was very cleverly incorporated into the acronym Odeon – Oscar Deutsch Entertains Our Nation. His chain was bought by J. Arthur Rank in 1942 and was part of the Rank Organisation until 1998.

Interiors were equally as exotic as exteriors with large foyers, luxurious powder rooms, cafés, restaurants, and sometimes ballrooms. The auditoriums were described as 'acres of seats in a garden of dreams'.

A wealth of new stars appeared and were idolized, such as Clarke Gable, Vivien Leigh, Rita Hayworth, Robert Mitchum, Elizabeth Taylor, Richard Burton – the list was endless – but many already established in the silent films adapted to the talkies. Greta Garbo's fans must have waited with bated breath to hear her voice for the first time; they were not disappointed. When she starred in her first sound film, *Anna Christie*, the 23 October 1929 issue of *Variety* announced, 'Garbo talks OK.' So great became her fame that from 12 April 1932 she was billed as just 'Garbo'. However, it was not until 1940 that Charlie Chaplin deviated from the character he created in his silent films.

Each programme consisted of a main *A* film, a supporting *B* film, a trailer, sometimes a serial usually on matinee performances, and a newsfilm – good value for money! With the rationing of many foods during the Second World War, the Ministry of Food controlled food supplies. Lord Woolton, Minister of Food, organized nutritionists to plan the nation's need. As well as newspapers, recipe leaflets and broadcasts on BBC radio, cinema screens were used to give the public information on the Food Facts. It wasn't until the early 1950s that television appeared in homes – many bought especially for viewing the coronation of Queen Elizabeth II – and so the newsreels, Pathe News and Gaumont-British, were the main source of pictorial news. 'To supply the news-films, operators were stationed all over the world, watching for events of local or general interest, and their films were sent in to their news service headquarters much as reporters gathered news for the daily papers. When something of unusual importance occurred, the films were dispatched with haste, developed, printed and distributed with such speed that audiences in cities hundreds of miles apart saw views of a great fire before the ruins had ceased smoking.'[2]

Over twenty cinemas in and around Swansea existed at one time. Many mushroomed in suburbia and nearby villages. There was The

---

2. *The Book Of Knowledge*, Vol. 5 (96-97 Farringdon Street, London E.C.4) p. 2088.

The Tivoli cinema, Pontarddulais.

Uplands Picture House in Uplands; The Maxime renamed The Odeon in Sketty; The Tower in Townhill; The Tivoli and The Regent in Mumbles; The Regal and The Gem in Morriston; The Tivoli in Cwmbwrla; The Electra in Gorseinon; The Tivoli in Pontarddulais; The Pictorium in St. Thomas.

Rose Young – Usherette

In 1948, Rose Young worked for a short time as an usherette in The Manor cinema in Manselton. "I went to watch a film in The Manor and saw an advert on the screen, 'Usherettes wanted,' and I thought I'd give it a try. It was a very modern cinema with two different programmes every week. I started my working day in the morning, travelling there by bus. Every morning I swept the floor of the cinema and once a week scrubbed it on my hands and knees; it was not an easy job sweeping and cleaning underneath all those seats. During the performances, I watched the kids; they were very naughty and created so much noise. The cinema had a shop in the foyer so I didn't sell sweets, etc. on a tray. One holiday, the front of the building and foyer flooded and I had to get rid of all that water. The job was very hard work with very poor pay, and so I left after a few months and went to work in Mettoys where I stayed for twenty-five years."

Frank Firth, proprietor of Twin Radios Supplies, an electrical repair shop in Pontarddulais Road, Gorseinon, recounts the origin of Gorseinon's Lido cinema. "My grandparents, Thomas and Martha Richards moved from Swansea to Weston-Super-Mare, in Devon. He built a few houses there, but was enticed back to the booming industry and increasing population of South Wales, and settled in Gorseinon. He leased some land in Western Square, West Street and built a roller skating rink – roller-skating being the craze at the time – and named it The Palace. His three children, Thomas, Frank and my mother, Phoebe Amanda were involved in the business; Thomas became known locally as *Tommy the Rink*. With the advent of the silent pictures, the building was converted into a cinema, and live entertainment hall. The family continued their involvement in the new venture; my mother used to play the piano to accompany the silent films. With the coming of the talkies, the building was given an Art Deco makeover, and renamed The Lido."

Penclawdd's first cinema was owned by Frank Hayward. It was housed in a zinc and wood lean-to at the back of Tom Booley's bicycle shop in Belle Vue, and contained about fifty, hard, wooden seats. Griff Rees spent many happy hours there. "It only had silent films: it was before the time of talkies. Mr Hayward's wife played appropriate music on the piano to accompany the film during the performance. Mr. Hayward was in charge of sound effects: thunder and lightning were simulated by pounding metal sheets; and the sound of rain was produced by throwing rice on metal sheet. It was very effective and worked well. I used to go with my mother and grandmother. My grandmother couldn't see, so my mother used to read the subtitles out to her." Win Walters, née Eaton, was also a fan. "The cinema was open once a week – on Saturday afternoons I think. Serials were shown, and at a very exciting moment – such as a train falling off a bridge – up would flash on the screen, 'to be continued,' and we would have to hold our breath for another week."

By the early 1920s, Booley had closed his shop. The premises became the home of Ernest Ratti and family and also housed his business – an ice-cream parlour. His oldest son Rudolph remembers, "We lived at the back of the premises and on the first floor. Only a curtain separated Frank Hayward's cinema from the kitchen, and when a breeze blew the curtain, we would be immediately transported from the kitchen to the cinema. When the cinema closed, my father bought the whole premises, and later, when I was about eleven, the house next door as well."

A venue for the talkies posed no problem for Penclawdd. A purpose-built cinema was not needed as the larger of two Memorial Halls, situated in the centre of the village, was utilized. The halls had been erected in 1921 by Penclawdd Miners' Welfare Association – later operating as Penclawdd Welfare Association – in memory of the men of the village who had been killed in the First World War. In the early 1930s, the Gower Rural District Council, in compliance with the Cinematography Act of 1909, granted a cinematography licence to William John Morgan in respect of the Memorial Hall, Penclawdd, and the cinema was born.

It was simply known as the Pictures. Ruby Skinner, when a pupil at Penclawdd Elementary School, remembers teacher, Gwynfor Jenkins, announcing, "The talkies have come to Penclawdd; they start tomorrow night but you can't go because it's a war film and not suitable for children." Gwynfor gave good advice as the cinema's maiden performance was *All Quiet on the Western Front*. The film was a dramatization of Erich Maria Remarque's book *Im Westen Nichts Neues* (Nothing New on the Western Front). Its subject was the First World War: in 1914, a group of German teenagers volunteered for action on the Western Front – between France and Flanders – but they became disillusioned however, and tragically, none survived. Made in 1930, and starring Lew Ayres, Louise Wolheim, Slim Summerville, John Wray, Raymond Griffiths, Russell Gleason, Ben Alexander and Beryl Mercer, it was a landmark of American cinema, and Universal's biggest and most serious undertaking until the 1960s. It seems that the film fixed in millions of minds the popular image of what it was like in the trenches. Erich Maria Remarque wrote of his work, 'This book is intended neither as an accusation nor as a confession, but simply as an attempt to account of a generation that was destroyed by the war – even those of it who survived the shelling.' Born in Osnabrück in 1899, he was exiled from Nazi Germany and deprived of his citizenship. He lived in America and Switzerland until his death in 1970.

Many projectionists were employed during the cinema's nearly thirty-year life span. Edna Jenkins recalls, "My brother, Charles Lewis was a projectionist in Penclawdd cinema at the very beginning. He, Glanrhyd Austin and two other friends, all in their teens, formed a group – like the 'Beatles' – and entertained the audience half-an-hour before the film performances; they were very popular and filled the hall. As did the majority of village children, Kathleen Guy, née Williams, attended the cinema regularly. "I can remember Mr. Morgan being in the pay-box. Although we were still in school he made us buy adult tickets. We used to dress up to go to the Pictures and he probably thought we looked older than we actually were. We thought this unfair and my friend, Gwenda, said to him, *'Ond wi'n mynd i'r ysgol!'* (But I go to school.) He replied, *'Mae Mr. James yn mynd i'r ysgol hefyd.'* (Mr. James goes to school as well). Mr. James was the headmaster of Penclawdd Elementary School." Miriam Lewis, Kathleen's twin sister adds, "We only went to the Pictures on Saturdays: we were not cinema people." John Henry Evans worked as projectionist, before being killed in action serving his country in the Second World War. Hubert Jenkins, brother of Gwynfor, operated the machines, and was later employed as manager in the public hall cinema in Brynamman. Kathleen remembers projectionist and manager, Robert Henry (Bob) Beckett. "As a young man, Mr. Beckett was a postman in Penclawdd. He was a fine chap. My Aunty Kate (Hagan) was employed to clean the cinema. She was a very hard worker and used to scrub the wooden floors on her hands and knees. Mr. Beckett used to help her clean; it was not his job so he didn't have to." When in his early twenties, Gilbert Davies started working in the Pictures. "I cut the audience's tickets in half and gave half back to them, when they came in, and showed them to their seats with a torch. I was, I suppose, an usherette. I also used to spray air freshener in the hall with those old-fashioned sprays that were used for fly killer; it was a nice smell but the audience would often have wet hair! I worked with Mr Beckett, and afterwards with Ivor Howells, who lived in Barham House. He was caretaker of Bethel Chapel, but also worked as a projectionist. On fine summer evenings the Pictures was full. They were not down the beaches; I couldn't work it out as it was boiling outside. But of course, it was a way of life, and the films were so good then – with Errol Flynn, Alan Ladd."

Eileen Foote, née Humphries – Book-keeper, Typist and Cashier

By the early 1940s, Eileen was greatly involved in the running of the cinema. "When I started, my salary was just over one pound a week, and when I finished in the early 1950s, it had increased to two pounds and nineteen shillings. Saturday morning seats cost six pence; at the two evening performances, the wooden front seats cost one shilling and the back comfortable seats, known as *the plush*, cost one shilling and nine pence. Our local policeman, Sergeant Lord, took an active interest in the smooth running of the cinema. He stood at the door checking that all who entered had tickets, which he ripped in half on entry. One evening, he had another appointment and he asked me to, 'Cut the tickets Eileen, until I come back.' I considered it a great honour that he trusted me to do so."

During the war years, soldiers of many regiments were stationed consecutively at the camps situated at the west-end of the village. Coupled with the Royal Artillery Regiment stationed on Salthouse Point in Crofty, they greatly swelled the population of Penclawdd, and cinema attendance. On Saturday night – the busiest night – the queues were often fifty yards long, and many were disappointed in failing to obtain seats. Eileen talks of one cold winter's night when American soldiers were stationed at the camps. "*Snow White and the Seven Dwarfs* was showing at the cinema. It was snowing so heavily that we couldn't open the main door for them to come in, so we opened the anteroom door. They were like children: they hadn't seen snow before. They were skating up the road and only little black faces could be seen; they were covered in snow. It was so appropriate that we were showing *Snow White*." 'The latter was Walt Disney's first feature cartoon, a mammoth enterprise which no one in the business thought would work. The romantic leads were wishy-washy but the splendid songs and the marvellous comic and villainous characters turned the film into a world-wide box-office bombshell, which is almost as fresh today as when it was made.'[3]

By the late 1950s, the price of cinema seats had increased to:

'Prices of Admission: 2/-, 1/6 and 1/-
Half Price for Children First House Saturdays only
No Half Price for School Children over 16
No Half Price for Children under 16 who are working'

On Friday and Saturday, 23 and 24 May 1958, the Pictures featured *Fire Down Below*. Made by Columbia/Warwick in 1957 in Technicolor, produced by Irving Allen and Albert R. Broccoli and directed by Robert Parrish, it was a screen play by Irwin Shaw based on a novel by Max Catto. It starred:

Rita Hayworth as Irena
Robert Mitchum[4] as Felix Bowers

---

3. *Halliwell's Film & Video Guide 2001* (77-85 Fulham Palace Road, Hammersmith, London W6 8JB), p. 750.
4. (1917-1997) Born in Bridgeport, Connecticut, he has been described as a sleepy-eyed American star, sometimes hiding his considerable talents behind a pretence of carelessness.

Rear view of the Pictures – larger building in the background, facing terraced houses.

Jack Lemmon[5] as Tony
Herbert Lom as Harbour Master
Bonar Colleano as Lieutenant Sellers
Bernard Lee as Doctor Sam Blake
Edric Connor as Jimmy Jean

Rita Hayworth was born Margarita Carmen Cansino, in Brooklyn, New York to an American mother and a Spanish gypsy father. Starting her career as her father's dancing partner, she was often ill at ease with dialogue, and best in film roles that exploited her dancer's expressive movement. It was one of her great frustrations that the studio insisted she be dubbed in musical numbers, but to her credit, she mastered synchronizing her motions with each *vocal ghost* she ever had. She was unquestionably one of the most beautiful actresses ever to grace the silver screen and became known as *The Love Goddess*. Following her role

---

5. (1925-2001) Born in an elevator at a Newton, Massachusetts Hospital, he was the son of a president of a doughnut company. He starred in many films winning an Oscar for his role in *Save the Tiger* (1973). An accomplished self-taught pianist, he wrote the theme for the movie *Tribute* (1980).

Rita Hayworth – The Love Goddess.

in *Miss Sadie Thompson* in 1953, Rita was absent from the screen for four years. Staying in Paris at the time, she was lured back to work by the director who gave her the script and offered her the role of Irena, originally intended for Ava Gardener. It seems the friendships she developed with Parrish, Mitchum and Lemmon must have alleviated her fears of stepping before the camera again. Her costumes were by Balmain of Paris and Bermans of London. Shot on location in Trinidad and at Warwick Film Studios in London, *Fire Down Below* was a fast-paced adventure yarn laced around a taut interlude of high drama: partners in a Caribbean fishing and smuggling business fall out over a woman. The song *Fire Down Below* – made famous by the film – was composed by Lester Lee and Ned Washington and sung by Peggy Lee.

The village proprietors advertised the forthcoming films in their shops. The poster of week commencing 19 May 1958, the property of Morgan and Kathleen Guy, is a legacy of those times. Kathleen explains, "We'd have the posters on the Monday to display in the window of our shoe shop. As a 'thank you' we'd have two complementary tickets for the cinema, but to be used mid-week only, and not on Saturdays."

Penclawdd Welfare Association

MEMORIAL HALL

Week Commencing MAY 19th, 1958

MONDAY and TUESDAY

Continuous Performance Mondays from 4.45 p.m.   (Tuesday 6.45 p.m.)

George Nader, Phyllis Thoxter and Tim Hovey in

MAN AFRIAD

Also Zizi Jean Marie, Eddie Constantine in FOLIES BERGERE - Technicolor

WEDNESDAY and THURSDAY (6.45p.m.)

Richard Conte, Diane Foster and Cary Grant in

THE BROTHERS RICO

ALSO FULL SUPPORTING PROGRAMME

FRIDAY (6.30) and SATURDAY (3.45 p.m. & 7 p.m.)

Rita Hayworth and Robert Mitchum in

FIRE DOWN BELOW

Also Charles Starret in TAKING SIDES

Prices of Admission: 2/-., 1/6 and 1/-

Half Price for Children First House Saturdays' only.   No Half Price for School Children over 16

No Half Price for Children under 16 who are working

Note misspelling of AFRAID.

With more and more homes boasting televisions in the late 1950s, cinema audience figures decreased in number. Many of its faithful attendees hoped that the Pictures would continue operating, but it was, by now, running at a loss and so in about 1960, they had to accept its inevitable closure.

Ivor Lloyd – Cinema Projectionist

Before the First World War, Tom Foy erected a small picture house near Gowerton South Railway Station. The building was acquired in 1920 by F. Harry Thomas who reopened it in 1921, naming it The Tivoli. About two years later, the new cinema proprietor employed young Ivor Lloyd.

Ivor Lloyd lived his formative years in Mill Street, Gowerton. "When I was a young boy in Gowerton School, I saved up to buy a projector for seven shillings and six pence. I saved more pennies and bought a second projector the next Christmas. I used to run shows in my big kitchen. I heard that Harry Thomas, who owned The Tivoli cinema in Gowerton, had some cinema films for sale. So, I saved again and bought two shillings worth of films from him. Eventually, I was buying so many films that he said, 'You'd better have a job with me in case I have competition.'

My first job at the cinema was selling chocolates; I was a chocolate boy. My boss owned horses, which he kept in a field he hired, by the GWR (Great Western Railway) Station in Gowerton. A corner of the field was boggy and he made me dig trenches to drain away the water. I started at the bottom and I went up to the very top: you couldn't get a larger cinema than The Plaza, in Swansea, where I later worked – it seated three thousand.

I was never trained as a projectionist: it was just in me. At The Tivoli, I worked from nine in the morning to eleven at night, for less than two pounds a week. On Monday mornings, I joined the different parts of the film: one film could be in twelve boxes. Parts one and two were put on one projector and parts three and four on the next, and so on. The performances were three hours long and consisted of a top feature film, a second feature film, the news and two serials. The only films I really used to enjoy were the musicals, such as Fred Astaire[6] and Ginger Rogers[7] in *Top Hat*.[8]

---

6. (1899-1987) Born Frederick Austerlitz, in Omaha, Nebraska, he delighted two generations with his dancing, half-spoken singing and good humour.
7. (1911-1995). Born Virginia McNath, American actress, comedienne and dancer, famous for her partnership with Fred Astaire in 1930s musicals.
8. RKO's 1935 film of true love, complicated by mistaken identities. It made famous the song, *Cheek to Cheek*.

The silent films were accompanied by a piano on the balcony, and on Saturday nights, an orchestra. In the first talkies, the action on the screen was synchronized to sound via sixteen-inch gramophone records attached to the projector. Later, sound on film was devised. The Tivoli had all sorts of sound equipment – a bit of this and a bit of that.

Harry Thomas decided to enlarge the cinema and add a billiard hall with full-size tables. I was involved in the alterations: I did everything there. He bought wooden panels from the *Canopic* – a White Star liner – docked at the ship breaking-up yard, Giant's Grave, in Briton Ferry. I drove an old Ford to Swansea to collect cement and sand. When we started fixing the panels to the walls we realized that we had a problem: the contour of a ship is not straight and the panels were made to follow the rake of the ship, so we could only use half of them.

Some nights the floor was cleared of chairs and roller-skating took place.

During the war, I was carrying a film to the projection room one Monday morning when a blue plane flew over. I waved and somebody in the plane waved back. Within a quarter of an hour, they had bombed Llandarcy Refinery.

I was getting ready to go to work one morning when a neighbour informed me that The Tivoli had burned down overnight. I arrived to find Harry Thomas in the midst of the ruins. He said, 'Oh! What we have worked for has all gone.'

Now unemployed, I was asked to train two fellows to be projectionists in Scard's cinema – The Astoria – in Milford Haven. The Germans were bombing Neyland and the two Irishmen who worked in the cinema had returned home. The cinema had good sound equipment – Western Electric. I had been there for about a year, when I had a phone call from Sid Griffiths, the manager of The Plaza in Swansea, offering me the job of projectionist there. When I told Scard that I was leaving, he nearly had a fit. I was married to Lavinia by now and living in Llotrog, Penclawdd. 'Stay and I'll build you a bungalow and you can live here,' he told me. But I was not interested and took the job in Swansea."

The centre of Swansea boasted many picture houses. The Swansea Pavilion, a flat-iron shaped building, filling the wedge shape created by the Prince of Wales Road filtering off High Street, was built in 1888 at a cost of ten thousand pounds. In 1892 it was renamed The Swansea Empire Music Hall. 1900 saw the opening of another Empire Theatre in Oxford Street, and so in about 1904 the former became known as The Palace of Varieties. 1911 saw yet another change of name, The People's Bioscope Palace,[9] when it became one of the early pioneers of moving

---

9. A kind of early film projector and is also a South African name for cinema.

films. It continued as a cinema until 1930 when it alternated between variety and cinema. Finally closing as a cinema in the early 1950s, it reverted to The Palace again in 1953. Saturday, 11 April 1914 saw the opening of The Elysium on the east-side of High Street as part of the capacious Dockers Union Hall. In the latter half of 1929, it seems that it had the distinction of featuring the first all-talkie film to be shown in

High Street and Empire Theatre.

The People's Bioscope Palace.

The Palace as it is today – awaiting its fate.

The Elysium – First World War.

The Picture House.

The Star Theatre – later The Rialto.

Swansea – *The Donovan Affair*. Closing as a cinema on 12 August 1960, it was then used as a bingo hall. A little further down the street southwards was The Picture House. Set back from the road, it was approached by a corridor just north of Henry A. Chapman, Photographer and Artist. Chapman's was first opened in 1853, and during its ninety-eight years, established fame throughout Wales. The Empire Theatre occasionally featured films during the Second World War. The Star Theatre, in Wind Street, was later used as a cinema and named The Rialto.

Saturday, 4 February 1931 saw the opening of The Plaza cinema in Northampton Place/Picton Place – later The Kingsway – with an impressive ceremony. It seems that the invited dignitaries of Swansea were unaware of how narrowly they missed viewing a blank screen. Dangerously near the commencement of the show, the chosen film *King of Jazz* starring Paul Whiteman, and his band, John Boles, Laura La Plante and Jeanie Lang, could not be found. It was eighteen-year-old Ted Hopkins, a previous employee of The Rialto cinema, who saved the day. The opening date had been brought forward before the interior was completed, and Ted found the film under a bag of cement. He managed to fix it into the projector just in the nick of time.

The largest cinema in Wales – seating three thousand – and considered the poshest in Swansea, The Plaza was a splendid example of Italian

The Plaza café.

South Wales Evening Post, Saturday, 2 September 1939.

The Plaza cinema photographed by Fred Neal. Note relief bus on right.

Tom Jenkins at the organ of The Plaza cinema.

Renaissance-style architecture. From the entrance, a grand marble staircase swept up to a first floor foyer graced with an illuminated glass fountain, plush seating, a gleaming polished wood floor, and huge chandeliers hanging from gilded ceilings. All were enhanced by light streaming in through stained glass windows. On a wall hung a metal plaque which retold the poem, *The Women of Mumbles Head*, by the noted poet, Clement Scott, whose dramatic text achieved considerable acclaim. The poem immortalized the heroism of Jessie Ace, and her sister, daughters of the Mumbles lighthouse keeper, Abraham Ace, off Mumbles Head, in the late nineteenth century:

> 'Bring novelists, your note book, bring dramatists, your pen,
> And I'll tell you a simple story of what women do for men.
> It's only a tale of a lifeboat, the dying and the dead,
> Of a terrible storm and shipwreck, that happened off Mumbles Head.
> . . .
> There by the rocks in the breakers these sisters, hand in hand,
> Beheld once more that desperate man, who struggled to reach the land,
> 'Twas only aid he wanted to help him across the wave,
> What are a couple of women? Well more than three craven men
> Who stood by the shore with chattering teeth, refusing to stir – and then
> Off went the women's shawls, sir, in a second they're torn and rent,
> Then knotting them into a rope of love, straight into the sea they went.
>
> "Come back," cried the lighthouse-keeper, "for God's sake, girls, come back."
> As they caught the waves on their foreheads, resisting the fierce attack.
> "Come back," moaned the grey-haired mother, as she stood by the angry sea.
> "If the waves take you my darlings, there's nobody left but me."
> "Come back," said the three strong soldiers, who still stood faint and pale,
> "You will drown if you face the breakers, you will fail if you brave the gale."
> "Come back," said the girls, "we will not, go tell it to all the town,
> We'll lose our lives, God willing, before that man shall drown."
>
> "Give one more knot to the shawls, Bess, give one strong clutch of your hand,
> Just follow me, brave, to the shingle, and we'll bring him safe to land.
> Wait for the next wave, darling, only a minute more,
> And I'll have him safe in my arms, dear, and we'll drag him safe to shore."
> Up to the arms in the water, fighting it breast to breast
> They caught and saved a brother alive, God bless us, you know the rest –

Well, many a heart beat stronger, and many a tear was shed,
And many a glass was tossed right off to – 'The Women of Mumbles Head'.'

Apart from sweets, chocolates and ice-cream served by chocolate girls, food was not for sale in the cinema halls, but The Plaza boasted an excellent café situated off the first floor foyer. The majority of the populace smoked: in a sense it was considered an initiation into adulthood. It is only in latter years that smoking has been prohibited in cinemas. As the films rolled in the cavernous hall, smoke from countless cigarettes curled up through the beams of the projection lights, and disappeared silently into the lofty heights. In those far off days, the huge crowds that attended The Plaza were well entertained for the princely sum of six pence, or those that really wanted to *push the boat out* for better viewing, paid two shillings and four pence.

Lionel Thompson – Pageboy

Lionel Thompson – pageboy, with usherette.

Joan Pye, Lionel's sister, reminisces, "My dad found Lionel his first job as a can boy – making teas for the men building The Plaza. When the cinema opened, my brother was then fifteen and employed as a pageboy. When he was about sixteen, he left The Plaza to become a regular in the Army. He spent seven years in India, serving in the King's Shropshire Light Infantry. During the Second World War, he was evacuated from Dunkirk, came home, and later fought for his country in North Africa."

Ivor Lloyd – Projectionist

With the advent of the Second World War, Ted Hopkins was conscripted into the RAF, where he ferried aeroplanes to and from Gibraltar.

Ivor enjoyed working in The Plaza. "Stan Rees was the chief projectionist before my time there and his assistant, Ted Hopkins, had been called up. Tom Jenkins and some other men owned The Plaza and a few cinemas in the valleys, Barry, Porthcawl and Cardiff; Tom was the cinemas' area manager. A man called Arthur Austin came every so often to service the sound projectors in the Swansea area."

Arthur had been invited by Western Electric to convert silent cinemas in Britain and Ireland. He was one of eight to have helped pioneer the talkies, giving so much enjoyment to so many people. In 2003, he was awarded the heraldic shield by the Institution of Electrical Engineers (IEE) of which he had been a member since 1935. He died at the age of one hundred years in December 2003.

Cinema audience figures for 1935 were twenty million per week. Initially instructed to close, cinemas remained open during the war years and their attendance, at thirty million, was at an all-time high, whether to see flag-wavers such as *Went the Day Well*, or escapism such as *Gone With the Wind*. The most popular films were those from the United States, with lavish costumes and Technicolor. However, Hollywood's romanticized attempts to reflect the realities of life in occupied Europe and Britain, such as *Mrs. Miniver* starring Greer Garson,[10] were sometimes met with understandable derision and contempt.

"The first night I worked, the sirens sounded," says Ivor, "and I thought, 'I'm in a pickle now but nothing can happen to Ivor Lloyd; a bomb wouldn't drop on his head.' The sirens were to sound many nights. When they did, I superimposed a slide on the film stating that the sirens had sounded, but the show would continue, and those who wanted to leave were free to do so, but very few did: they probably thought they were safer inside than out. When the all-clear sounded – which was usually in about an hour's time – I superimposed another slide stating so. I often used to think of the consequences of a bomb dropping on the cinema, with all those people there. America had entered the war by then, and there were many American servicemen in Swansea. One night, a land mine exploded nearby; it was a terrific bang and shook the building. I had two boys helping me rewind the films, etc. One of them went white. I said, 'Don't worry. I go to chapel and a bomb won't drop on us.'

'Do you think so?' he said.

'Positive,' I replied, and that seemed to put him right.

I was paid eight pounds a week. This was the top rate as in some

---

10. (1903-1996) Red-headed Anglo-Irish leading lady, born in Essex. Her stage role, Mrs. Chipping in *Goodbye Mr. Chips* instigated a move to Hollywood where her gentle aristocratic good looks remained popular for ten years.

instances the projectionists were paid according to the seating – the capacity of the cinema – and this was the case in The Plaza. As I was a cinema projectionist, and over thirty-five years of age, I was in a reserved occupation: public entertainment was important for the morale of the people. But I did sign for the RAF, and did two fire watch nights, as well as my job.

Cinema work was always interesting but it entailed long hours: all Monday morning was involved in preparing the programme for the week; there were also the machines to look after and the fans to check. I worked six days a week from half-past nine in the morning and was not home until half-past eleven at night. During the war years, the films finished at half-past nine sharp because of the blackout regulations, and the streets were very dark.

I didn't have a dinner hour as such, but the cook in the café was very kind. She used to send me down a dinner in the lift and I used to stop it halfway near the projection room; I had it free, as my salary was so little. She phoned me in a panic one day. 'Come up quick!' she said, 'there's a rat in the freezer and I'm afraid to open it.' Up I went with my screwdriver. I removed the back of the freezer and there was the rat with her young; it was a big freezer with a powerful gas jet and the rat had made her nest there in the warm. I wouldn't touch them and phoned for the commissionaire to deal with it.

The two boys who worked with me operated the spotlights; two shone on the organist, Handel Evans, who played in-between performances. The organ rose from the basement on a lift, but stopped short of the stage. One night there was a Conservative meeting and I overran the trippers so that the organ and stage were parallel – a gap would have been dangerous. I told Handel to press the switch to let himself down, as I was busy. I was having a cup of tea later when Sid Griffiths burst into my room and shouted, 'He's still up there; he hasn't come down!' So I went under the screen and shouted to Handel, 'Press the switch!' and down he came. I wondered if they could hear me in the front seats. But that was not all: he had played five minutes more that his allocated time and we had to finish promptly because of the blackout.

There were three Belgian usherettes working there. Their families were fishing people and had sailed over before the start of war, anticipating Hitler's occupation of their country." Mary Richards[11] remembers seeing the film *The Snake Pit*, starring Olivia de Havilland, thanks to her aunt, Doreen Reisley, working as an usherette at the Plaza. "I was fourteen, and underage to see the film. It was about a girl becom-

---

11. See Chapter 4, pp. 165-170.

ing mentally deranged and having horrifying experiences in an institution.[12] I went with my mother, and my aunt told me to walk in on tip toes."

Occasionally, Ivor had a breath of fresh air during his working hours. "I sometimes used to go for a stroll around the town. One day, there were about half-a-dozen soldiers outside The Castle cinema: there was a large unexploded bomb in the middle of the road. I heard later that it had exploded and killed all the soldiers. Tom Jenkins was also the manager of The Elysium. He phoned me from his home in Llanelli and asked me to go and check the cinema as some bombs had fallen near it. I went to High Street and found that a bomb had dropped by the G.W.R. Station, the windows of W. H. Smith had blown out and the books were all over the road.

I was cycling home one evening, as usual, on the Three Crosses-Penclawdd road. Just before Brynhir, I was stopped by the flashing lights of a big lorry. Somebody shouted, 'Who goes there? I jumped off my bike and was faced by two RAF men pointing guns at me. 'Where are you going?' I was asked.

'I work in The Plaza in Swansea,' I replied.

The other fellow said, 'We'd better take him to the commanding officer.'

'Well, hurry up then,' I said, 'I want to go home.'

The next day I told Sid Griffiths of the incident and he gave me a roll of complementary tickets warning me to issue only three at a time. That night I was stopped by three RAF men – they were stationed at Fairwood Aerodrome – and I gave them the tickets. This continued for a few nights but soon the number of RAF men increased: word had got around that I was handing out complementary tickets. I continued to give them tickets during the war years, but, as instructed by Sid Griffiths, only three at a time.

At the end of the war, I gave notice and said that I was retiring from the cinema as I had a wife at home who never saw me until half-past eleven at night. I went to the Elba Steelworks in Gowerton and asked the chief engineer for a job.

He said, 'You have a good job in Swansea; you're the chief projectionist at The Plaza.'

I replied, 'Yes, but for the last twenty years I have hardly been home.'

---

12. 'A headline-hitting film, which made a stirring plea for more sympathetic treatment of mental illness. Very well made, and arrestingly acted, but somehow nobody's favourite movie.' *Halliwell's Film & Video Guide 2001* (77-85 Fulham Palace Road, Hammersmith, London W6 8JB), p. 750.

Sid Griffiths wouldn't accept my notice and phoned the owners in Cardiff. They said, 'Don't accept it until we come to Swansea.' They *flew* down and offered me more money.

I said, 'No. I've made up my mind that I'm going to leave the cinema business. I have a wife at home and I want to be with her.'

They asked me, 'Leave it for a fortnight so that we can send two fellows down to take over.' I did, and they were very thankful; that was the end of my cinema career."

Ray Stock – Assistant Projectionist

A year before Ivor retired, Ray Stock became one of his assistants. Like Ivor, Ray, a native of Swansea now residing in Penclawdd, acquired an interest in cinematography while still a schoolboy.

"My first experience of a projector was through a neighbour of mine – Austin Taylor – who was the chief projectionist at The Grand Theatre. Films were shown during the war years and for a little while afterwards; later, it was closed for a short time and then the Swansea City Council took over. While a pupil at Swansea Grammar School, I used to visit Austin in the evenings and help out in the projection room, which was in the top circle – *the gods*, as it was known in the theatre. One of the perks of the job was having free passes for the Swansea cinemas and other theatres. I went to The Empire Theatre regularly – it was marvellous. I remember the big Irishman outside – Con Murphy – who was the commissionaire.

I left school and went to work full-time at The Plaza. I should have stayed in school longer I suppose, but I got hooked on the cinema and enjoyed it. The Plaza was the most modern, up-market cinema in Swansea – a beautiful building inside and outside. Upstairs, above the entrance, was a mezzanine floor furnished with plush seating and many palm plants. At the end of the seat rows, and at the back of the hall, were double seats like small settees for couples – a unique feature of cinemas.

Kiosks in the foyer sold sweets, chocolates and ice-cream. During the intervals in-between films, the lights were switched on, the organ played, and chocolate girls sold chocolates, etc., and the usherettes shone torches to help the audience to their seats.

For about the first year, I worked with Ivor Lloyd. We shared our news films with The Rialto in Wind Street, and as junior, it was one of my jobs to take the reels down there. It was a tiny little place that had previously been The Star Theatre. The owner organized a band, and although the members were local ragamuffins, he transformed them into a smart group. I remember the projectionist at The Rialto – Fred – who used crutches.

I worked long hours. The first show started at two o'clock in the afternoon and the last finished at about ten o'clock; I worked through with a half-hour break. I had some evenings off and every Sunday. Cinemas were closed on Sundays. Every reel had to be rewound by hand and that was a devil of a job. I held the reel between fingers and thumb; they had to touch the sides of the film to feel for imperfections. At first they used to be cut by the sharp edge of the film, but fortunately in time they hardened. Where an imperfection occurred, the film was cut with a guillotine and joined by acetone. Sometimes the film would break in the projector and the film would have to be stopped and repaired. The audience would immediately start booing and whistling loudly, and so we had to work quickly to rethread the film. A great popular genre was the cowboy films – a wonderful subject – and at the end of the war, war films. We featured shorts – films of about a quarter of an hour – particularly at matinee performances.

Ted Hopkins returned after the war, and I worked with him for a couple of years until I left and joined the Royal Navy. I did not return to the cinema because I appreciated my evenings off too much."

Ted's service days over, he was re-employed by The Plaza on 2 October 1945, and promoted to being in charge of the projection room. The first film featured was *National Velvet* starring Elizabeth Taylor, his favourite film star. He was to stay there until the cinema's closure in 1965.

Early March 1951 saw the advent of the Sunday opening of Swansea cinemas. The *South Wales Evening Post* newspaper reported on 5 March 1951, 'Queues formed outside some of the Swansea cinemas, which opened yesterday for the first time on a Sunday. At one cinema – The Plaza – there was queuing for more than an hour, and the attendance was somewhere in the region of two thousand. . . . For many of these Sunday cinema-goers however, there was a disappointment to come. Sunday bus services in Swansea were not intended to cope with large numbers of people returning home late, and there were many who had to walk home, thus losing some of the spirit of entertainment.'

On 7 April 1965, the newspaper published the following article, 'For Swansea picture-goers, the coming Saturday will be a sad one, with The Plaza closing its doors to make way for modernization. . . . In post-war years the cinema industry has faced the competition of television and later, bingo. . . . Demolition starts on 20 April.'

Fred Neal, now eighty-four years of age and the oldest existing member of Swansea Camera Club, has lived in Pentregethin Road, Manselton, Swansea, since the age of four. It seems that Fred's photograph of The Plaza was the last to be taken. He recalls the occasion. "My wife, Violet, read in the local paper that The Plaza was shortly to be demolished. I thought that I'd better take a photograph of it before it was too late – one of my purposes in photography is to record buildings, etc. I went to The Plaza and the sign was still there advertising the cinema's last performance on 10th April 1965 – the Certificate A film, *A Shot in the Dark*, starring Peter Sellers and Elke Sommer. In photography it is very important to get the exposure absolutely right; if it's not so, it can't be printed. I was using a Rolleiflex twin lens reflex camera at the time, and a hand-held exposure meter to evaluate the light. I set up my camera but unknown to me, by the time I had taken the photograph, the clouds had come over the sun and the lighting was wrong. I had underexposed the negative. The following day I developed the picture in my dark room at home, but my wife realizing that something was wrong asked, 'What's the matter, love?'

I replied, 'I've underexposed it; I can't print it,' because in those days, only soft, normal or hard paper existed and the underexposed negative would not have printed on them.

Now, how am I convinced that that photograph was one of the last, if not the last that was taken of The Plaza? When I took my photograph, only the façade of the cinema was left: the back had been demolished. I went down the following day to re-take my photo but when I arrived, there was no Plaza: it had all been knocked down. Because of the traffic, the road would have to have been cordoned off, and that could only have been done at night.

Fortunately we now have multigrade paper, and so years and years after taking my photograph of The Plaza I have been able to print it off, putting multigrade on maximum hard grade."

In Fred's opinion Swansea Camera Club is the oldest camera club in the world. He feels that its origins were instigated by an article in the *Cambrian* newspaper. He explains, "A few business men who had been running a small camera club featured an article in the *Cambrian* newspaper on 3rd February 1861 inquiring if any were interested in enlarging their club for Swansea and District."

The Grand Theatre was built upon the site of the former Drill Hall in Singleton Street. It was officially opened by the renowned prima donna, Madam Adelina Patti on Monday, 26 July 1897. It closed as a *live* theatre with a production of the pantomime *Babes in the Wood* on 12 January 1934, except for a week in the following March when the Swansea Drama Society performed – a previous arrangement. It seems the reasons for closing were dwindling numbers in audiences and a very severe 'flu epidemic. It was bought by Globe Cinema Co. Ltd., Cardiff, owned by the Willis family, well-known Cardiff cinema owners. Reopening on 15 January 1934 as The New Grand Cinema, it was sometimes called The Swansea Cinema in the late 1930s. However, The Grand continued to play host to the Swansea Welsh Drama Society's Drama Week until 1939. On week commencing 4 September 1939, The Grand featured *The Mikado*, the first Gilbert and Sullivan opera to be brought to the screen. Late December 1947 saw its demise as a cinema when it reverted to *live* theatre again – apart from featuring a few films between 1959 and 1963.

The Music Hall, later renamed The Albert Hall – situated at the corner of Craddock Street and De la Beche Road – officially opened in May 1864 for every conceivable occasion: public meetings, banquets, concerts, etc. On 1 April 1929, *The Jazz Singer* was featured and within a month was booked at The Regent in Mumbles. Frank Firth (of Twin Radio Supplies, Gorseinon) remembers, "As a young child, I was taken to see *The Jazz Singer* in Mumbles, by my father. I wasn't really interested in the film as it was nearly all singing and I preferred cowboy films." 1977 saw the demise of The Albert Hall as a cinema with the

The Music Hall, later The Albert Hall cinema.

The Carlton cinema advertising film 'Fifty Fathoms Deep'.

showing of *Suspiria* – a thriller starring Jessica Harper, Alida Valli and Joan Bennett. It is now a bingo hall.

The Carlton cinema in Oxford Street opened on 31 January 1914. It was described as the most sumptuous picture palace in Wales. In the style of the theatre of the period, it is the finest of the four large buildings that the notable Welsh architect, Sir Charles Tamlin Ruthen, designed for Swansea. The front section was purpose-built to house a shop, dining room, and tearoom, on five floors – a unique feature in early cinema history. It closed on 29 October 1977 with the film *Sinbad and the Eye of the Tiger* starring Patrick Wayne, Taryn Power and Jane Seymour. The building lay empty for many years before housing Waterstones bookshop.

With the exception of The Picture House, the cinemas in Swansea miraculously survived the German bombings of the town.

Gwyneth Crowley – Usherette

In 1934, Gwyneth's career in the Swansea cinemas happened by chance – being in the right place at the right time.

"I lived in Colliers Row in Cockett, Swansea. My father had an accident in Garngoch Colliery No. 1 on my fifth birthday; a lump of coal fell on his back and broke his spine. He died three weeks later in the old Swansea Hospital. A few years later, my mother remarried and we went to live in St. Thomas. I was very lucky in having a wonderful stepfather.

After my grandfather died, my grandmother opened a little shop – selling sweets and groceries – in her front parlour in her house in St. Thomas. One day, I went to her shop and found Jack Rees, the projectionist of The Grand, sitting there. He asked my grandmother, 'Who is this lady?'

'My granddaughter,' she replied.

'Would you like to work in the cinema?' he said to me.

'Yes,' I said, 'I think I would.'

'How old are you?'

'Eighteen on Saturday.'

He told me that if he put a word in for me, would I be prepared to go for an interview. I agreed.

My mother bought her meat from Mr. Nichollas' stall in Swansea Market. On a Saturday, I used to help out on the stall – sweep up and scrub the boards. The other girl who worked there was paid twelve shillings and six pence, but he didn't pay me: I liked working there; I did it for the fun of it. I had only just put on my overalls one day when my mother came to the stall and told me, 'There's a letter for you from The Grand asking you to go for an interview. I've brought your frock, shoes, hat and gloves.' I went to the market toilet, quickly changed, and went.

I was taken on as an usherette. I cleaned every morning. I swept the wooden floors, mopped them, and cleaned the brass. I went home and my mother would have dinner ready for me; I had a bath, and went back for the afternoon performance. My uniform was a blue frock with silver buttons down the front; it was made by a woman who lived near The Grand. I had a photograph taken in my uniform, with my cousin, John Rosser, who was going in for his apprenticeship as an upholsterer. I showed the audience to their seats; they always wanted to go down the centre aisle. Sometimes some were standing at the back during a film, so I found a seat for them; there were usually single ones available, especially if it was somebody you knew. I left about eleven o'clock after tipping up the seats. There were a few St. Thomas girls working in The Grand and we'd all walk home after work – perhaps with a few boyfriends as well.

We had a tidy audience – but not packed. Before three o'clock the tickets cost six pence – old money – downstairs and nine pence in the circle; after three o'clock they were full price.

Gwyneth, usherette, with her cousin.

The Grand was owned by Mr. Willis. His nephew, Mr. Turtle was the manager. His wife was tall, blonde and very beautiful; she carried herself so well and was like a film star. Mr Taylor was the commissionaire.

One afternoon, I walked across the back of the cinema, for no reason that I can think of: it was not something I usually did. I was near the gents' toilets when I smelt an unfamiliar smell. It was not that of the disinfectant that Mr. Taylor used to clean the toilets and I wondered what it was. I looked towards the seats and saw a young couple slumped over the seats in front of them. They were drinking Lysol – trying to commit suicide! I went in the row behind and pulled the girl back shouting, 'What are you doing? What's the matter? Where's the bottle?' He had it, so I sat him up, and took the bottle. I quickly told the boss and the ambulance and police were called. I had to give particulars and it was to be a court case. I was shy and backward in those days and one of the girls liked the limelight. I said to her, 'Peggy, I'm not going up the police station. If I tell you word for word what happened will you go for me?' She did, and enjoyed it.

I'll never forget the film, *Birth of a Baby* and boy did they show the birth! It was the story of a mother's pregnancy, and then her actually giving birth, with nothing covering her. It was so very unusual to show that sort of thing in those days. The cinema was full on that first night, and when they showed the confinement the audience came out collapsing everywhere; you'd think war had been declared. The men were fainting and you couldn't put your foot between them to walk. The film was shown for a week and they kept coming to see it in their droves – husbands and wives, youngsters. It was crazy, crazy!

I sometimes worked in the cash desk with a friend. We'd pack up at nine o'clock, give the money to the boss, and run up to The Plaza. We'd have tea and something to eat in the café, and then watch a film with complementary tickets that we were issued through working in The Grand.

I earned just over one pound a week. We had Thursday afternoons and all day Sunday off. In the summer, Millie and I would go by bus to Caswell Bay on Sundays. There was a mansion in Caswell Valley that served delicious food. We'd have lunch there – with fresh garden produce – and strawberries and cream for tea. The bus queues were always long to go home, and if somebody touched us on the shoulder offering a lift, we'd think we were royalty.

After a few years I was forced to leave through ill health. I had suffered with my chest since I was thirteen when I nearly died of bronchial pneumonia. It was Christmas, and I was so ill that the doctor came twice and the priest stayed with me all day.

About a year later I went to work in The Plaza as an usherette and cleaner – no heavy work, only dusting and polishing. I wore a maroon uniform with gold braid trims around the collar and cuffs; they were tailor-made uniforms – class.

The Plaza was a beautiful cinema. Every Monday, fresh flowers were displayed at the foot of the railings surrounding the well on the first floor; they were a sight and must have cost a fortune.

The Plaza had two commissionaires, Tommy Andrews and Tommy Jones. They also wore smart maroon uniforms. Tom Jenkins was the manager. He was a very strict boss, a military man, but I was happy with that – you knew where you were with him. He played the organ and dressed in his tails for the evening performance. He became area manager. Sid Griffiths took over from him as manager, and Handel Evans played the organ. Sid Griffiths came from The Pictorium (later renamed The Scala) cinema in St. Thomas. When I was about sixteen, us local girls and boys used to hang around outside, under the glass canopy. Sid would shout, 'Go away girls!'

We'd say, 'But its raining, and we've nowhere to go. We're not making any noise.' But he was good to the boys and let them go in his projection box. Mrs. Ace worked there as an usherette; she was in her seventies and no bigger than sixpenn'orth of coppers. On a Thursday, we'd give Mrs. Ace a tuppenny bar of chocolate and she'd keep the back row for us.

When the film *Maytime* was featured at The Plaza, starring Janette McDonald and Nelson Eddy, after the first performance Handel Evans asked me, 'What did you think of the film Miss Thomas?'

'Oh! It was beautiful; I cried all the way through it,' I replied.

'Be prepared for a busy week,' he told me.

A few weeks later, I married from The Plaza on 30th of July 1938.

I had been married to Fred for nearly three years when I discovered I was pregnant. I told my neighbour and she said, 'Oh my God, Gwyneth! I'll give you something to get rid of it: we don't know what's in front of us.'

'No,' I replied, 'I've waited a long time for this baby. I'll take my chances.' Brian was born in 1941.

By the early 1950s we had two sons: Brian was ten and Wynford five. I went to The Carlton cinema with my sister and it came up on the screen, 'Part-time usherette wanted'. I said, 'I'm going to apply for that, Jean.'

'Fred will kill you,' she said, but I took the job.

The Carlton was rat-infested. When having our sandwiches in the staff room, we'd keep tapping the table, and stamping our feet to ward them off; they were brazen when food was around. One weekend, poison was put on the stage. When the curtains were pulled back on the Monday morning, the stage was covered with dead rats; you couldn't put a pin between them!

When I told my husband that I was going to work again, he didn't talk to me for three weeks, but it didn't bother me as I was happy in my work. I loved working in the cinema."

In September 1998, Gwyneth, with chocolate girl Sylvia Jones, attended The Grand as VIP guests to re-kindle old memories, on the invitation of

Mr. Gary Isles, manager of the theatre. The evening took the form of a buffet meal followed by a performance of Frank Vickery's comedy *Pullin the Wool*. Gwyneth comments, "We had a beautiful buffet. Afterwards, we were presented with a programme and a box of chocolates and had our photographs taken. It was a wonderful evening; one I'll never forget."

Freda Arnould – Usherette

It was through Freda's determination at a young age to swell the family purse, that she became employed at The Grand.

"I was only fifteen – just come out of school. My dad had died when I was twelve and my mum had to bring up a big family on her own. I had done well when I was in St. Helens Elementary School in Swansea; I was usually top of the class and was head girl. My mother had wanted me to try scholarship and continue my education, but I couldn't wait to leave school and work to earn money for her.

I went to The Grand, which was showing films at the time, and asked if I could work there as an usherette. A Mr. Willis from Cardiff owned The Grand then. When he interviewed me he said, 'You're too young; you're only fifteen and should be sixteen to start work.'

I replied, 'I can do it, I'm sure.' I was young and fancied my chances in those days.

'Alright,' he said, 'you can start by taking the tray around in the intervals,' and so I became a chocolate girl.

I went around with my tray on all the floors. I was only earning ten shillings a week and worked six days from two o'clock in the afternoon until eleven o'clock in the night, with two early nights a week – finishing at nine o'clock. The cinema employed cleaners in the morning who also worked as usherettes during film performances. I thought that if I could have a cleaning job as well, I would have twenty-one shillings a week, which was an awful lot of money then, and would be wonderful for my mother. When I asked Mr. Willis he said, 'But you're only a little girl.' I begged him to let me do it and he agreed. The rest of the girls were older than me – about twenty – and stayed there for donkey's years. I started cleaning at nine o'clock and finished at half-past eleven. I brushed up all the rubbish – ice-cream cartons, pop bottles, cigarette ends – with a pan and brush: there were no hoovers then. I'd go home and get myself washed and changed – no showers – into my uniform and be back at the cinema for the afternoon performance.

My mother wasn't happy for me to do the cleaning. My brother, Cyril Jones, was four years older than me. Before I went to work at The Grand he was a pageboy there, and later succeeded Mr. Taylor as commissionaire. He stood at the door, and organized the queues and parked the toffs' cars for them. He discouraged me to work there as he said it was very hard work.

Mrs. Willis used to come to measure us for our uniforms. We were all slim and I can remember her commenting, 'Oh! Twenty-four inch waist.' We had quite a few different uniforms; they were all nice. At one time we had maroon skirts, cream shantung blouses with bishop sleeves and a maroon satin bow at the neck, and matching maroon satin berets. Skirts were always worn just below the knee: we hadn't heard of mini skirts then. The military uniforms – pageboys' uniforms – were also in maroon, with three rows of brass buttons down the front of the jacket and a pillar-box hat. Princess Marina – wife of the King's brother, Prince George – was our icon of fashion then as Princess Diana became later. We fashioned our hair on Princess Marina's: we had waves in the front and Princess Marina curls all the way up to the pillar-box hat.

The cinemas were closed on Sundays, thank goodness, but the only other day we closed was Christmas Day. We had one week's holiday a year.

It's hard now to remember how low the money was. I feel privileged that I have lived so long. I have seen so many changes in my lifetime. Tickets for the front stalls – the pits – were six pence old money; back stalls, one shilling; front circle, one shilling and six pence; back circle, one shilling and thruppence; and *the gods*, six pence. I'm amazed when my daughter tells me that now the films sometimes don't start until eight o'clock in the evening and that she books her ticket over the phone in advance. It was so different when I was young: there was a continuous performance from two o'clock in the afternoon to eleven o'clock in the evening and we queued to go in – sometimes for hours. If the cinema was full, some would stand through all the performance.

War broke out when I was eighteen. Bob (Robert John) Arnould had come from Blackwood, in Monmouthshire (now Gwent), to Swansea to work, before the war. He was employed as a groomsman by Lord and Lady Edwards, of Hendrefoilan House. They entered their horses in posh races, which the royal family's horses rode in. The animals had beautiful rugs and ribbons. Bob lived in the staff quarters of the house and was provided with his keep, a uniform, and one pound a week. His uniform was very smart: olive green jodhpurs, a matching cut-away coat, black boots, and a trilby – Oh, he looked lovely. He often came to

Freda, sporting a Vera Lynn hairstyle.

The Grand with Sir Clive, the son of his employers, and if they had been riding, came in his uniform.

One day he came on his own. I asked him to move up a seat away from the pillar and he teased me that he would not. Another time he asked me to sit by him. I said, 'Don't be so soft.' You know how you are when you're young: give cheek back to them. He later asked me for a date.

He said, 'I know where you live. I traipsed you home one night.' I lived in Beach Street by the old Swansea Hospital. He arranged to meet me at the Hospital Square, but I had no intention of going. However, when I came home from church that night, my brother was in the front room with his girl friend. She said, 'I thought you had a date?'

I replied, 'I have.'

'Why aren't you going then?' she said.

I was so annoyed with her that I thought, 'Blow you!' and went. Bob was waiting for me. We were soon engaged and did all our quarrelling before we were married.

Bob volunteered for the Army when he was nineteen. The poster, 'We need you' tempted many young men to join up. He was stationed in Liverpool as a dispatch rider. The city was very badly bombed before the Swansea Blitz. He was injured during one of the terrible raids and fractured his leg when he was blown across the road into a shop window. They kept him in Liverpool for a while until his plaster was removed, and he was then transferred to the military hospital in Brynmill – in the large houses in Bryn Road.

I was working during the first night of the Blitz. The cinema was full. It was a way of life then; now all the youngsters go to the pubs. Everybody used to go to the pictures, old and young alike. They were lovely films we used to have then, with lovely stories. When the sirens sounded, 'The sirens have sounded. Please remain in your seats until the all-clear', appeared on the screen. Well, that night we were waiting for the all-clear when all of a sudden a bomb came through the roof onto the stage. It broke the screen and we had a power cut. We were in darkness apart from the gaslights, which lit the floor of the aisles. The loudspeaker sounded, 'You cannot go out. You must remain where you are.' Despite the warnings there was panic, and people were in the aisles and climbing over the seats desperate to leave, but they couldn't, as there were soldiers on guard outside preventing them. We staff had to stay in the building until all the audience had left. I thought that while all this was going on my boyfriend was safely in my mother's, as he was still hobbling on crutches, but I heard his voice cry, 'Freda! Freda! Where are you?' My mother had told me that if ever I was involved in a raid I was to stand in a corner against a solid wall. I shouted back, 'I'm downstairs in a corner by the ladies' toilets.' All the lights were out and the water cut off. It was the only time that my boss was generous – people were fainting and he ordered, 'Give them ice-cream,' which was kept in a fridge in his room. When we eventually got out I looked up and saw Townhill all a-blaze, and the bombs were still dropping. I was so frightened and wanted to run but Bob said, 'Stop love. I can't run. Catch on my arm and we'll get home just the same.'

Bob wanted to break off our engagement as he felt he was a cripple: his legs were terribly twisted. I'd have married him anyway. I loved him. However, he was sent to Portsmouth and when I saw him on his return I couldn't believe it: he was striding from the bus with his bag over his shoulder.

By then more and more women were doing men's jobs to relieve them for active service. I was prepared to go into the forces but not the ammunitions. My four brothers were in the Army and my mother pleaded with the authorities, 'Freda is my right hand man. Please don't take her away from me.' I was told that I could work in Fletchers Garage in Swansea – the first and only girl amongst fifty men!

Bob and I were married in September 1941 when I was twenty and he twenty-one. We would never have married so young if it hadn't been for the war, as we had no money; some couples courted for seven years. About six months later, Bob was posted abroad. He served in Montgomery's Eighth Army in North Africa and fought in the great Battle of El Alamein. He was a tank driver throughout the war, fighting through Sicily, Italy and then the Rhine in Germany.

I enjoyed working in Fletchers and got on well with all the men. Every month, thirty-five soldiers came to train on MT courses to learn to service their own lorries. The soldiers would say to me, 'Hello sunshine. Have a date with me darlin'?'

I used to show them Bob's photo that I wore in a fob brooch on my overall and say, 'He's watching you mind,' and remained faithful to Bob.

Sid Parkhouse, of R. Parkhouse and Sons, a transport firm in Penclawdd, often came to the garage. A few weeks after we were married he gave me a present saying, 'Here you are handsome.' It was a lovely tablecloth with matching napkins. He was as good as gold.

After four years in the Army, Bob came home for a short leave. I became pregnant and was so thrilled at the thought of having our baby. I continued working but sadly had a miscarriage. I left Fletchers, and Bob was demobbed in May 1946. We were later blessed with two loving children, a daughter, Julia and a son, Brian."

George Bean – Projectionist

In his formative years, George Bean, a native of Bonymaen, acquired a keen interest in films and acting. He was fortunate that in later years, his hobbies and his careers became one.

"When my parents were first married, they lived in a caravan while looking for a house in Swansea. They had come from Kent: my father from Ashford and my mother from Dartford. My father owned a magic lantern and many silent films including some of the first cowboy films starring Tom Mix. In those days, arc lamps were used in projectors. The negative was touched to the positive, which split them apart about four inches giving off a white light. My father was showing my mother a film when the magic lantern blew up and the caravan was burnt to the ground.

He bought another magic lantern. When I was about eleven or twelve, my friend, John Bowden and I used to put a white sheet on the kitchen wall and show my father's films to the local kids – Don Hamlyn, who now lives in Langland, was one of them. I operated the projector while John made the sound effects: he simulated horses running by banging two coconut shells together. Sometimes I'd stop the film and run it backwards; the horses would be running in reverse, which caused a bit of fun for the kids. We charged an entrance fee of a safety pin – it was all some could afford – until my mother got fed up of all those safety pins in the house, so we let them in free. Years later, when I was living in Chelsea, I was taken back to those days when television featured a series based on male murderers called *A Pin to see the Peep Show*. I saw a programme based on silent films. I thought, 'My films in the bathroom cupboard in Swansea must be worth a fortune.' When next at home, I asked my mother if they were still there. On her replying yes, I excitedly rushed upstairs, but when I opened the tins, I discovered that the films had turned to dust. It was such a waste as there had been newsreels of the Klu-Klux Klan from 1914/15 and early clips of Charlie Chaplin that nobody had seen. Ironically, a method of preserving them had existed but wasn't available to me at the time.

When I was about seventeen, I also used to entertain the local kids in our garden by playing my mouth organ and guitar. It used to drive my mother mad but I told her that the kids were only having a little sing-song and they were safe there. One day, a little seven-year-old boy tugged at my shirt. He said, 'Georgie, have you got an old mouth organ you don't want?' I gave him one as I had quite a few: they were only about two shillings then. Off he went skipping through the houses and lanes playing his mouth organ. It was the only time I saw him. In 1987, I was giving a concert for the elderly in the old Truant School in Bony-maen, by then a community centre. I was approached by an elderly lady who said, 'If I had known you when you were a teenager, I would have strangled you.'

'Why?' I answered.

'Because I'm Spencer Davis' mother and you gave him a mouth organ and he used to drive us mad with it; he played it in the bath, on the toilet, he wouldn't put it down.'

'But,' I said, 'it got him interested in music and he did very well.' He was of course, Spencer Davis of, The Spencer Davis Group.

'You're quite right,' she replied, 'and if he knew that I was talking to you he'd say, tell Georgie to get on a plane to Los Angeles and have a free holiday in my home for as long as he wants.'

In my youth, I realized the enjoyment I gave the local children through music and films; it taught me a great compassion for children, and I have loved them ever since.

When I was about eighteen, I thought I'd look for a job in a Swansea cinema. In 1945, I inquired at The Grand Theatre, which was featuring films at the time. They said they wanted someone to rewind the films and so I was employed as a rewind boy.

I learned how the projection machines worked: how to put films in them and how they got the film to operate. The chief projectionist – they were always called chief – was Austin Taylor. We were three of us working in the operating box and we had plenty of laughter. Each reel of film lasted about twenty minutes running alternately on two projectors. We had a signal from the film to start the first reel and then a second signal to slap over – it was known as slapping over – to the other projector with the second reel, and so on. While the film was running, we'd sometimes play cards. We'd hear the rumbling of feet from the audience and we'd look up to see a blank screen: the film had run out and we hadn't noticed. We'd then have to rush to get the film started again.

We'd make a small bonus between the three of us. The Grand had a Saturday morning performance for children and the cinema used to get packed. The children sat in *the gods*, which they entered through a side door. When *the gods* were three-quarters-full, we'd shout down to the girl at the cash box, 'Full up! Full up!' She'd close her window and disappear. One of us would go down and tell the kids, 'Come on! Come in!' and charge them half price. We'd fill the place up and share the money between us. The children had a habit of putting their hands up into the beam of the film so one of us would open the box window, and shout, 'Sit down! Sit down!' and squirt oil over them.

I became interested in musicals; I saw *The Wizard of Oz* about fifty times. I saw the films so many times that I learned them off by heart. Because of this, I was later to memorize scripts easily.

I was at The Grand for about two years when I discovered that there was a vacancy for a second projectionist at The Carlton cinema, next to The Empire Theatre.

I got the job and while there learned that The Carlton and The Albert Hall were owned by the same company. They shared the same news-

George Bean, aged 21 years, 1948.

reels at different times of the day: The Albert Hall featured one at three o'clock in the afternoon and so somebody would then stick it in a tin and rush it down to The Carlton for the evening performance. The staff was also shared between the two cinemas: if a projectionist was away at The Albert Hall we'd go and help out, and vice versa. My chief at The Carlton was David Thomas from Bonymaen.

So that was more or less my life in the cinema box, and looking back on it now, it was a wonderful time. So many excellent films stick in my mind: *Arsenic and Old Lace* – a black comedy with a classic script, starring Cary Grant and Raymond Massey; *Captains Courageous* starring Spencer Tracy, Lionel Barrymore, Freddie Bartholomew and Mickey Rooney. Apart from the acting, directing, etc., I realized later that *Captains Courageous* was so good because the author of the original story – a spoiled rich boy falls off a cruise liner and lives for a while among fisherfolk who teach him how to live – was Rudyard Kipling.

I entered a singing competition in The Empire Theatre and I had a few shows there. I was approached by an agent and asked if I was interested in work in London. I obtained an audition and stayed in London for the next twenty-five years. In the early 1960s I was compère singer at the most famous public house in London – The Rising Sun in Bethnal Green. The theatres were closed on Sundays and the stars used to ask the taxi drivers, 'Where can we go to get some fun?' and were directed to The Rising Sun. I worked there for four years, six nights a week, and met many famous stars – Barbara Windsor and her husband Ronnie, Kim Novak, Eddie Albert, Ian McShane of Lovejoy fame. I was invited to one of Ian McShane's engagements at a club in Sloane Square. Everybody there was famous – Deborah Kerr, Lance Percival, Julian Holloway (son of Stan) – except me.

I returned to live in Bonymaen, and today I get a great thrill in visiting the elderly in homes, sheltered accommodation, church halls, community centres, etc. where I give free concerts; playing my keyboard, singing nice songs and relating a few anecdotes from some of the famous films."

Olive Hackford – Chocolate Girl, Usherette, Cashier

The Castle cinema, built in 1913, was aptly named, having been built on the site of Swansea's original Norman castle. It remains an entertainment centre, but not a cinema.

Olive Hackford, born in Mayhill, Swansea and of Irish/Welsh descent, obtained her job in The Castle cinema through family connections.

"My father, Will Malloy, and his family had come over from County Wexford, Southern Ireland to work in Swansea. He married my mother, Mary, one of seventeen children. My mother's family were all in cinemas. One of her brothers was a projectionist in The Regal in Morriston; her sister was a cashier there; another sister worked in The Elysium; and her brother, Fred, was a projectionist in The Castle cinema.

I attended Mayhill Elementary School and then, because my father was Catholic, I went to St. David's Catholic School in Swansea. My youngest sister and I were evacuated to Pontyates, in Carmarthenshire, during the war. The people we lived with had a small daughter. We learned Welsh from her and she English from us, but I have forgotten the Welsh now. I lived there until I finished my education in 1944. I have stayed in touch with the daughter.

We were a houseful of eleven children, and when I left school my mother said, 'Uncle Freddie's got a job for you in The Castle cinema.' I left school on the Friday and started work the following Monday: you did as you were told in those days.

I had my first coat of my own and a Shirley Temple hat with a peak in the front; I thought I was cheese. My mother bought it from the Co-op and paid so much a week for it. She had a very hard life, but she always did her best for us children.

I went as a chocolate and cigarette girl. It was the war years, and chocolates and cigarettes were on coupons and in short supply, so I also trained as an assistant cashier. My father used to ask me to try and get some tobacco for him, but we didn't sell it. The owner of The Posada pub in Wind Street (on the corner of Castle Lane) used to come to The Castle and sometimes brought tobacco for my father. The usherettes worked the side aisles. When the service men came in, the usherettes on one side would say to me, 'Tell the usherettes over there to bring some service men our side.' I didn't have a uniform. Mr. Rees, the under-manager was a lovely gentleman and very kind to me. I can remember teasing him, 'I always thought chocolate and cigarette girls had a nice uniform.'

He replied, 'Do you want a bunny tail as well?'

He also used to say to me, 'The spivs are in the market. Take a couple of passes (complementary tickets) down there and get some stockings.' They were seconds, and the seams were usually in the wrong place, or only at the top of the stocking; you never had a decent pair, but they were beautiful silk.

The Andrew brothers owned The Castle; they also owned David Evans Departmental Store. They were very elderly and later the sons took over. Mr. Taylor was the commissionaire when I started there. He seemed quite elderly to me and had a big moustache – a proper army type but very fatherly. Mr. Bill Jones, from Townhill, came after him. They wore dark uniforms with caps – navy or black.

Swansea was full of servicemen then: sailors from the docks and white and coloured Americans. I used to finish work at eight o'clock and walk over the bombed sites to catch my bus home to Mayhill, but nobody bothered me; I felt quite safe. However, one incident frightened me a little. I had a cocoa tin on my tray to keep the coupons and one evening a soldier put a ten-shilling note in it. I called Mr. Rees to tell him. I had an awful feeling that the soldier would be waiting for me outside. I needn't have worried; there was nothing to it and he probably thought I was collecting for something.

The Castle Café – Belli – near the *Evening Post* office, used to be a popular meeting place for the servicemen and the GPO girls working in

Castle cinema staff outing.
Left to right, front row: Olive Malloy, Bill Jones (commissionaire).
1st row, standing: Teddy Hawkins, ?, ?, ?, Mrs. Loy (cleaner), Mrs. Evans (cleaner),
?, ?, Iris Bidder (usherette), Doris (usherette), Lily Nea, ?, ?,
Raymond White (projectionist), Watkin, Marie, driver.

Wind Street. The Italian Belli brothers were lovely – so friendly. My friend, Betty – such a beautiful girl – worked in the GPO. She married an officer in the Navy, went to America to live, and had a wonderful life there.

All the buildings in the centre of the town had been flattened in the Blitz. It was a very bad experience living in Swansea through the rest of the bombings. I still get quite nervous when I hear thunder. We lived near Teilo Crescent where most of the houses in the street were burned, and many, many people killed. We had a fire in one of the bedrooms in our house and my father was in bed with the 'flu at the time. My mother tried to explain away the bombing of Mayhill by saying, 'The Germans think that Mayhill School is a fort,' but of course they were trying for the docks.

Of an evening, my mother and father used to stand in the garden and look out to the wonderful view over Swansea Bay. My father would say, 'I've got a couple of passes,' – he worked on the railways – 'how about going to Ireland?' and off they'd go by train to Fishguard at twelve o'clock at night, sail to Ireland, travel by train to Ballycullane and visit his family at Saltmills, his home village.

Swansea was beautiful before it was bombed in the war. I remember Ben Evans – such a wonderful store. My mother-in-law, Gertie Hackford – she was Morris then – worked there as a tailoress, and her sister, Aida Tucker also worked there as a tailoress. I also remember Edwards the Eagle – a big store in Swansea when I was in school; I used to buy tins of toffees there for Christmas.

The photograph was of a staff outing; it was the only one I went on. I can remember the photograph being taken but I can't remember where we were going. I'd just come off the boat from a holiday in Ireland at about six o'clock in the morning and it was raining. Well, I was rushing and put a few curlers in my hair and covered them with a turban.

When I was a little older I became an usherette. In time, I was promoted to cashier and worked at The Castle for nearly five years, until my son was on the way. I thoroughly enjoyed my time there, and worked with some lovely people."

Inevitably, progress has caught up with cinema-going: multi-screen complexes provide audiences with a choice of viewing within the same building; seats can be booked in advance, over the phone or on the internet, eliminating vast queues; smoking is prohibited. However, the magic of *going to the flicks* has gone. Usherettes guiding to seats have been replaced by ticket collectors pointing to doors. Double seats are no more. Kissing and cuddling has given way to eating, and drinking soft drinks. Filmfood counters in the foyers offer popcorns, hot dogs, combo meals, which are nachos – a type of spicy crisp – with dips of cheese or salsa, and soft drinks – always in oversize cardboard containers. Consequently, all viewers are subjected to the smell of others' indulgence. Exteriors and interiors of cinemas are no longer things of great beauty. The glamour and sense of occasion has disappeared.

There are still about fifty original cinemas working in the UK, having survived change – The Coliseum in Porthmadog, Gwynedd, The Dome in Worthing, West Sussex, The Electric Palace in Harwich, Essex, etc. Most have experienced interrupted lives, but the Duke of York's in Brighton boasts to be the oldest continuously working cinema in Britain.

4.

Working at Bens

Ben Evans & Co. Ltd. – known as Bens – has been described as the most magnificent and exclusive of Swansea's departmental stores. The proverb *From small beginnings come great things* is certainly applicable to the growth of the business.

In 1865, Evan Evans, a native of Llansadwrn, Carmarthenshire, opened a shop at 3 Temple Street. The next year, the business was taken over by his brother, Ben.

Over the next thirty years, Ben Evans extended his premises by gradually buying adjacent properties and building new. This expansion reached its zenith when, in 1894, a fine new block of commercial architecture, housing the new frontage of the store in Castle Bailey Street was completed. By then, the store almost filled the huge square site bounded by Caer Street, Castle Bailey Street, Goat Street and Temple Street – now Castle Square.

At the time, Ben Evans, his wife, Maria, and family were residing in Corrymor, a large house, set in grounds, in Uplands and by 1906, were living at Llanfair Grange, Llandovery.

In 1895, he floated Ben Evans and Co. Ltd. on the Stock Exchange, raising share capital of one hundred and three thousand pounds.

The store's excellence was promoted in the *Cambrian* newspaper in December 1898:

Ben Evans & Co. Ltd.

GRAND CHRISTMAS SHOW

> We confess we do not feel equal to the task of adequately describing Ben Evans and Co.'s grand Christmas show and bazaar. It is unquestionably one of the 'sights' of the season. There are toys and dolls and games by the thousand – in fact, everything and anything which child-life loves. Ben Evans and Co. can supply you with dolls that sleep, dolls that walk, dolls that talk, dolls that

Bens, Wind Street.

Bens.

use the feeding bottle, and also with dolls' houses. . . . The bazaar may be approached from all parts of Ben Evans and Co.'s premises, although the chief entrances are in Castle Bailey Street and Caer Street. Seeing is believing! To see the grand Christmas show is to believe our statement that it is not equalled outside London, and only by a very few of the great London houses.

. . . Not only is Ben Evans and Co.'s Christmas show and bazaar worth visiting, but also the other departments, all of which may now be seen at their best. . . . We have set before us in the most charming manner in-door and out-door dresses, splendid furs, real sealskin jackets, boas, and warm and comely and fashionable attire. Here we may have, too, the widest range of choice of the thousand and one things of an ornate and delicate and tasteful nature that are needed to make beautiful the already more beautiful-endowed half of the human family. . . .

There is also an exceptionally elaborate selection of goods for eveningwear. Not even in London have we seen a finer display of reception, dance, and dinner gowns, evening bodices and blouses, and Misses and children's dance dresses. Also, materials for evening wear in silk, satin, sequin lisse,[1] gauze, tarlatan,[2] net, and accordeon chiffon;[3] the newest style in evening cloaks and wraps, fans, flowers, coiffures, gloves with evening shoes to match.

In the same issue, the *Cambrian* advertised:

Ben Evans & Co. Ltd.

Would respectfully recommend a visit to their
shops and show-rooms

TOMORROW SATURDAY AND FOLLOWING DAYS,

when

MOST EXTRAORDINARY VALUE WILL BE OFFERED.

They have been enabled to purchase for cash immense

CONSIGNMENTS OF NEW GOODS

At from 30 to 50 per cent. below current prices, and as the full benefit is given to customers, an opportunity is presented that very rarely occurs, which should at once be taken advantage of.

---

1. Smooth sequined material.
2. Thin stiff open-weave muslin, used especially for ball-dresses.
3. Pleated chiffon.

45 doz.⁴ striped & fancy flannelette shirts, special price 1/11, 2/11.

15 doz. striped & figured flannelette blouses, special price 1/11.

20 doz. striped golf jerseys, in all colours, special price 1/11, 2/11.

Special purchase – 150 doz. fur circlets & necklets, in black and sable colour, hare, goat, mink, chinchilla and fox, 8¾, 1/0½, 1/6½, 1/11½.

25 coats and skirts, new frieze cloth and heather-mixtures, special price 10/11.

10 doz. flannelette petticoats (with shaped bands), 1/11 each.

37 pieces Venetian costume cloth (all colours), 48 inches wide, 1/0¾.

21 boxes corde-du-roi velveteen (new shades), 27 inches wide, 1/0¾.

350 pieces REAL WELSH FLANNELS for costumes, skirts and shirts.

Mary Ada Higgs

In 1902, Mary Ada Higgs commenced her career at Bens. Her daughter, Averil Price, recalls in an article featured in the *South Wales Evening Post*, 'My mother, Mary Ada Higgs, was always talking of Ben Evans. At the age of twenty-two, she left the Rhondda Valley for Swansea to work as an assistant there. Her department was haberdashery, then hats. In those days, they slept in and on St. David's Day, they all had to dress in Welsh costumes. She returned to her home in 1910, after eight of the happiest years of her life, to get married.'⁵

Although salaries and conditions were poor, it was considered a privilege to work in Bens. But 1911 saw unrest in the store. 'Twenty-five Swansea dressmakers – all employees of Ben Evans – went on strike for better pay and conditions. The girls gained support from several quarters and there were mass demonstrations of five to six thousand people. Mary McArthur, founder of the National Federation of Women Workers, travelled down from London to be of assistance. Most supportive of all was a local industrialist, Amy Dillwyn,⁶ who urged shoppers to boycott

---

4. Abbreviation of dozen – twelve in number.
5. *South Wales Evening Post*, Thursday 18 February 1999, p. 22.
6. Amy Elizabeth Dillwyn (1845-1935) was the daughter of Lewis Llywelyn Dillwyn of Hendrefoilan estate in Sketty, Swansea. On her father's death, she inherited Llansamlet Spelter Works, which was in debt to around one hundred thousand pounds. By improving productivity, she paid the debt in seven years.

Exceptional Value in Boots for Lads and Lassies.

Style, Quality, and Price alike give Satisfaction

Every parent realises the futility of buying "Cheap" Footwear for school use. We can thoroughly recommend the lines here quoted as embodying sound materials and reliable workmanship.

Boy's Strong Box Calf Boots, leather lined— 4/11½ pair.

Boys' Calf Boots, studded soles, ¼-iron tips, Sizes 11—1, **7/11**; Sizes 2—5, **8/11** pair.

Boys' Fine Box Calf Boots for best wear, Sizes 11—1, **8/11**; Sizes 2—5, **9/11** pair.

Maids' Glace Kid or Box Calf Boots, button or lace, full round toes, square heels; Sizes 2—5, **6/11** pair.

Maids' Box Calf and Tan Willow Calf 'Rinking' Boots. Cut extra high, splendid protection in wet weather; Studded all the way up, easy to fasten: Sizes 2—5, **10/11** pair.

Ben. Evans & Co., Ltd.
—: SWANSEA. :—

Summer sale 1916, showing entrance in Temple Street.

Summer sale 1916, showing corner of mantle department.

the store and persuaded her family and friends to withdraw their custom. At a meeting, Amy was reported to have said: Employers have no right to grind them (poor people) down to take unfair wages. . . . Is five shillings a living wage? If twenty girls had an increase of two shillings a week, it would mean a lot to them . . . I cannot see my way to deal with Messrs. Ben Evans and I hope everyone else will feel likewise.'[7]

Bens secured the enviable contract of supplying uniforms to those involved in the Great War. Two young girls, both natives of Llanrhidian, North Gower, had occasion to visit the stores at the time. 'Violet Morgan

---

7. Derek Draisey, *Women in Welsh History* (77 Geirol Road, Townhill, Swansea, SA1 6QR, 2004) p. 118.

(later Davies) and Annie Austin (later Williams) volunteered as part-time nurses in World War One joining the Voluntary Aid Detachment (VAD) of the Red Cross. They did spells of duty at the hospital at Horton, in South Gower – a very large house, converted for the purpose. The wounded soldiers there had already received treatment and were placed at Horton for care and recuperation. . . . Violet recalled going in to Ben Evans store in Swansea (a very posh shop, she remembers) to buy a long navy nurse's coat, and being greeted by a 'shopwalker' who was wearing a dress with a yard-long train!'[8]

The basement of the Goat Street premises was used as a packing and receiving room for Bens' wares. The incoming goods and deliveries to customers were transported initially by horse and cart, and later by horse-drawn vans. Joyce Bidder, of Blackpill, Swansea wrote to the *South Wales Evening Post* of her memories of Bens, 'In the 1920s, my father, Bill French, was in charge of the receiving room, where all the goods going into the store were delivered, checked and then distributed to the different departments. I remember every Friday, pay day, my mum would walk me from our home in St. Thomas, to go and get my dad's wages, when we would then go and do the shopping.

I got to know a lot of the staff, especially the men who delivered the goods to the customers – it was very high class. They delivered by horse and van and stabled their horses opposite St. Mary's Church. One driver I remember in particular was Bob, who I called the Mumbles Apple Man as he delivered to Mumbles and always gave me apples.

Apart from working in the receiving room, every Christmas my dad was Father Christmas in the bazaar, and my mum always took me to see him so I could tell him what I wanted for Christmas. I always thought there was something familiar about him but I never guessed who he was. I always wondered how he knew so much about me, especially my misdemeanours.'[9]

'I knew the wireless-department boss as George the Wireless; most staff had house names. When the new wirelesses came in with valves, George came to my home in Sebastopol Street and helped my dad to build his own set. He had a kit, and I remember being fascinated by the blueprint.

. . . There was a night watchman, and every year when he had his annual holiday, my dad would stand in for him. There were a lot of rats about and the watchman had a dog called Peggy, to help catch them.

---

8. *Our Memories of Llanrhidian*. Compiled by Pat Williams for Llanrhidian Local History Group (Rawlings Road, Llandybie, Carmarthenshire, SA18 3YD, 2004). p. 18.
9. *South Wales Evening Post*, Thursday 21 January 1999, p. 6.

Dad told stories of how he used to set a trap with a big laundry basket to entice them inside, and then put Peggy in to kill them off.

Young apprentices who worked there used to live in on the top floor, and they employed a housekeeper to look after them."[10]

Rosie Lloyd

Rosie Lloyd's parents had the unenviable task of bringing up ten children during the years of the Depression. Bens played a part in alleviating their problem – to a certain extent: it provided their five daughters with employment. Rosie their only daughter whose name did not begin with an M, tells the story.

"I lived in Plasmarl near the Smuggler's Arms pub. I went to work in Bens when I was fourteen, in 1928. I worked in the curtain department with Dolly Bidder. Mr. Price was our boss, but he died young. It was lovely working there. We sold every kind of material imaginable. I remember the heavy velvet with a thick nap. We sold by the yard, and measured with a three-foot wooden measure.

I didn't have a uniform, but wore anything I liked under my overall, of sorts – it wasn't posh. I could wear any sort of shoes; I was lucky to get a bit of sole. St. David's Day was special; the women dressed up in full Welsh costume with the tall hats, and I had a doll, also in Welsh costume, by my side while I served. The men wore daffodils in their coat lapels.

I was given my wages in an envelope, and when I first took it home, my mother couldn't get over it – she thought it was a lot. My sisters were a crowd: there were five of us – Muriel, Megan, May, Maggie – and we all worked in Bens. Muriel worked as waitress in the café. She wore makeup and nail varnish, but old fashioned she was. I used to go there during my dinner hour to have a snack. They had wonderful cream slices. My mother made dinner for all of us, after work, in the evening.

Bens held wonderful mannequin parades, with a bride and groom and all.

We sisters all went to and from Bens by bus, if we were lucky, and if not, we walked. It sometimes took us an hour and a half to get home.

I worked there for years and years until I married. I was sorry to leave; I enjoyed it so much."

---

10. *South Wales Evening Post,* Thursday 18 February 1999, p. 23.

Sydney Rumbelow

Bens' stables provided accommodation for about fourteen horses, and the van shed about twenty vans. The manager, Charles Reed, from Norwood in Devon, with his wife, Annie, and six children, lived in an adjacent house.

By the late 1920s, Sydney Rumbelow, and his wife, Laura, occupied the premises. Their only child, Gillian (Yates), born in 1933, remembers her early childhood there.

"We lived in Ben Evans House, which was in 12A St. Mary's Square, opposite St. Mary's Church. It was situated next door to Rutland Street School. When the war came, the school closed and it became a food office. Iceland store is there now. It was a very large, three-storeyed house, where we lived rent-free, and had all our gas, light, and coal provided for us free of charge. There was a huge yard, which was entered through large double doors spanned by an arch. The vans were garaged in what used to be the stables. The petrol room was adjacent to our house; it was like a big garage. Carpets were sold in the store, and in a room above the petrol room, girls cut and sewed them for the customers' requirements. I spent many happy hours watching the girls sew the carpets. Before starting their day's work, the van boys and the drivers ate their sandwiches in the old harness room: it was warm and cosy, always having a big fire.

My father was in transport, as had his father been before him. My grandfather, Jim, had been a deliveryman, and on Saturdays, my father used to go out with him on his horse and cart. Later, with motorization, my father became his father's boss. My father was chauffeur to the managing director, and we were allowed to use the firm's cars to go on family holidays. He was also involved in the firm's funeral service, attending the funerals, and possibly, driving the hearses. Because many of the staff came from far afield, such as West Wales, Bens provided them with staff living accommodation on the premises. It was part of my father's job to see that all were in safely every night, and lock the doors. He opened them at six each morning for the store's cleaners.

Bens was my playground, my palace, and the neighbourhood, my world. As a little girl, I used to run around the store freely. I could go anywhere: everybody knew me. I used to go in the lifts and became friendly with the girls in uniforms operating them. I think their uniform was brown with coffee-coloured lapels. I would visit my Aunty Amy, a buyer in the china department on the top floor, and remember seeing a

In Ben Evans House before staff dance.
Standing: Sydney Rumbelow. Sitting, left to right: Elsie Davies, Cliff Davies, Laura Rumbelow.

Bens' staff dance – early war years.
Left to right, on floor: Bill Thompson (Thomas), Sydney Rumbelow, Mark Parkhouse,
Bert C. Millard. 1st row seated: Dulcie Thomas (wife of Bill Thompson), Laura Rumbelow,
Mr. Jolliffe (Jones), Mrs. Jones (wife of Mr. Jolliffe), Mr. Wheatley, Miss Dorman, Mrs. Millard.

Gillian on her first birthday with mother and family. Van possibly reads 'Get it at Bens'.

Gillian with her aunt, Amy Rumbelow and Bens' car.

Sydney and Laura Rumbelow with friend on left – Bens' car.

Sydney and Laura Rumbelow in Bens' car.

Swansea Carnival from there. There was a large wooden horse in George the Leather's department, which I loved to ride. George must have sold harnesses, etc.

Bens organized staff dances every year. My parents always attended, and my father was usually MC. I remember my aunty taking me to watch the dancing in The Park Hotel, in Park Street – about where Mothercare is situated now. All the ladies wore long evening dresses, and the men were in tails. It was a great thrill for me then, as a little girl.

Bert Millard was the secretary. Bill Thompson was a floorwalker; his real name was Thomas, but as that was a common name among the staff, he was renamed Thompson. Mark Parkhouse worked in the furniture department; he was the father of the well-known cricketer, Gilbert Parkhouse. The managing director was Mr. R. G. Lewis; he was a big man with a moustache. I remember going to his house in Gower Road, I think it was. His cook – always in cap and apron – served me the most wonderful meringues that I have ever tasted. I enjoyed my visits there so much. He was succeeded by the manager, Mr. Wheatley, who in turn, was replaced by the head floorwalker, Mr. Jolliffe, who was really Mr. Jones – another common name."

Meg Phillips of Cwmdu, Swansea also has happy childhood memories of Bens – in the early 1930s. Her story was published in the *South Wales*

Evening Post. 'I am in my mid-70s but have a vivid memory of being taken to Bens to see the *Bwthyn Bach* (Little Cottage) which the people of Wales presented to the little Princesses Elizabeth and Margaret. It was on exhibition at the store before being taken to London. There was a wonderful staircase at the store and the house was placed in the well of the stairs. You walked around to see the bottom part of the house then climbed the stairs to see the upper floors. It was a wonderful *Bwthyn Bach* with every item done on a small scale.

I also recollect Monk's the pork butchers in Wind Street – going there every Saturday for pork sausages, and sometimes a pork joint. I always thought it a long way to walk, but coming back we would enter the back of Bens and walk through the store, which shortened the journey back to the market to continue our shopping.'[11]

Dora Evans

In the early 1930s, Dora commenced her two-year apprenticeship at Bens. She was born to Henry Owen Evan and Ann Rogers, of Gowerton, in November 1915. Having tried her scholarship examination, she was told that she had narrowly missed a place in Gowerton County School, but a vacancy was available for her in Llanelly Grammar School. It was given with the proviso that she might later be transferred to the Gowerton school, but this, however, did not transpire.

When Dora completed her education, she informed her mother that she was prepared to work in the local steelworks in Gowerton, but her mother had other plans. The Reverend Able, a Gowerton minister, had a cousin who was a director of Ben Evans & Co. Ltd. Dora's mother approached the minister, and it was through his cousin's influence in the store that Dora obtained an apprenticeship. Dora was pleased with her new employment.

"The Reverend Able's daughter worked in Ben Evans on the handkerchief counter. She used to talk of her work and I used to think that I would like to work there too. I didn't ask to go: in those days, your mother arranged everything, and we did as we were told. I wore a brown skirt, a fawn top, and a brown and fawn hat, for my first interview with Mr. Able, in his office. I always wore a hat in those days: most women did. He called Miss Rosser, the buyer, to his office and she looked me over. I was quite tall then and she said that they wanted tall girls. I had thick, long, brown, wavy hair and every one used to pass remarks on

---

11. *South Wales Evening Post*, Thursday 18 February 1999, p. 22.

it, and say how gorgeous it was. I looked after it well and wore a net to bed every night. Miss Rosser must have approved of me as I had my interview on the Friday, and I started work on the following Monday.

I was seventeen. I was so nervous on my first day. I found the entrance on my own, and was told to sit on a velvet ottoman until someone could help me. I didn't know a soul, but soon got into the swing of it. We apprentices worked for two years for almost nothing. Our only income was thruppence in the pound on the garments we sold, and we were not allowed to sell unless the buyers and sales ladies were already selling to a customer at the time. Our uniforms were long, green frocks down to our ankles. We were given material cheaply, and had to have them made up ourselves.

Ben Evans was a beautiful place situated where Castle Gardens are now. The other departmental stores, David Evans, Lewis Lewis, Edwards, etc. were lovely, but Ben Evans was the most exclusive in Swansea. All the lords and ladies used to shop there – the *crachach* (snobs). I particularly remember Sir William and Lady Jenkins and Lady Edwards. They were easy to talk to and made us feel that we were all on the same level. The husbands usually came with their wives, and I used to be fascinated by their smart spats, which were fashionable at the time.

The showroom where I worked covered a very large area, with separate compartments for coats, frocks, gowns, millinery, knitwear and shoes. There was also a hairdressing salon on the same floor. The coats, etc. were not on rails as they are today, but in individual glass cases. The roof of the store was made of glass, and the carpet was very beautiful – in fawn, brown, and autumn shades – but it used to get red-hot in sunny weather, and it was terrible for our feet. My mother had bought me a beautiful pair of black patent shoes, but they were a disaster in that heat. I said, 'Mam, I can't go back. I can't stand it anymore. My feet are too bad.'

She pasted the soles of my feet with salt butter every night and said, 'Promise me to try it for a month and see how you get on.' So I carried on working, and soon my feet got acclimatized. Our employers were very understanding, and we were able to wear comfortable shoes, as they could not be seen much below our long frocks.

Our first job every morning was to hoover the carpet, clean inside the glass cases, and dust the shoulders of the coats and the top of the glass cases. We worked in each department, coats, frocks, etc. for six months to gain experience in each. I preferred the coat department as the buyer was nicer, and when working in the frock department, we had to sew on loose buttons. I hated sewing; I was hopeless at it. It was our job to fetch the boxes of garments from downstairs, in the packing department, to our floor, for the buyers to price them.

When we were not actually doing anything, we had to parade around the floor like mannequins; we were not allowed to sit down at work. Once the lift opened and a customer came out, we had to approach them and say, 'Good morning, Madam. Can I help you? Would you come this way Madam? Please take a seat Madam.' We'd then fetch the buyer to help them.

I often think of the way many shop assistants serve today. When you ask them where a certain something is they don't move, but just point and say, 'Over there.'

When we were allowed to serve, we'd take the customer into a fitting room and bring a variety of the type of garment she wanted. Sometimes we'd bring every one in the department and the customer still couldn't make up her mind. We'd say, 'I think it looks lovely on you Madam, but don't take my word for it because we want you to be comfortable in it, and it is you that has to wear it – but I think it makes you look slimmer.' Well, that would usually do the trick. But if we did fail to make the sale, we dare not let her go out empty handed, so we'd fetch the buyer to have a word with her, and if she failed, well, that was that.

We didn't deal with money: most of the customers had accounts with club cards. When a purchase was agreed, we'd make a note of it, with the customer's name and address, and then take it to the counting house. We waited for the sale to be confirmed before wrapping the garment. We had two counting houses. I'm not sure what the system was on the lower floors, but I expect they dealt in cash, as the items were small – handkerchiefs, gloves, etc. We were taught how to fold the garments to their advantage and to place them in boxes with loads and loads of tissue paper. I remember selling my first fur coat. I was so excited that I nearly tried to put my customer off as I thought, 'How am I going to handle this?' but in fact it was easy, as she made up her mind so quickly. I was not very experienced at the time and I was quickly counting up how many thruppences I had earned.

Our customers used to go on cruises. I was in the throes of selling lots of clothes to one such customer when Miss Paton, the senior sales assistant, brushed me aside telling me that it was too much for me. Of course, she wanted the commission, but I didn't dislike her for it: it was the system. She always wore her black hair plaited into two coils over her ears.

The store had genuine sales. I can remember buying coats for my mother and sister, and a suit for my other sister, but never anything for myself: I was surrounded by clothes and so was uninterested. I had a little discount during sales, about tuppence in the pound, I think. When most of the garments were sold in our department, we were told to help out downstairs. We hated it, as we didn't earn much money selling handkerchiefs and gloves.

We used to have mannequin parades, and as apprentices, we helped the mannequins to dress. It did used to make me laugh because as a reward, we were allowed to have a nice little tea free of charge in the tearooms, but of course, this meant that we missed the opportunity of a sale – the thruppence in the pound.

A friend of mine was a window dresser; she used drapes, etc. from the different departments. She was only a little person but her work was excellent. If we were slack in the showroom, the buyer would tell me to go down and help her. We sometimes used to wave to the bank clerks in the bank opposite; we used to do a lot of naughty things that we shouldn't have done. When she was off from work, I was asked to dress a window in her stead. It was only a small side window but the stores also had huge windows.

I was always addressed as Miss Rogers: we were never called by our Christian names. If two people had the same surname – a common occurrence – one would be given a fictitious name. My friend's name was Miss Griffiths; there was another girl of that name so she was re-named Miss Gibbon.

Our managing director, Mr. Able was an extremely nice man. Every morning he came to see us, entering the floor by lift. It was a treat to see him as he always wore a suit with matching bowler hat – one day in brown, another in grey, etc. He passed each of us saying, 'Good morning ladies. Good morning ladies.'

The sons and daughters of many influential people worked there but they had no side. It was a wonderful place to work – a magical place: there was not one person that I disliked; I can't remember having words with anybody; they were all lovely; we worked together like one big happy family. I never once got up in the morning thinking, 'Oh, I have got to go to work today.' We used to have Christmas presents from the senior staff. It was considered an honour to work in Ben Evans.

Miss Scott worked downstairs in the lace department. She was ninety years of age and as long as she wanted to work, she was allowed to do so. I can see her now slowly going up the stairs. She was such a dear old lady.

The stores had beautiful luncheon and tearooms for its customers, and it was there that the senior staff ate their lunch. At the top of the building were two rooms for our use: one where we hung our coats and another where we ate lunch. They were very austere with nails for our coats and a long, old, plain, wooden table on which to eat our sandwiches. We brought our sandwiches from home, and if we felt a bit flush, we'd go out and buy a couple of chips.

Miss Paton, first sales in the coat department, and Miss James, first sales in the frock and gown department, lived in. I think their quarters must have been austere as well, as I heard at the time that they were looking for a flat in Swansea.

The store was open Mondays to Wednesdays, nine to six o'clock; Thursdays, nine to one o'clock; Fridays, nine to eight o'clock; and Saturdays, nine to nine o'clock.

I got up at seven-thirty and caught the eight-twenty train from the top station in Gowerton to Victoria Station[12] in Swansea: I suffered from travel sickness on buses. On Saturday night, I caught the last train home. My husband, Stan Evans – then my boyfriend – would be keeping my mother and father company. He used to meet me off the train and we'd go straight home. It wasn't long before my mother would say, 'Your bus is due Stan; it's time to go.' That was our Saturday night together. I always had to be home by ten o'clock. When Stan and I were courting, we used to sit in the front room. I had known Stan for four years before he came to my home. We had to keep the door open for my mother to spy on us in the mirror over the fireplace. I can honestly say that I was definitely a virgin when I married. How Stan ever married me I'll never know: my mother was so strict.

The coaches of the train I travelled in had no corridors. When coming home, I never went into a compartment that had just one man in it, or an empty compartment, in case a man would come in at the next stop. One evening, I entered a compartment with two men and a woman. At the next stop, one man and the woman got out. The man left started chatting to me, and asked me if I would go out with him, promising that he would buy me a fur coat if I did. I didn't know what to do, whether to pull down the window and shout, or what. I was terrified. I was so glad to get out at Gowerton, and very thankful that he didn't try to stop me. I eventually conquered my bus travel sickness and travelled on a South Wales Transport single decker after that.

In summer, on Thursday afternoons, our afternoon off, all us girls

---

12. Part of the station's buildings have been used to house the Swansea Industrial and Maritime Museum.

from the showroom would go down to Crawley Woods in South Gower. I remember it like it was yesterday. We'd never bathe, just paddle. Afterwards, we'd go to Nicholston Hall for high tea and we thought we were it. We'd have bacon and as many eggs as we wanted all for half-a-crown. We thought it was wonderful.

I remember my first staff dance. Phyllis Harris, from Penclawdd, worked in the hairdressing department – she later married John Morgan, who worked in the carpet department. They were a very handsome couple. She'd often sneak me into the salon and do my hair for nothing. A staff dance had been arranged. I had never been to a dance and did not possess a dance frock. Phyllis asked me if I was going. I said that I'd love to go but didn't have a dance frock.

'Well,' she said, 'you're looking the same size as me. You can have one of mine.'

It was a skirt and a top. So that is how I went to my first dance. I'll remember her kindness to me all my life."

Inevitably, romances occurred amongst the staff. Dora remembers one incident clearly. "There was a fellow working in the gents' department who was a lot older that me. He went to Devonshire on holiday. One day, while he was away, I was told, 'There's a card for you Miss Rogers.' I couldn't think who it could have been from; well, it was from this fellow. There was a photo of a house on the card and the words, 'I'm contemplating purchase. How about it?' I had such a surprise as I had no idea of his feelings for me, as he never talked to me of them. He had dark, horned-rimmed glasses and dark receding hair. He must have been well in his forties, and I was only seventeen. He was due back on the Monday, but I didn't see him after that card: he contracted peritonitis and died.

Dorothy, my oldest sister, was married to Harry Thomas, owner of The Tivoli cinema in Gowerton. I didn't like him as he was always making a fool of himself. He was the first man to own a car in the village. He also owned horses, some quite wild. Miss Rosser, my buyer, used to go riding. Something happened to her horse and she asked me if I knew where she could buy another one. I thought, 'I'm not going to connect that silly bugger with Miss Rosser,' so I said I didn't. One evening, he told Dorothy that he was going to play chess in Swansea. He played the game often, but not that night. He went down to Loughor Bridge, took off his watch, and threw himself over and drowned.

After my two-year apprenticeship was completed, I earned eighteen shilling a week; it was very difficult financially for my mother. One day it came to me that this was getting beyond. I caught the director quietly on his own and we arranged to meet in his office. I explained my situation; I was shaking like a leaf, but I thought I'd have to make a stand.

'Alright,' he said, 'I'll give you an extra five shilling.' I kept this to myself and never told my colleagues.

After a while, the long frocks went out of fashion, and we had short black frocks, and then short brown frocks. We were expected to wear smarter shoes with the shorter lengths.

Clock presented to Dora from Bens.

Married women were not allowed to work in those days. When my husband asked me to marry him I said, 'Oh, I'll have to leave Ben Evans.' I didn't want to leave, but I did marry him, and left Bens. I was presented with a clock with a silver plated inscription:

'Presented to Miss Rogers
From Ben Evans & Co. 1940'.

Working in Ben Evans was the happiest time of my single life."

John and Phyllis Morgan

John and Phyllis' story is one of Bens' many romances.

John commenced his employment at the store in 1930, when seventeen years of age.

"I lived near Dyfatty, in Swansea, and travelled to work on my motor bike. I sold carpets in the store and when laying carpets for its customers, cycled to their homes, carrying my tools in the panniers of my bike. I didn't have a uniform; I could wear what I liked. The carpet

John Morgan.

Phyllis Morgan.

department was on the bottom floor, and every Armistice Day the store was closed in the morning, and a remembrance service held in the department.

All Bens' customers were proud to say that they had bought at Bens. The management was very strict: we dare not step out of turn; we weren't even allowed to go to the lavatory, only during break times – but we had a terrific staff."

Phyllis was born in 1918 to Thomas James Harris and Mary Fry, of Brynfa Terrace, Penclawdd. She attended Gowerton County School for three years before commencing her two-year apprenticeship in the hairdressing salon of Bens in 1934.

"I started working at Bens when I was sixteen. My grandfather, John Fry, paid twenty guineas for my apprenticeship. My other grandfather, Thomas Harris, was a deacon in Bethel Chapel, Penclawdd. He had three children when he married my grandmother, Nurse Elizabeth Harris. She was the village midwife and delivered – it was reported – two thousand babies. She was always in her uniform: a long blue twill frock; a white starched pinafore with a bib, waistband, and skirt down to the floor; a stiffly starched white collar with a stud; a little round hat; and a long navy cloak. She was always carrying her Gladstone bag. As children, we thought her appearance quite awesome, and when she looked at us, we'd be cowering in the corner. Her first language was Welsh; she spoke very little English and, when at work, would say only, 'Water, please.' This was well before the National Health Service and her patients paid her when she delivered their babies. She was not a nasty woman, but very strict. However, she had a very gentle side. After my grandfather died my sisters and I used to take it in turns to sleep in my grandmother's house. When it was my turn, she'd sit in the chair by the side of the fire all night. She didn't go to bed and so I had to sit in the chair the other side of the fire. One night, I saw her stroking something on her lap: it was a little mouse. It must have been a common occurrence, as the mouse had become quite tame. They used to say to me in the village, 'Nurse Harris will never die while you are alive,' as I had the same walk as her. She retired before I had my daughter, Rosalind, in 1941.

During the two years of my apprenticeship at Bens, I earned nothing; I relied only on tips. Fortunately, our clients were kind, wealthy ladies and even if I only washed hair, or swept the floor, I would be given a tip of two shillings. After two years, I earned ten shillings a week and paid one shilling and four pence on insurance; after another two years, my wages went up to fifteen shilling a week, less one shilling and eight pence.

I went to work by bus, which only cost me a pound a month. We had to buy our own white cotton overalls; I had three a week which my mother laundered for me.

I learned to cut hair very well at Bens, and had an excellent teacher in my manager, Mr. Watts. I used to perm hair and our customers were all strung up in those machines; clamps were put in their hair, which were attached by wires to a machine at their side. Some of my customers had their hair washed and set every week. Peroxide hair was very fashionable then, and although I was a brunette when I started work, I was a blonde for many years afterwards. I never let my hair grow long; I always wore it in a shingle, and still do. Every Friday evening, Louie Delve and I cleaned the two hundred brushes used in the salon with soap and water.

Louie started her apprenticeship a week before me, and we became great friends. Her son, David Wilkinson, now the Area Dean of Gower, was in college with Rowan Williams, now the Archbishop of Canterbury. About two years ago, when the latter was the Archbishop of Wales, he was invited to a communal service of the churches and chapels of Gower, held in Bethel Chapel. David Wilkinson introduced Rowan

Williams to the congregation. They were both so interested to hear that I had learned my trade with David's mother in Ben Evans.

You were somebody if you worked in Bens, but we worked hard and we dare not put a foot wrong. If we didn't have a customer, we were not allowed to sit down, and our seniors would soon find us something to do. Each department had its own floor manager or managers – ours was Mr. Lewis – immaculately dressed in tails and white tie, always watching that nobody misbehaved. Mr. Able was the big boss in the office and never walked the floors. His wife was one of my regular customers.

The salon was on the same floor as the gowns, shoes and millinery. Bens had the most beautiful hats sold by Miss Wilks, the sales assistant. Mannequin parades were held about twice a year in the gown department where a stage was erected. It was a large area – as big as Bethel Chapel. I modelled a few times with the other girls from the gowns department.

My manager, Mr. Watts – a tall, pot-bellied man – was about fifty-five. Everyday he went out for lunch and always had a little drink. When he returned he used to say to me, 'You've got pretty little ears, Miss Hawkins.' Because there was already a Miss Harris working in the department, I was renamed Miss Hawkins – what a horrible name!

John Morgan, dressed for staff dance.

I enjoyed my work in Bens and we had some good times there. Every summer we had a staff trip; we went to Tenby one year. We also had staff dinner-dances held in different venues in Swansea, such as the Mackworth Hotel in High Street. They were always well attended by the staff and managers.

John won the swimming championship of Swansea and his photo was prominently displayed in a window of the store. All the girls were after John, and when he went to his chapel in Swansea, they used to queue on the stairs to see him. I didn't know him well at the time. I worked with a girl called Vennie Ewing who had a soft spot for him. John was a big rugby player and played for the Swansea Baa-baas (Barbarians). I heard that he was to play in Penclawdd and decided to arrange a meeting between John and Vennie. My sister, Lizzie Ann had a farm in-between Penclawdd and Three Crosses. I said to Vennie, 'I'll invite John to my sister's for supper and you can come as well,' and that was how John and I started courting. But Vennie and I remained friends, and she came to our wedding.

   I took sandwiches for lunch, but sometimes I'd have lunch in the tearooms. I'd only pay a shilling: John's sister, Minnie, was the head-waitress; and his brother, Arthur, who worked in the carpet department, married a girl who was a waitress. It was quite a family affair as John's brother, Theo, made curtains in the soft furnishing department.

   When John and I were courting, we went to the pictures in Swansea on John's motorbike. I was wearing a lovely new dress that Olga Clark had made for me; it was green with a long bodice and pleated skirt. I was sitting on the back of the bike and as we were going down the hill by Park Beck (Sketty), a car came towards us and our bike skidded. Oh! How we weren't killed I'll never know. My dress was ripped, and my mother didn't half say it.

   One of my customers was a wealthy lady named Mrs. Morgan, who, I understand, owned a colliery in Glyncorrwg. Her husband held a very important position in a bank; he was a bank manager. Mrs. Morgan came to the salon every week, and her daughter, Mary, occasionally: Mary was at boarding school so came in her school holidays. I also used to manicure Mary's nails. We used to chat and she often confided in me. They always gave me five shillings tip, which was a lot of money then. When I told them I was getting married, they gave me a beautiful white tablecloth of linen with crochet insets; I treasure it greatly. During the Whitsun Walks on Whit Monday I kept a table at the Whitsun tea in Bethel vestry. I always used my special tablecloth, and have never used it on any other occasion. A few years ago, my son Robert – he followed his father in the trade – was laying a carpet for a lady in Mumbles. It transpired that she was Mary Morgan. She had married a dentist, but was then widowed. She was so interested to hear about me, and Robert took her a photo of John and me.

   As was the ruling, I had to leave Bens when John and I married in April 1939. I wore a long white dress, which was made for me by Evelyn Jenkins of Penlan, sister of Gwen, the teacher. I bought the material in Bens, and also my veil and headdress. The ceremony was in Bethel Chapel, and we went to Aberystwyth on honeymoon. Afterwards, we went to live in my family home in Penclawdd."

Ron Tooney

Dennis Evans, a native of Mumbles and a great friend of Ron, reminisces. "Ron lived in Newton, in Mumbles and later moved to Queens Road. He worked in Ben Evans as a gents' hairdresser – a very high class business. During the war, Ron, then about thirty, was aware that he would soon be called up. He decided on a change of career and in 1940, went to work in the offshoot of Cwmfelin Steelworks owned by Richard Thomas and Baldwins where I also worked. It had press shops making Jerry cans, parts for armaments and ammunition boxes. Ron was a good entertainer – a tap dancer – and became one of the concert party in the works. Ron and I travelled to work on the Mumbles Train for the duration of the war until I went into the Army in 1944."

Kath Jones

Kath Jones, née Slade, lived at the top of Constitution Hill – the steepest hill in Swansea. At the age of fifteen, she started her two-year apprenticeship at Bens, in October 1940. It was, however, to be short-lived.

"I started in the haberdashery (haby) department. The buyer, Miss Dorman, was also the buyer for jewellery and belts, etc. and I often worked on that counter as well," says Kath. "I received no salary, only a commission of thruppence in the pound. I wore a black frock and when taking a coffee break in the store's restaurant, was expected to wear a hat, as did all the customers. I worked there until February 1941."

The Early War Years

Tragically, Bens was completely destroyed by fire on 21 February 1941 – the last night of the Swansea Blitz.

Although then a young child, Gillian, the Rumbelow's daughter, still vividly remembers the trauma of the war years in Swansea. "During the war, Bens constructed a huge air-raid shelter in the yard for its staff; it was also used by local inhabitants, who used to bring their beds with them, such as old Mrs. Coakley – the fish merchant in Goat Street – and her two daughters. It was a close-knit community; there were many houses as well as shops around Bens. When the bombing was at its height, my father moved all the big vans from the yard and parked them outside. One night, my mother, grandmother, the dog and the budgie, my mother's fur coat and I went into a van for safety. Apparently, the bells fell from St. Mary's Church, and the vibration lifted the van up from the ground. A soldier got in and said in amazement, 'What are you all doing in here?' and drove us off. He took us to the shelter at the gas works and it was hours before my father found us.

Mrs. Coakley – fish merchant.

Ben Evans House miraculously remained undamaged and the offices of Bens were relocated there. We moved out to live with my mother's sister, and later to a flat in Uplands. My father, still employed by Bens, worked as retail petrol distributor until he was called up to join the Army in – I think – 1943."

Dora recalls, "My friend, Sylvia, was still working during the Blitz. She went to see the store the next morning: she had to find out if work was possible. She told me, 'It was terrible; there were arms and legs strewn everywhere.' What a waste! Ben Evans was down to the ground and all that beautiful stock.

The Tivoli cinema, in Gowerton, was hit by shrapnel and also burned down. My sister told me and we both went to tell my mother the bad news. It was later rebuilt."

After her marriage, Dora remained in Gowerton. "We rented two rooms in a house in Cecil Road, in Gowerton, just behind my mother's house. Our landlady was a retired nurse from London; she had a little Pekinese dog that she used to take to bed with her.

During the war, I worked full-time, and Stan worked part-time for the Auxiliary Fire Service in the fireman's training station in Gorseinon. I was a switch board operator and enjoyed the work, but not as much as I did at Ben Evans."

John left Bens in 1939 when he was conscripted into the RAF. "My mother had eight boys and two girls. All us boys went to the forces and only five returned. Just before the war started, I bought a new bike, a maroon Triumph Speed Twin, in Brayleys motorbike shop. It was expensive – ninety pounds and we didn't have much money. I went away to the forces and stored my bike in Brayleys, but during the Blitz, my bike went up in the air, and I never saw it again, but I did have compensation." Phyllis adds, "And I bought a dining table suite in Bens when we were married. I discovered woodworm in one of the leaves of the table. Bens asked me to return it for it to be treated, but it disappeared during the Blitz."

Kath remembers, "We usually congregated for lunch in a café behind the stores. I was there when the first unexploded bomb went off in Castle Street and we all dived under the table. Seven soldiers were killed. During the first two days of the Blitz we couldn't go into the store as it was damaged; we just stood about in the basement. On the morning after the third night I met Gwyn Morris, who was on materials, coming from Bens. He said to me, 'There's no point in you going to the shop: there's nothing left.' Having no employment, I went to Weston-Super-Mare that summer, to look after my relative's children."

The Post-Blitz Years

The three consecutive large-scale bombing attacks by the Germans on 19, 20 and 21 of February 1941, destroyed the retail centre of Swansea. Although Bens' building was damaged beyond repair, the firm was soon trading again. It relocated briefly to a small premises in Woodfield Street, Morriston, about ten miles north-east of Swansea, and by September 1941, had returned to Swansea – to 22/25 Walters Road, originally the residential area of the town.

Sydney Rumbelow returned from the forces and continued to work for Bens as transport manager, based in St. Mary's Square – all the vans were still there.

SERVICE WITH A SMILE

BEN EVANS & CO. LTD.

12, ST. MARY'S SQ.
SWANSEA

Beg to announce the

OPENING OF
TWO MORE OF
THEIR BRANCHES

137 and 138 WOODFIELD STREET

MORRISTON

Where they will offer a further New Delivery of—

GENERAL DRAPERY
HOUSEHOLD LINENS
FURNISHING FABRICS
WOOLLEN AND SILK
DRESS MATERIALS

We are now able to offer our New

SPRING MILLINERY
KNITWEAR AND
FANCY GOODS AT

5 WOODFIELD STREET

Visit our

FURNITURE, CARPET
CHINA AND HARDWARE
SECTIONS .. ALSO MEN'S
WEAR SECTION AT

12 ST. MARY'S SQUARE

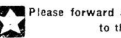 Please forward all Inquiries and Remittances to the above Address.

South Wales Evening Post,
Thursday, 15 November 1945.

Telephone—5015

BEN EVANS & Co. Ltd.
22, 23, 24 & 25, WALTERS ROAD
SWANSEA

For Ladies and Childrens Wear, Mens and Boys.
Household Linens and Fancy Depts.

Complete Funeral Furnishers
(after hours Phone 6607)

ALSO AT 12, St. MARY'S SQUARE
For Furniture, Carpets and Hardware Depts.

Dora was anxious to work again. "I wanted to get out of the house: my mother had passed away and Stan was at work all day. I contacted Miss Rosser and asked her if it would be possible for me to be re-employed. She first asked me if my husband was still alive. When I said yes, she said there was no work for me, but if I had been widowed, it would have been different."

Home from the forces, John returned to his trade, but became self-employed. He worked for the warehouses J. T. Morgan and Thomas Thomas, the Co-operative Store, and the carpet stores, Baileys and Arthur Llewellyn Jenkins. He comments, "A. L. Jenkins was an excellent firm to work for. I was fortunate in being their mainstay at the time."

Kath Jones

Kath returned to Swansea in October 1941. "I was in Bens one day visiting old friends. Miss Dorman happened to spot me and said, 'We've been looking for you everywhere. Where have you been?' I explained that I had been living away from Swansea. I started back in the store straight away and never looked back.

Three weeks later, the government introduced legislation that all employees were to be paid; it was the end of shop apprenticeships.

I hadn't been back very long before Miss Lilian Shapland, the buyer of needlework asked me to join her. I was pleased, as I had always been interested in needlework, and still enjoy working complicated embroideries.

We all loved Mr. Wheatley the managing director. My first fiancé was in the Army and when he was home on leave Mr. Wheatley would say to me, 'You can take time off to see him.'

I worked in Bens until 1944, when I was called up.

All the services were full, and I was given the option of nursing, or working in a factory. I had no wish to do factory work, and as I used to belong to the Junior Red Cross said, 'I'll go nursing.' I had a severe two-week training in Cefn Coed Hospital, in Swansea where I had to live in. The mentally ill patients had been moved out into the country, and the military had taken over, renaming it the Princess Royal Hospital. I was then posted to a maternity hospital in Ruthin near Wrexham, in North Wales. It was a maternity hospital for Londoners who had been evacuated to escape the doodlebugs. The hospital consisted of two lovely big houses: one for the prenatal patients and the other for the births and recovery.

Kath Slade, St. Woolaston Hospital, Newport, Monmouth, 1945.

There were two other nurses from Swansea there, Alma Markley and Betty Wellington, and although we had some fun, were fed up out in the country, and so asked for transfers. I was only there for about seven weeks before being transferred to St. Woolaston House Hospital in Newport, where I nursed soldiers. The building had originally been built as a workhouse, and was being used as an old people's home before being taken over during the war for military personnel. One of my brothers had been killed in the RAF on 5th March 1944, before I went nursing. My other brother was killed in a motor accident – a booby trap – near Athens in Greece, four months after the war ended, on 19th September 1945, two weeks before he was to be demobbed. My parents were shattered so I asked to be transferred home. I worked in Cefn Coed for two weeks until the military section closed: there were fewer injured soldiers coming home by then. I spent the last six months of my nursing career in Morriston Hospital, which had four military wards.

Miss Shapland had died six months before my two-year nursing finished. At the time, Mr. Wheatley, the managing director had tried to get me exempt, but failed. Bens kept my job open for me and so, my nursing completed, I took over the buyership of Miss Shapland. It was a tiny department; it had probably been a little back bedroom in the original house. Mavis Williams and Barbara Davies – her shop name was Derry – worked with me at first. Barbara went to another department and Eileen Rushmere joined me in March 1948, straight from school. I had lots of juniors at different times but Eileen was the best. Mavis married in September 1948 and Catherine (Kitty) Thompson took her place as first sales. Kitty went to another department and was succeeded by Barbara, but by August 1950, Barbara left, and Kitty was back with me.

The furniture department was housed in Ben Evans House, which survived the Blitz. Mr. Parkhouse was the buyer.

I loved working at Bens; I had a good time and everyone enjoyed working there. During the last years of the war, and after the war, everything was in short supply. Goods were rationed, and coupons – which we received from customers – were sent with our orders to the warehouses to receive more goods, such as knitting wools. I used to go to visit the London firms and went to the British Industrial Fair there. I went to the Paton and Ballwen factory to see their patterns, etc.; it was very interesting. We bought patterns for tuppence and stranded cottons were the same price. While working at Bens, I kept a diary of all its social events:

1946	12 August	Mannequin Parade at the Masonic Hall, St. Helens Road, Swansea.
	26 September	Staff Outing to Hereford and the Wye Valley.
1947	1 January	Staff Dance at the Mackworth Hotel, High Street, Swansea.
	24 June	Staff Outing to Tenby.
1948	15 January	Staff Dance at the Mackworth Hotel, High Street, Swansea.

	28 January	Mr. Graham's retirement dinner, Mermaid Hotel, Mumbles. He was the buyer for linens and bedding.
	15 February	Mannequin Parade at the Grand cinema, Swansea.
	8 July	Staff Outing to Llandrindod Wells.
1949	6 January	Staff Dance at the Mackworth Hotel, High Street, Swansea.
	19 January	Drapers' Ball at the Brangwyn Hall, Swansea.
	28 May	Coupons for clothes finished.
	30 June	Staff Outing to Aberystwyth.
1950	22 March	Drapers' Ball at the Brangwyn Hall, Swansea.
	24 June	Staff Outing to Weston-Super-Mare.
	8 August	Party for Glamorgan Cricket Club player, Gilbert Parkhouse, son of Mark – employee buyer.
1951	14 February	Drapers' Ball at the Brangwyn Hall, Swansea.
	14 June	Staff Outing to Bourton-on-the-Water.

Bens' staff at Mr. Graham's retirement dinner at the Mermaid Hotel, Mumbles, 28 January 1948. Left to right, front row: Kath Slade, ?, Mr. Dawson, Mr. Millard, Mr. Graham, ?. Middle row, 5th from left: Mr. Rumbelow, Miss Regan, Amy Rumbelow.

*Bens' staff dance at the Mackworth Hotel, 6 January 1949.
Kath Slade 3rd row from front, 9th from left.*

The Staff Dances were for Bens' staff only, but we could invite guests. The Drapers' Balls were for many stores. Each one – David Evans, Lewis Lewis, Sidney Heath – had its own table. We used to dress up; we wore long dresses with long gloves, and the men were in evening dress.

Six months before I left, Hilda Hills – her surname was changed from Howells – was leaving to get married. I was asked to take over the baby department as well as my own. I argued that it was hardly worth it, but nevertheless, agreed to do so. I left Bens when I married Gordon Jones, who was from an old Gower family originally from Pwll Du, in September 1951, and Kitty – my first sales – took my job as buyer of the needlework department."

Catherine Wort

At the age of sixteen, Catherine Wort, née Thomas, left school and went to work in Bens. During the store's mannequin parades, she shared the catwalk with famous London models. Her early years, however, were a far cry from such glamour.

"My parents owned a butcher's shop in Brynhyfryd, Swansea, where we lived on the premises. It still traded under the name of Elias Thomas, my paternal grandfather – who had established the business. We had a slaughterhouse behind the shop. The slaughter men – sixteen of them – came to eat in our kitchen, with its long table, straight from the slaughterhouse, still in their bloody overalls. They would have the same food as us, and we often had steak for breakfast. The head slaughter man always kept the seat next to him for me, to make sure I behaved myself.

I have a brother, Elias, and two sisters Nancy and Jean. After the third night of the Swansea Blitz, my father packed us all off to Llandeilo, where we stayed with friends of my father, for about a month. My father then bought a farm, Tirllan, between Llandeilo and Carmarthen. My brother and I ran the farm between us; I was eleven and he was twelve. We did everything: we used to plough the fields with two horses; we had every animal imaginable and perhaps we'd sit up all night during calving; we'd get up early to milk, and then go straight to school. We walked the four miles there and back every day. My parents ran the shop in Brynhyfryd during the week and on Saturday night, came to the farm, and went back to the shop on Monday. Two maids lived with us on the farm during the week, and spent the weekend at the shop premises.

We left the farm after the war, and returned to our home in Brynhyfryd. When I was sixteen, my Aunty Jinny, who worked in Bens, got me a job there. I was told that I would be called Miss Thompson as there was another Miss Thomas working there. I started in shoes with Marian Palferman. We were still on rationing and could only buy two pairs of Clarks shoes a month for the shop. I'd sometimes buy the both for myself, until Mr. Herbert, my boss found out. They were sometimes too small and I'd squeeze my feet into them; I have the most terribly toes now. I later went to knitting wools and embroidery with Kath Slade, who was my boss.

Working in Bens was fun: everything was a dare. I was always in trouble, and so often threatened with the sack. There was a little baker's shop and café immediately behind the stores in Henrietta Street. Every morning at ten o'clock they'd have doughnuts – doughnuts that you've never tasted before. Of course, I was the one sent to buy them because nobody else would do it: it was a risk for us girls getting in and out of the shop unseen by Mr. Jolliffe, our manager. The girls would warn me of his movements. 'He's turning his back now,' they'd say, and off I'd go. While I was out, he'd be parading on the ground floor – up and down, up and down. He'd then go upstairs to the first floor and round every department to see who was there, and discover that I was missing. 'Where's Miss Thompson?' he'd ask. When I came back from the shop, I'd peep through the side window. Mr. Jolliffe would be downstairs again and I'd wait for him to turn his back so that I could slip in unseen. Sometimes he'd be talking to a customer, and I'd be standing there with these hot doughnuts, for ages.

Before Christmas, I'd put a drop from each of my father's bottles into one bottle and take it to work. We'd all share it, and by the end of the day would be quite tipsy. On one such occasion I fell against some packaging, which in turn fell against one of the large windows and broke it. Mr. Jolliffe was downstairs and said, 'That will be Miss Thompson.' He came upstairs and didn't ask how I was, although I had cut my finger.

I always wore stilettos; I never wore flat shoes. I was getting something down from a high shelf, and instead of using a chair, stepped on a glass display cabinet. My heel went through and I fell backwards. I was lucky as the glass was thick and I could have had a serious injury.

Everything had to be done properly at Bens, and we always had to speak politely to customers. I can remember Lady Kitty Glasbrook coming to Bens every morning in her chauffeur-driven car; she was a major shareholder. We had to go out of our way to serve her, and if we didn't have what she required we'd say, 'Perhaps we can order it for you, madam?' Mr. Wheatley was the director; he was a lovely man. Every afternoon at three o'clock, he did his rounds, going to every department. He had a nice word to say to everyone – 'Hello. How are you today?' Mr. Jolliffe was great, as long as you did your job properly, and didn't expect him to smile; but it was his job to make sure that everything was done correctly.

It was the post-war years, and so much was in short supply. Hazel Bevan – she's now Gambol – told me how she will never forget my giving her a length of green material that I had put away for myself. She was going to a special do and desperately wanted a new dress, which she made from the material.

I remember Miss Wylies who was on underwear – corsets. Betty Mac, now Radford, was always laughing; she was lovely. Rosemary Tucker was on gloves. I can remember the glass case with rows of gloves in the drawers. Miss Jones was the manageress of the restaurant, assisted by Nicky. Later Nicky took over. She liked me and gave me a gold necklace that she had been given by her mother; it had a pendant of the three monkeys – hear all, see all, say nought. I worked with Miss Elms on shoes for a while. She loved me; I don't know why. She also gave me one of her treasured possessions; it was a beautiful gold necklace with aquamarine stones. I treasured them both greatly.

I modelled the stores clothes for advertisements in the *Evening Post* paper, etc. Bens held their own mannequin parades at the Grand Theatre and the Masonic Hall. They were very popular and there was always a full house. Professional models came from London and some of us girls joined them on the catwalk. We were, of course, terrified. The models were made up to perfection with heavy makeup, and we were not. Mr. Jolliffe intervened at one show and said, 'For God's sake, put some make-up on them! They look like ghosts! And tell them to smile!' Dorothy Walker, one of the top models who modelled for elderly ladies, wanted me to go back to London with her to train as a model, but I refused: I was so young, but I wish I had now, with hindsight.

Many things happened in 1953: in January, strong winds and high tides caused floods in Eastern England, when three hundred people lost their lives, and many more were left homeless – the greatest British peacetime catastrophe; it was the Queen's Coronation; I married, left Bens, and went to live in Birmingham."

Group photograph of staff outing to Llandrindod Wells, 8 July 1948 – Henrietta Street.

Staff outing to Aberystwyth, 30 June 1949.
Kitty Thompson centre front.

Staff outing to Aberystwyth, 30 June 1949.
Front row, seated, left to right: Bill Thompson, Hilda Howells, Clement, Kath Slade, Jean Davies, Mary Gwyther, Peggy Clark, Dorothy Newell, Mr. Lewis.

Staff outing to Aberystwyth, 30 June 1949.
Front row, left to right: Kath Slade, Clement, Jean Davies, Kath Lloyd, ?.
Back row: ?, Nell, Miss Brogen, Kitty Thompson, Gwyn Morris, Marian Palferman, Norma Jones, Miss Regan, Joan Drury, Jean Maguire, ?.

Staff outing 1950s.

Staff outing 1950s.

Staff outing to Llandrindod Wells, 1950s.

Marian Slade

Marian Slade, née Palferman, commenced work at Bens in 1946, having learned her trade in the Swansea branch of the shoe shop, Stead and Simpsons.

"I left school in 1945, and worked in the children's department of Stead and Simpsons – Steads – in Alexandra Road, Swansea – the main shop was in High Street in the front of the ground floor of the Mackworth Hotel. I started by scrubbing the floors and then worked my way up. I measured the length and width of the children's feet by hand with a stick measure. Shoes came in widths A, B, C and D, the most common fitting then being A – the narrowest; and size three and a half the most common shoe size. Later, X-ray machines were invented which were used more for children's feet, than adults.

I then had a chance of going to work in the footwear department of Ben Evans; it was the best thing I ever did. I later became a buyer for the department. I did not travel away to buy, as the reps. came to Swansea – to the Mackworth Hotel or to a place in Alexandra Road – with their display of wares, and I would go to them; or they would come to Bens with samples in their cases.

Mr. Jolliffe, the manager, was at the door when we arrived in the morning and greeted us with a nod. We'd clock in and then polish and hoover our departments – I loved doing it. By half-past ten, we would have had our coffee, with a Penguin biscuit and a little cigarette; I had started smoking, which was against my parents' wishes – they were disgusted. Mr. Wheatley, the managing director, then came around. He'd stop at every department to say good morning, and he came again in the afternoon to say good afternoon. Mr. Millard was the secretary; I got on famously with him and his wife also.

We'd sneak up to the needlework room; we enjoyed that; it was such fun. Sometimes, we'd find out where Mr. Jolliffe was, and if he was in his office, we'd slip out on the sly. We'd come back by the side door praying that we had not been seen; and hoping that nobody would be at the boardroom door waiting for us. The members of the managerial staff were all lovely people, and we respected them highly; but we knew how far to go; we knew our boundaries.

There were quite a lot of staff there that had worked in the old Ben Evans: Miss Paton, Miss James, Miss Clayton, Mr. Jenner, Mr. Dawson, Mr. Jenkins, Miss Erwin, Miss Rosser, Mr. Neilsen, the tailor – a marvellous man.

I usually had my lunch in the store restaurant. Miss Jones was its manageress, and was later succeeded by Mrs. Nicholls – Nicky. My friend, Mary Morse, who worked on the cash desk next to my department, used to serve for me when I was on my coffee and dinner breaks. We all helped each other out in all the departments – we mucked in – unless, of course, we were serving a customer of our own.

Miss Clayton was one of the big shareholders. She lived in a house called Ryelands, in Bishopston, and used to come to Bens in a chauffeur-driven car. Everybody would stop for her. She went around every department and we gave her a lot of attention – I always knew what make of shoes she liked. Her sister, Mrs. Jenkins – a lovely lady – who lived next door to her in Heathlands, was also a customer. She loved hats and I can see her now trying them on in the millinery department. Many solicitors and their families had their accounts with us. They were all well-to-do, but lovely people; they were not snooty in any way.

My paternal grandfather, Samuel James Palferman, owned a shoe shop in pre-war Swansea. He joined with Mr. Roberts, and they had two shops – one in Goat Street. During the General Strike of 1926, the business met financial ruin: their customers could not afford to pay their bills, and unfortunately, the business collapsed. My grandfather went to work in Liptons, a grocery shop in Oxford Street. He was prepared to set me up in a shoe business of my own. My father was not keen, as he remembered his father's financial downfall. I didn't have enough confidence anyway, so I stayed at Bens.

In about 1951, an extension was built at the back of the store, a lift installed, and many of the departments moved to different floors.

We were, of course, situated out of town, and in the early 1950s, the centre of Swansea was being rebuilt after the war. We started having competition from new shoe shops that were opening – Lilley and Skinner, A. J. Meeks, Dolcis, etc. By 1956/57, the shareholders of Bens were dying off. The management started breaking up the departments and sending the goods to other stores all over the country. I assume that they didn't have enough money to keep going, but I didn't know a lot about it. It was such a shame, but I suppose they could never have brought Ben Evans back to how it was in its heyday.

I bought my wedding dress, headdress and veil at Bens, and Mary Morse was my bridesmaid. I worked there for nine years, and it was the happiest time of my life."

Mair Bowen

Mair Bowen, née Lloyd, lived her formative years in The Lodge, Penclawdd. An extremely attractive residence, with spectacular views of North Gower to Whiteford Sands, it was the original lodge of Brynhir House. After her years as a pupil of Three Crosses Junior School, she attended The Gregg School Secretarial Training College in Heathfield, Swansea, where she was taught Greggs' own form of shorthand. It was the college's policy to find employment for its students.

> **THE GREGG SCHOOL**
>
> **1 & 2 HEATHFIELD, SWANSEA**
>
> Telephone 3587.
>
> ———
>
> Secretarial Training College with Secondary Education Department.
>
> ———
>
> **Students Efficient** are placed in satisfactory positions on completion of their training.
>
> ———
>
> **Employers** in need of Secretarial Assistants, are invited to apply to :—
>
> **THE GREGG SCHOOL**
>
> The Principal is in attendance daily.

"They sent me to Bens as a shorthand typist,' recalls Mair, 'and I loved it. I found a job for my sister, Ann, there and also my friend in Greggs, Gwyneth Grove, from Landimore.

Our office was on the first floor. The shop had originally been houses and was very quaint. My boss was Miss Owen; she was lovely. She belonged to Manselton Choir and had a beautiful singing voice. We were about six of us in the typing pool. We'd be typing away and she'd start singing all of a sudden. I learned the words of all the oratorios from her, but the one that stuck in my mind was *I Dreamed I Dwelt in Marble Halls*. It snowed so much in the mid-1960s that a road had to be cut through the lanes near my farmhouse. As I walked through the walls of snow, that song came back to me.

When I started working, I wore my ordinary clothes. After I had been working there about a month Miss Owen said to me, 'If you look around, you will see that everybody is dressed in black.' My mother couldn't afford to buy me a black dress. She was talking to Verona Dalimore's mother, Sarann (Sarah Ann) next door, and Sarann said, 'Verona has a black dress; Mair can have that.' Well, I was so thin that Verona was twice my size, but Sarann took the dress in at the sides, and I wore that for the year that I worked in Bens. I felt terrible in it, but I thought, 'Needs must.'

There was a little baker's shop around the corner in Henrietta Street that sold the most beautiful cakes. Eleven o'clock would be coffee time and we'd go there and buy macaroons; they were what we liked in our office. On Fridays – payday – we could afford to have lunch in the restaurant; it was very nice. On the other days of the week we took our own sandwiches.

I loved the two ladies who worked in the curtain department and often went down to have a chat with them. I had an account there. I saved and bought curtains from the department for my mother. You had good value at Bens and they lasted for years and years. I also bought my mother a three-piece suite – from a shop down the road –and paid off something each week. Oh, you were proud to work in Bens.

Miss Amy Rumbelow in the china department was very friendly with my boss. The men were all very smartly dressed. I loved Mr. Jolliffe; he was such a nice man and my favourite. We were afraid – in awe – of the older ones; we felt we wanted to curtsey to them.

It was the rich that had accounts at Bens. I still remember them through their monthly accounts, but I never met them. Many of the solicitors, who had offices in Walter Road, used to have coffee in Bens.

In 1951, after I had been working in Bens for about a year, my sister was taken ill and had to have her appendix taken out. When I visited her in hospital I could see all these nurses fussing about and I thought, 'Oh, I'd like to do that.' I left Bens when I was sixteen. You had to be eighteen to work in Swansea Hospital – the old Swansea General – and so I went to Gorseinon Hospital to do my pre-nursing training before undertaking my full general training. I married my farmer-husband Elvet in 1957 and became a farmer's wife. In 1968, after I had my two daughters, I was approached by a lady from the health office and was offered the job of district nurse. My mother-in-law said that she would be prepared to look after my children and encouraged me to try it for a few weeks. I thought I'd try it for six weeks, but stayed for twenty-five years."

Mary Richards

In August 1949, Mary Richards, née Morse, was employed by Bens as a cashier.

"I went to work at Bens straight from school at the age of fifteen. I lived by the Grange School and my friend June Lewis lived in Norton Road, Mumbles. I always wanted to work in a shop, and so did June. We decided to approach Audrey Butt – she lived in Glen Road – who worked in Bens. She said that she'd make inquiries and let us know. It was not long before we had an interview with Miss Regan, who was in charge of the cash office.

It was the first time that I had worn stockings. I didn't have a suspender belt but kept them up with garters; but oh dear, it was not a success as they kept slipping down. I wore a black crepe frock and heavy black suede shoes, and I thought I looked like little Orphan Annie. June and I were both accepted on the staff and informed that we would be working on the cash desk for three months to learn money, etc. and then see what department we would like to work in after that.

June and I used to cycle to work. My great uncle, Alf Williams from St. Thomas, and my uncle, Terry Andrew from Mumbles, were drivers on the Mumbles Train and when they passed us on the Mumbles Road they used to beep the hooter at us. Mr. Sydney Rumbelow was in charge of transport and Bens' funeral service. He was assisted by Mr. Evans and Mr. Graig. They often used to wheel our bikes through the china department to the outside shed, not trusting us not to break any china. June left after about eight months, and so, not wanting to cycle on my own, I used to catch the Mumbles Train at Norton Road and run up Argyle Street to Walter Road. The train was great and always came to time. Later, I travelled by bus through Uplands to Walter Road: it was more convenient.

After I had been working for a while, I decided to smarten myself up and buy something more fashionable to add to my wardrobe. We were not provided with a uniform but bought our own clothes. We had a discount at Bens and could also buy during the sales. We were allowed to wear any skirt or frock in black, black or white jumpers, or a white blouse and black cardigan; later, we could replace black with navy if we so wished. And of course, it was stockings: no tights then.

Bens was not housed in a purpose-built building but in what must have previously been a few terraced houses. When I first worked there, the interior seemed unaltered, with many staircases and small room-size departments. At first, there were no escalators or lifts and customers had to climb the stairs. I doubt whether many would be happy doing so today.

My three months on the cash desk completed, I was asked by Miss Regan if I would like to continue working there. I quickly agreed and was to spend all the eight years of my time at Bens as a cashier. My desk was on the fashion floor, the first floor, which housed ladies' frocks and coats, etc., millinery, wools, underwear, the baby department and shoes. Marian Palferman – she's Slade now – from Bonymaen, was the buyer for the shoes. The buyers also served in the shop, and as well as being a cashier, I relieved Marian when she was away. I had no formal training – just picked it up as I went along. The cash office was a separate building built in the garden at the back of the store near Mr. Rumbelow's workshop. Every morning, I went there to collect my float – which was in a canvas bag – and the assistants' cash books for the day. They were hard, red or black backed books and quite heavy as I usually carried about fifteen at a time. The assistants entered every sale in their books. The customers were given the top copy, and I, the carbon copy. I entered every transaction in my big ledger, by hand, and at the close of business every day, balanced my cash, minus the amount of the float, with the balance in my ledger. There were no adding machines then and all had to be done in my head. The management was very strict and I had to balance to the nearest penny: a pound was a lot in those days. I then took the cash books and takings to the cash office. Cheques were seldom used: most people dealt in cash.

We had many wealthy customers – solicitors and doctors. We met some very nice people. I can remember Dr. Elwyn James and his wife, and Mr. and Mrs. Rhodri Harris. They had accounts at Bens, which they settled by cheque, but I was not involved in that: it was controlled by the counting house.

Every morning about ten o'clock, the manager, Mr. Jolliffe, came around the department. He'd always give a little cough to warn us that he was approaching. He'd say, 'Good morning Miss Morse. How are the takings today?' He also came around at three o'clock in the afternoon. He was a lovely man and quite shy. Mr. Thompson was the floorwalker, and Mr. Millard was the managing director by then. He and his wife had no children and during the Second World War had housed an evacuee girl – Phyllis West – from London. The war over, Phyllis didn't return to London, but stayed with the Millards – they were quite old then. She was a pupil at the private Convent School – St. Winifred's – in Swansea. When she visited the shop she used to brush the hats and say, 'I'm going to work here when I leave school.' She was granted her wish and worked in the millinery department, but was not given special treatment. Mr. Millard's nieces, Pat and Peggy Millard also worked in the stores.

The store was open from 9 a.m. to 5.30 p.m. every weekday, except Thursday – half-day in Swansea – when it closed at 1 p.m.; Saturday it remained open until 6 p.m. Being a cashier, every so often I had to take my turn of late duty for a week and wait until 5. 45 p.m. for every customer to vacate the premises. We had to clock in and clock out each day, putting our cards in a large machine to be stamped with the time.

We had no real staff room as such, just a small cloakroom at the top of the building with a small window and benches. The shop had a lovely restaurant on the ground floor. We were allowed a fifteen-minute break mid-morning and mid-afternoon when we usually had a tea or coffee there. We had an hour for lunch. We sometimes brought our own sandwiches, but if we wanted to buy chips, we had to run all the way up to Mount Pleasant and back, trying to keep them warm: there were few eating places near Walter Road in the Fifties. We ate in the cloakroom but it was not pleasant as some of the older girls used to smoke. Alternatively, we went to Joe's Ice-cream Parlour, by the old Swansea Hospital, or to Athertons' Café in Oxford Street next to Woolworth. Mr. Atherton didn't mind us eating our sandwiches there as long as we bought a cup of tea or coffee. I usually had lunch in the restaurant if I was going out straight from work. It was a lovely meal; only two shillings and six pence for soup, main course, sweet and a coffee. Mrs. Nicholls – we called her Nicky – was the manager and such a scream.

    I earned one pound and five shillings a week at first. I can't remember joining a union: I don't think there was one at Bens. But it was lovely working there and we were a nice bunch. We had super staff trips to a great variety of places: Weston, Symond's Yat, Llandrindod Wells, Stratford-on-Avon, and Llandudno.

    I still vividly remember many of the staff. The top floor, which was like an attic, housed the alteration hands – they were a lovely crowd. Mr. Jenner was the buyer for curtains and nets with Miss Clayton, his assistant. She was quite elderly and had probably came from the old Bens. I can see her now. She walked slowly, wearing little glasses and her white hair in a bun. The hosiery department was run by Miss Charles. It was a small area but there was such a choice of stocking colours. A girl used to come in on certain days of the week to repair nylon stockings; she must have had wonderful eyesight, but what a tedious job! Miss Rosser was the buyer for ladies' fashion and Miss Paton was first sales. She wore her black hair – and I don't think it was dyed – in plaited coils over her ears. It so happened that many of the girls had unusual surnames, but if there was a duplication of names – usually Welsh ones – they were given a shop name: Elaine Williams for instance, who worked in the fashion department, was renamed Wilmot. Val Thyer was on knitwear and Miss Erwin was on ladies' underwear. Aida Tossell was the buyer for millinery and her assistant was Miss Elms. Miss Amy Rumbelow – sister of Sydney Rumbelow – was sweet; she was a sweet little lady in charge of the china department on the ground floor. Her assistant was Val Pickard – she later married Morris on materials – who, I thought, was lovely. Val's father was an inspector on the Mumbles Trains. The switchboard – operated by Glenys Harris – was also in that department but later relocated to the top floor. Mary Gwyther was on

Front: Elaine Williams.
Back, left to right: Mary Morse, Sheila Gay, Pat Rowlands.

haberdashery. Miss Owen was in charge of the office where Meirwen Morgan, Dorothy Jones, Pat, and Mair Lloyd from Penclawdd worked. Rose Edwards, Joan Drury, Mary Ball, Ann Pimm, Vicky, Dorothy Paniers and Dorothy Newell worked in the cash office with Miss Regan in charge. We were very few married women on the staff. Mr. Neilson was Bens' tailor. It was so different then as most suits were not bought off the peg, but made to measure. Mr. Hayward –on the ground floor – was the buyer for the gents' department and his assistant was Rosemary Tucker from Llanrhidian. Mr. Davies – Denis – from Bonymaen was the buyer for the boys' department and Malcolm Evans worked on materials. I can't remember much about the basement. Mr. Reed was the buyer for kitchens and hardware. Mr. George was in the sports department with Mark Parkhouse, father of the famous cricketer Gilbert Parkhouse. We used to love to hug Stanley Lewis who worked there; he was a slight little boy with black eyes and black curly hair. There were nice boys on the vans with Mr. Rumbelow: Frank was one of them; he was gorgeous but so shy; he married Peggy Clarke on leather goods.

By the mid-1950s we were conscious that Bens was coming to an end. I knew that I would have a good reference from Bens and was fortunate in being quickly employed as a cashier by Co-operative House in Oxford Street."

Left to right: Glenys Harris, Kathy Gibbins, Dorothy Newell, Mary Morse, Val Thyer.

In July 1955, a takeover bid was made by GUS (Great Universal Stores). After controlling Bens for about a year they decided to hold a sale to clear out old stock and make way for new developments. This preceded a store closure of two weeks for modernization. The old carpet shop was to be completely transformed into a first-class fashion and underwear shop under the then present manageress, Aida Tossell. J. E. Jolliffe, who had been with Bens for fifteen years, was to be retained as manager and B. C. Millard as general secretary.

Despite the efforts of GUS, as it was too far from the town's post-war shopping centre – Kingsway, Princess Way and Oxford Street – Ben Evans & Co. Ltd. went out of business in the late 1950s.

Immediately before and after its demise, most of the staff of Bens found employment elsewhere. Sydney Rumbelow was employed by Co-operative House and Miss Paton by D. C. Jones in Wind Street. Miss Charles transferred to Lewis Lewis, situated outside the pre-war town centre, in High Street – the only Swansea departmental store to survive the Blitz. Miss Amy Rumbelow joined the staff of David Evans.

5.

All with Good Grace

Win Henry – Milliner

> 'The term millinery is generally used to designate women's hats and their trimmings – ribbons, lace, feathers, artificial flowers, etc. – and is also applied to the art of making and trimming hats and bonnets. Originally the word meant *Milan goods* such as textiles, fabrics, gloves, ribbons, *Milan bonnets*, and needles. Many articles of millinery are sold by haberdashers and drapers. Milliners are those who make and trim hats and headgear of all descriptions for women and children, and are nearly all women.'[1]

Over the centuries, women's hats have been worn for practical reasons – to protect the head from heat, cold and rain, and the complexion from sun. However, they also played a large part in fashion, and a woman would never be seen out without a hat. It was considered essential for a woman to wear a hat in church and chapel: it was mistakenly thought that St. Paul had commanded women to keep their heads covered in church.[2] Today, headgear is worn to protect from the cold and sun, but as far as fashion is concerned, hats are worn rarely – for weddings, ladies' lunches and posh occasions.

Millinery played a large part in instigating the screen career of Greta Garbo – the legendary Swedish film star. When about sixteen, she was employed in the millinery department of Paul U. Bergstrom (PUB), a large departmental store in Stockholm. Selected to model hats for the store's 1921 spring mail order catalogue and then appearing in a pro-

---

1. *Everyman's Encyclopaedia*, Volume 8 (Milan, Italy. 1967) p. 336.
2. St. Paul's reputation as a woman-hater is a twisted version of what he really felt and preached. It was not the age of woman's lib and women had to do as they were told; if that was to be subservient and be a plaything of men, then so be it. St. Paul, however, realized that a woman was the creation of God just as a man was, and so she must have the final say, and should be honoured and set apart. She must be allowed to say 'No' if she wished to, and if she wished to cover her hair in the presence of men, then she should be allowed to do that as well.

motional film *How Not To Dress*, she was invited to star in her first film, *Peter and the Tramp*.

Coco Chanel the famous French designer was described as not just being ahead of her time, but ahead of herself. She began her fashion revolution against society by aiming at the head; millinery was her first business.

Swansea boasted its own famous milliner, Gina Davies, chairman of the Millinery Guild for nine years. She was born in Walter Road, Swansea. Leaving school at fifteen, she served her apprenticeship in Theophilus, one of the town's exclusive fashion shops. During the Depression she obtained a job in London, and was soon one of the city's renowned milliners and of international fame. Stars of stage and screen – Elizabeth Taylor, Ava Gardner – became clients in her salon behind Claridge's. In post-war years, the ladies of Swansea experienced a flavour of her hats when Gina showed her collections in Swansea's departmental store, David Evans, in Princess Way. Her first royal commission was a hat for Queen Elizabeth, the Queen Mother, for the state funeral of her husband King George VI. She was the first of many royal clients – Queen Elizabeth II, Princess Margaret, Princess Alexandra and Princess Michael.

"My mother thought that I was rather flighty, which I was of course," says Win. "She decided to put me in millinery to make a lady out of me; looking back, I think she succeeded. She was a wonderful woman with lovely violet eyes and very black lashes. She was very aristocratic with titled people in her family and was a hundred and one when she died. My grandfather, Henry Martin had an important job down the docks and was knighted for his work. My parents, sisters Dorothy and Gwen, and I lived with him in his home – a large thirteen-roomed house, No. 57, St. Helens Road. My father was an invalid, having been gassed in the First World War; it eventually resulted in his death. He was horribly ill; it was awful for my mother.

In 1928, I went straight from Oxford Street School at the age of fourteen, to learn my trade in a little millinery shop called Simons, in St. Helens Road, opposite the YMCA – there was also a branch in Oxford Street. It was a small shop but very exclusive. We were about four or five on staff and displayed only one or two hats in the window: a small number was more eye-catching. I loved my work and our customers were the well-to-do of Swansea. I remember Sir William and Lady Jenkins – she was very smart and loved her hats. They lived in a big house in Gower Road.

I sometimes used a wooden model to sew my hats, but mostly, I used my own head and front and back mirrors. Quartered crown hats were sewn by machine, but all the rest were sewn by hand – hats with big brims and small brims. It was important to use materials that were easily workable; crêpe was not, and I favoured pure silk, as did my mother. When a customer was buying a hat I liked to put it on her head myself, giving her a mirror with a handle for her to see the back of her head.

I took a lot of care over my appearance. I loved my hair looking good, but I was lucky, as it was easy hair to look after. I was possibly the first in Swansea to have a perm; I loved them. My make-up was as thick as porridge. I wore brilliant red or orange lipstick but did conform and wore pale pink nail varnish to please my mother. I never wore black as we had had a lot of deaths in our family and always seemed to be in deep mourning; also, black drained me of colour, although I was always sunburned, living near the sea and being a sun baby. My working clothes were always navy. I wore pure silk stockings; they were a dream to wear. I loved to dress well and never went out without a hat. My mother was a clever dressmaker and made all our clothes, and there was always a bit of material over to make a hat. My sisters and I had a lot of fun together. Dorothy was a lady like my mother, but Gwen was more like me – a tomboy. Although my mother tried to tame me, I used to make her laugh. I think she was proud of me really, but she tried not to show it.

I occasionally went to the cinema in Swansea – The Plaza, The Albert Hall, The Grand – but dancing was my first love. I couldn't walk anywhere; I always danced. Dances were held in the Patti Pavilion[3] nearly every night throughout the Second World War. It had a wonderful wooden block floor; it was like glass, but you'd never fall on it. I couldn't resist going most nights; girls could go to dances on their own, then. My mother wasn't very happy about it as she thought the Patti common – but she made me dance dresses to go. I usually wore flat shoes, but my longing was to wear high heels; I was

South Wales Evening Post,
15 August 1945.

---

3. The famous Anglo-Italian opera diva, Madam Patti (1843-1919), who lived in Craig-y-Nos, in the Swansea Valley, donated her winter garden to the people of Swansea. It was transported piece by piece to be reconstructed in Victoria Park, Swansea, as the Patti Pavilion.

daring and did sometimes, but was always afraid that I might break my neck! I loved all the dances, but I especially loved the Charleston – it was really me. The war years were sad, but we had a whale of a time. There were a lot of men – in the forces – around and they were all good dancers. I was never taught to dance; I was just a natural dancer.

One night I saw a man twirling a girl around and around. The floor had cleared to watch them. 'Oh!' I thought. 'I've got to have him: I meant to dance with not to marry, but I did both. Many met their husbands and wives in the Patti.

My mother didn't want me to marry, but nevertheless, we got engaged; you had to get engaged before you married then. Later, she was pleased that I had married Ted as he was strict, but I had married a dancer and we kept on dancing. We went to live in Wembley, in London, for a while: Ted had a job there. We loved Wembley because there were lots of wonderful dance halls in the area. Ted and I danced the waltz, etc. but the tango was our favourite. I can see us dancing now with a circle of spectators around. They used to go off the floor to watch us and we usually ended up doing an exhibition. The men wore suits, and the ladies short frocks, but the men usually hired evening dress for posh dances and the ladies wore long frocks. They were wonderful years.

We returned to Swansea. By then, our daughter, Jean was born. She was a doll of a baby; she was very beautiful and my mother was happy to look after her for me to go back to work. She was always afraid that Jean would turn out to be a tomboy like me. I was employed in the new David Evans in the handkerchief department. I loved handkerchiefs and fashioned them into flowers and displayed them on a silver tree stand. The store was owned by two cousins, David and Edward Andrews. One of the Mr. Andrews – a very good-looking man – used to say to me, 'And how is my handkerchief lady today? Your display is wonderful.' I loved working there but I was always a milliner, and always a fool.

I've had a wonderful life. I used to break all the rules and hope for the best. It seemed to work."

Edna Jenkins – Shoe-Shop Assistant

Footwear has always been an essential part of one's apparel.

It has gone down in history such as the Wellington boot, introduced by, or named after Arthur Wellesley, the famous first Duke of Wellington, British general and statesman.

Footwear has also been the subject of stories, films, poems and songs. In 1845, Hans Christian Andersen, the Danish son of a cobbler, wrote *The Red Shoes*. It was a tragic fairy tale about a pair of magical shoes that made their wearer dance uncontrollably without stopping; the consequences were disasterous. The film *The Red Shoes,* made in 1948 and starring Moira Shearer, Anton Walbrook and Marius Goring was based on the fairy tale. It was Moira Shearer, the Sadler's Wells ballerina's debut as an actress, and the greatest ballet melodrama film of all time.

The short-story writer and poet, Joseph Rudyard Kipling inspired by the Boer War, wrote in 1903:

> 'We're foot – slog – slog – slog –sloggin' over Africa –
> Foot – foot – foot – foot – sloggin' over Africa –
> (Boots – boots – boots – boots – movin' up an' down again!)
> There's no discharge in the war!'

The title of his poem was *Boots*.

Over half a century later, Nancy, daughter of the famous Frank Sinatra, used the same title for her hit song, in 1966.

Today, footwear is a riot of colour and styles -- round toes, pointed toes, square toes, flat heels, chunky heels, wedge heels, stiletto heels, etc.; however, when Edna was a young girl, heavy black or brown foot gear was all the rage.

Like many young people of her time, Edna Jenkins, née Lewis, was unable to pursue her chosen career through lack of parental finances. Instead, she worked in R. Smith's shoe shop for two years. Established in 1920, the shop, at No. 12 Union Street, was recognized by its distinctive outdoor display of every type of footwear hanging in abundance from racks either side of its door. The hard work, long hours, and low salary, coupled with a boss with whom she shared little empathy, proved to be an unenviable experience.

"We lived in one of the last remaining thatched cottages in Penclawdd. It was situated in Banc Bach – the other was in Cefn Bychan. We later moved to No. 10, Sea View.

When we were in school, Eurfryn Preston and I were the first children in Penclawdd to go around the houses selling the Labour newspaper, the *Daily Herald*, from Philip John Davies' shop, Gower Stores.

I wanted to be a missionary, but my parents didn't have the money as my father was a miner, and so I had to go out to work. Having said that, on leaving Penclawdd Elementary School, my parents put me in Pagefield College – it was later called Clarke's College – where the fees were four guineas a term. I was doing very well at shorthand and typing, but it was then 1926 and the Miners' (and General) Strike, so after only being there a year, I had to leave.

I went to work in Ebenezer Evans' confectionery shop in Sea View, Penclawdd. A baker-boy from Gowerton used to deliver bread to the shop. He had a connection with an assistant working in R. Smith's shoe shop in Union Street, Swansea. 'Listen,' he said to me, 'There's a job in Swansea. Do you want it?'

When I was interviewed by Mr. Smith, he wanted to know about my education; it held me in good stead that I had attended Pagefield College – and just to be a shop assistant! Jobs were hard to come by; it was a terrible situation.

At first, I worked in the shop in Union Street next-but-one to the No. 10 pub, with the owner, Mr. Smith – a very nice man. It was a small shop but always very busy. I had only been working for a short time, when Mr. Smith opened another shop in High Street Arcade. I went to work there with the manager – he was a deacon in chapel but I didn't like him very much. An old lady came in one day. She tried on a pair of shoes that she liked. 'I think I'll have them,' she said.

'But you'll never be able to wear them,' I told her. 'They'll slip off.'

The manager was listening and gave me a row after because I had stopped her buying the shoes; he didn't care that the shoes were a bad fit.

I served both male and female customers but mostly female. There was a boy assistant – Kenneth Connibeer – as well as myself. I was very polite to the customers; I'd meet them with a smile as they came in, take them to a seat, and ask them what they wanted – brown, black shoes, etc. The shoes were in boxes piled high and I had to go up and down, up and down the ladder; it was a killer, but I didn't really mind and it was expected. I sat on a stool at the customer's feet, measured them and used a shoe lift to put the shoes on. Lace-up shoes – rather like brogues – with a short chunky heel, were very fashionable and so also were boots and clogs. I was taught how to pack: I wrapped the shoes in tissue paper; put them in their box; covered the box with brown paper and tied it with cord. I was taught to cut cord with my hands; it was a knack, and I can still do it. I took the customer's payment to the till and returned with the receipt. It was all cash then; I never saw a cheque. I bought a pair of clogs, but had to pay for them; I had no concession.

Shoes were cheap: they were mostly four (shillings) and elevenpence-halfpenny, but some at six (shillings) and elevenpence were a terrific price. Later when I got married, my uncle, Horace Thorold, treated me to a pair of shoes at Dolcis that were the dearest shoes in the shop. They were made of lizard skin and cost one guinea – twenty-one shillings – and lasted for years and years.

At first, I went to work by train from Penclawdd Station; I didn't have much time and had to almost run from Victoria Station to get to Smiths by half-past nine. Later, I travelled by bus with my friend, Win Eaton, as she then was. She lived in Clifford House, Penlan, and worked as a tailoress in Swansea. I worked long hours: I started work every morning at half-past nine – except Sunday when the shop was closed; Monday, Tuesday and Wednesday I finished work at ten to six; Thursday – half-day – the shop closed at one o'clock; Friday it closed at eight o'clock and Saturday nine o'clock. During my lunch-hour, I ate my sandwiches in the kitchen and I also used to go to Swansea Market to shop for my mother. I didn't wear a uniform, but a dark overall that my mother bought for me. I earned seven (shillings) and sixpence a week and my weekly train fare cost five shillings. My father was earning very little at the time; they were bad times.

After I had been working there a while, I was asked to live in during the week, and for about three months, slept in a bedroom above the shop. I went down to the shop in the mornings before the rest of the staff came in, and put the gas on. My boyfriend, Mel Jenkins, who later became my husband, used to meet me after work on a Saturday night and we'd go to Gowerton on the ten o'clock train; I would carry on to Penclawdd and he to Loughor.

I first met Mel at Ship Bank, in Penclawdd; he was very handsome and from Loughor. I was with my friend, Sis Davies, and he had a date with her elder sister, Marion. I was only fourteen then, but I met him again two years later and we never parted. We had been courting for four years before he came to my house, and all the family liked him.

I left Smiths after two years, as the pay was so poor. If I had continued working with Mr. Smith, I know I would have enjoyed my job more.

After we were married, Mel bought a second-hand motorbike. One day we went on the bike to see his mother in Loughor. When we were travelling up the hill in Kingsbridge – Loughor Road – the bike was going slower and slower. The children came out of school laughing and shouting hooray and chased us up to the top of the hill; I have never felt so ashamed in all my life. Mel fancied a new bike – a Silver Star. 'How much is it?' I asked him.

'Ninety pounds,' he replied.

'I've got ninety pounds.' I told him. 'You can have it to buy the bike.'

The tears came to his eyes as money was so hard to come by then, but I was a saver. Then we had a lovely time; we went to Carmarthen, and down Port Eynon bathing on a Sunday. I bought a pair of trousers, and wore them on Sundays; I'd put a frock on at home and only change into my trousers after I'd left Penclawdd."

Edna undertook much committee work in Penclawdd, which she greatly enjoyed. After the Second World War, Penclawdd Rugby Club was in dire straits financially and needed all the support possible. The Ladies Supporters Club was formed under the chairmanship of Carys Hughes, the local doctor's daughter. They were an extremely hard-working bunch undertaking many tasks, from laundering and mending the team's kit to organizing rugby dinners. Edna continues, "I was an active member of the club and on the committee of the WI for years. In about 1957, I was a founder member of Tabernacle Sisterhood with Phyllis Griffiths and Martha Guy. Phyllis wanted to call it Sisterhood and Martha, Guild; I preferred Sisterhood, and so it was carried. I was its treasurer and secretary for many years."

Alice Draper – Dressmaker

'Glamour is what makes a man ask for your telephone number. But it also is what makes a woman ask for the name of your dressmaker.'[4] There was usually a dressmaker or two in town or village, sewing garments to fit the individual to perfection whatever be their shape and size. Today, they are few and far between and women mostly have to rely on *off the peg* clothes – not always to their satisfaction. Moreover, alteration hands are extremely hard to come by.

Alice was born to Trevor Edwin and Able Winifred Garmey in 1919. She was initiated into the Rag Trade when just a child: Nellie England involved her young niece in the tailoring business at the tender age of ten years. Alice recounts her chequered career.

"I was born in Vicarage Terrace, St. Thomas, but later lived in Foxhole. Biblical names from the Old Testament were very prevalent in the area: Canaan Chapel, All Saints Church, Canaan Terrace, Jericho Row, Lambs Row, Lions Row – 'The lamb laid down with the lion' – and we

---

4. Lily Dache, *Woman's Home Companion,* July 1955.

lived in Ahi Cottages, the oldest houses in that part of Foxhole. We lived in a semi-detached cottage and had semi-detached toilets. The two cottages shared the cleaning of the toilets and they were always spotless; I can remember the wooden seats were always gleaming white. It was one of my jobs to clean them and I used to think I was privileged to do so because it was a grown-up job. My mother used to say to me, 'If you don't behave yourself, you're not going to clean the toilets!' There is very little of Foxhole left now; slum clearance they called it, but I didn't think they were.

They were hard times for my parents financially; they had thirty shillings a week – ten shillings from the government, and my father's one pound pension for losing the sight of his eye – to bring up four kids. My father was in the Army during the First World War and had lost the sight of his left eye when hit by a piece of shrapnel; as a result, he lost his job as a tube inspector in the German-owned Mannesmann[5] Copper Tube Works in Swansea. My parents were subjected to the cruel, humiliating, means test,[6] which was an awful experience and so unfair; like my father, so many involved had served their country in the First World War. When my parents anticipated a visit from the means test representative, they hid the wall clock in a cupboard. I can remember one occasion: the man said, 'I know you have a clock; I can see the mark on the wallpaper.'

My father replied, 'During the war, I was expected to kill men for six pence a day; if you touch my clock, I will kill you for nothing.'

The Mission Hall – originally a school – is on Kilvey Hill. When I was a child, it was run by a little dwarf-girl, called Jane. She had come into money from her dad and being very religious, put all her money and effort into the building. It was the time of the Temperance Movement, and I was saved so many times! Us children signed the pledge never to drink – to become Temperance boys and girls; but after we signed, we'd have a cup of cocoa – and a certificate – so we signed many times! We were bribed of course, but we didn't care: we just wanted the cocoa. Half of Foxhole signed.

In the parish hall in Foxhole Road, we'd have magic lantern shows, again on the Temperance Movement; we'd be shown slides of the drunken father spending all the family wages on the demon drink, with his downtrodden wife and starving children.

Viewing the dead was a popular pastime. We'd say, 'Jim Kilt is dead.'

---

5. Reinhardt Mannesmann was a German inventor and industrialist (1856-1922).
6. Part of the savage measures adopted by the Labour Government to cope with the economic crisis following their return to power in 1929.

'Is he in his coffin?'

'Yes.'

So we'd go and knock on the door – quite a crowd of us – and say, 'Please, Mrs. Kilt, can we see Mr. Kilt, to pay our respects?' He'd be in the front room with candles burning. We didn't like the candles and would have preferred the gas lights to be lit; but we knew there would be sandwiches in the back room. The dead always had a net over their faces to protect them from the cats; everybody had cats to kill the mice. The net would be drawn aside and we'd say, 'Oh, don't he look nice; oh, don't he look lovely; he looks as if he's sleeping,' – we'd heard our parents make these comments. 'Well, we're going now.'

'Would you like a sandwich?'

'Yes please!'

We'd go to The Pictorium cinema in St. Thomas on a Saturday afternoon, for tuppence. We'd be given a ticket, which allowed us to go straight from school on a Wednesday, for one penny; there would be a different performance then. I earned the money through running errands: shopping for my mother; going to the chemist and buying paraffin oil for elderly neighbours; delivering sewing for my aunt to the Jews, who lived near The Albert Hall. My Aunty Nellie used to say, 'Oh, give her an umbrella; she'll go to hell and back with an umbrella,' so my mother gave me an umbrella, and off I'd go in all weathers.

Voting day of local elections was an important event in Foxhole, and all, adults and children alike, took it very seriously. Shop-owners were mostly Liberal, and the rest were Labour; I never remember Conservatives. Photos of the candidates were placed in the windows of the front room of the houses. The women dressed in their best clothes to vote; it was probably the only time they went out with their husbands – apart from going to chapel.

We – the Labour kids – used to form a band: we covered combs with paper and blew through them; and banged on toffee tins. We dressed in the Labour colours, red and yellow, and marched back and forth from Foxhole to Pentrechwyth playing our instruments and singing:

> 'Vote, vote, vote for Mr. Williams
> He's the one that's going to win,
> For we have a salmon tin, and we'll put old Jonesy in,
> And then he won't see daylight anymore.'

The Liberal kids – they were in green and white – used to try and make a procession, but we'd do anything to stop them – even pelting them with stones! We'd be very grubby by teatime, but we would have had a wonderful day. We knew, of course, that Labour would win, but the Liberals used to come very close though.

We'd be allowed to stay up for the count. Our man would have got in and there would be celebrations. We'd go to the successful candidate's house and enjoy the spread: ham sandwiches would be served, and once we had fresh salmon; we didn't know what it was as we had only seen tinned.

When I left school at fourteen, I was fortunate in having a job in a sewing factory – Struttons – in Cockett; it was a clothing factory, and the only one of its type in Swansea – apart from Jones' and you'd have to be pretty desperate to work there. Struttons was originally housed in Mansel Street in Swansea. The Mormon Church – Jesus Christ of Latterday Saints – is now built on the site of Struttons in Cockett; they sing praises now where there were plenty of curses before. The owners of the factory are buried in the churchyard of St. Peters Church; their monumental grave overlooks the old factory site, and has a swirl of material fashioned around it. They were not nice people to work for, and were out to squeeze every drop of sweat that they could get out of you. These factories were known as sweat shops.

My aunt – Nellie Watkins she was, but married a man called England – was a tailoress; using Weldon's pattern books she made tailored suits and costumes in serge and tweed; they'd last you for the rest of your life. I'd been helping her – tacking, basting, making buttonholes – since I was ten, and my payment would be collecting enough of the unwanted scraps of material to make little purses; so I was already quite knowledgeable in dressmaking before I went to work in the factory. There were about two hundred and fifty industrial sewing machines in the factory and they were very heavy. I found it quite natural to adjust to these fast, powerful machines, and soon became very competent. I was good at my job: my aunt had taught me well.

I earned three shillings and six pence a week, and out of that my mother paid for a one shilling and sixpenny weekly return train ticket from High Street Station to Cockett; later, I bought a bike, a Royal Enfield Roadster model – the people who made rifles – and cycled to work. It was an excellent bike but didn't have the Halford's drop-handle-bars that were becoming popular then; we used to call them, *Head down, ass up, bikes*. It was hard work cycling up Carmarthen Road, especially against the wind; I had to pedal like mad, as the bike had no gears. I dare not be late so always hoped to hang on behind a lorry – especially up the steep part. I cycled to work in all weathers; I had no special clothing and was often absolutely saturated by the time I reached Struttons. I'd leave my bike in the bike rack and if I was lucky, the boiler-man would be in a good mood and take my coat to dry, otherwise, it would still be wet when I went home. I had to be careful of the tramlines in Cwmbwrla: if the wheels went on them they would twist, and I would be off-balanced.

After I'd been working there for about six weeks, they put me on piecework. The manageress was tall, and very strict. She said that I was worth twelve shillings and six pence a week, so I had to earn that before I made any money; if I earned less than that, it would be deducted from my wages. I would have a bundle of all the separate parts of one dozen blouses to sew up; I did not cut the material, or sew on the buttons. There were organdie blouses with frilly fronts, ordered by Marks and Spencer – then a small shop in High Street Arcade. It was hard going as I was expected to make the one dozen blouses in one day; if I was very lucky, I'd make an extra half dozen. Marks and Spencer later opened up in the centre of Swansea; they were very particular, and if they stated that they wanted fourteen stitches to the inch, no other number would do.

You never skived off work then; every day was a working day; but once I was in work it was a different world, and I loved it.

My friends and I used to go to the dances at the Patti Pavilion on a Saturday night. Occasionally, we walked to the dances at the Pier Hotel, in Mumbles, hoping for a lift home; if we did not have one, we caught the last Mumbles Train home, very rarely paying.

With the declaration of war, my salary increased: I earned about three pounds and ten shillings a week making army uniforms – officers' mess jackets – which was fantastic."

Rationing was enforced on 8 January 1940, organized by the Ministry of Food headed by Lord Woolton. Ration books were issued to each citizen. People had to register their name with one retailer from whom they obtained their rationed food. Purchases were exchanged for the equivalent cost in coupons, which were extracted from the book; an empty book meant exhaustion of the ration quota. Food was the first commodity to be rationed.

May 1941 saw a point system adopted for the rationing of clothes: materials were in great demand for military uniforms, blankets, etc. The government also introduced utility garments to save material and control prices. Clothes, blankets, sheets, etc. were made to 'basic' standards and limited range of designs: ladies' skirts were cut straight and worn just below the knee; men's trousers had no turn-ups; jackets were single-breasted; a limit was put on pockets and buttons. Handing clothes down and sewing home-made garments, was encouraged. Women were advised to compromise, and to be inventive through the Sew and Save campaign. It was supported in newspaper articles regularly featuring Mrs. SEW-and-SEW, a rag doll. She demonstrated how to turn old clothes into new – a lady's dress into two children's frocks, or a new shirtfront from a shirttail, and so on.

Alice talks of her war years. "Charles Eleazer – nicknamed Champagne Charlie – and I were married in 1939, and went to live with my husband's parents. I left my work, as my in-laws didn't approve of married women working; also, it was considered a bit common to work in these factories. A few of the girls were a bit *rough and tumble* – the first time I saw a girl smoking was in the factory – but on the whole they were excellent workers.

I bought a machine and spent a good many years dressmaking at home – *taking in* sewing. I was fortunate that I was a dressmaker, as clothes were in short supply, and also rationed. If you had a brother in the Navy that was great: they were issued with off-white blankets, which made beautiful topcoats; I made many swagger coats out of them. Skirts were short – just below the knee – and tight, all through the war: it saved material.

I sewed for many of the girls working in Marks and Spencer: I'd polish the lino, measure my customers, and then cut the garment pieces out of the material, on the floor; I didn't use a pattern. The cinemas played a big part in our lives and, apart from the entertain-

The Observer, 11 June 1944.

Alice wearing hand-me-down costume from friend, and utility shoes.

ment, were used to keep up with fashion. My customers would go to the cinema and say to me, 'Go to The Castle' or, 'Go to The Plaza and look what she (the film star) is wearing; I want a dress/coat like that,' and they'd pay for me to go."

Greta Garbo featured in many films of the time. Coupled with John Gilbert, she starred as the eponymous heroine of the period film, *Queen Christina*. Made in 1933, it was based on the colourful life of Queen Christina, sovereign of seventeenth century Sweden. One of Garbo's topcoats proved very popular and Alice copied it for her customers. "It was a military style garment with huge shoulders, full sleeves, three front buttons, a flared skirt, a ruched back with an inset belt that tied in the front, and a Duchess of Windsor-type collar. Stiffening material was not to be had at the time so I soaked the hem, rubbed ordinary Sunlight soap on the turn-up, pressed it, and then hemmed it with big looping stitches: the skirts were cut on the bias and would have sagged if I had just sewn the hem. I used grey, French bouclé wool material, which cost six shillings and eleven pence per yard; they were quite expensive, as I needed at least four yards. I must have made dozens of them, with a toque hat to match. I also made one for myself, which I loved, and wore for years and years.

Stockings were very scarce. Being a red-head, I didn't tan easily and so painted my legs brown, and also painted a seam at the back of my legs – seamless stockings hadn't been invented.

Soldiers were billeted in our house after Dunkirk in 1940; we had no choice. They slept three to a bedroom; one was a Londoner called Sharpy; one was from way up north of Scotland – we couldn't understand a word he said – and the third was from Perth. When they arrived they were soaking and full of sand. We were later asked to accommodate a sergeant, so I had to give up my bedroom and sleep in a camp bed at the bottom of my in-laws' bed – my husband was by now away in the Army. My in-laws slept in a brass bedstead with big knobs on the posts. My father-in-law snored so loudly that he would have frightened Hitler; and my mother-in-law was just as bad. Every time they snored, the knobs would shake. After a few nights, the soldiers said that they would rather go back to Dunkirk. I could stand it no longer, and went downstairs to sleep on the settee in the back parlour, with the two dogs. Living in Fabian Street I had become used to the hooting of the tugs and ships, the trams going like mad around the corner to East Docks Station, the shunting of the railway trucks opposite going bang, bang, bang, and the whistling of the trains. But I couldn't stand the snoring.

My father-in-law owned an asbestos bungalow in Pennard, which we used as a weekend holiday home. The roof of our house was damaged during bombing and so we all piled into the bungalow. My mother-in-law couldn't exist without Swansea Market – she'd go every day even if it were just to buy a pound of apples – and so, when the roof was mended, she and my father-in-law went back to Fabian Street – and the bombing. My husband and I stayed, as he had just been discharged from the Army through injury in Northern Ireland, and it was quiet for him there. I had to sign up and would have liked to be a Wren, but I was told that my job was to nurse my husband. He later had a job in Swansea Docks and travelled back and forth to his work every day by Swan Buses – yellow buses.

It was hard work, but I loved living in Pennard. I carried our water through three fields from Browns Farm. The bungalow had no electricity and we used paraffin lamps and heaters. The winters were so cold that the paraffin sometimes froze; the milk was always frozen. I used to scrounge around the farms looking for food: I had rabbits from Jack Sandy, in Sandy Lane; they were nine pence each and if I brought the skins back, I had a tuppenny refund; I became quite an expert at skinning them. I used to sew for the farmers and was never paid in cash, but always with goods – two eggs, etc. I patched one of the farmer's trousers and sewed some heavy stuff. The farmer's wife said, 'There's a nice shoulder of lamb for you, for Sunday.' So I invited my mother and father-in-law for a roast lamb dinner.

'Oh,' they said, 'a shoulder of lamb,' and were thrilled to bits.

I stuffed it with thyme, parsley, breadcrumbs and a beaten egg and we enjoyed it; it was beautiful. My mother-in-law said to me, 'There's something different about farm lamb.' Well, we discovered later that it wasn't lamb; it was a shoulder of goat. I didn't guess as it had been such a long time since I had seen a shoulder of lamb, I'd forgotten what it looked like. I used to get up at seven o'clock in the morning and come back with about eight or nine mushrooms; I'd fry them with some Welsh bacon – perhaps it was all fat – from Winnie Neath's farm, or scrounge an egg to make an omelette. I'd walk the golf links looking for a particular mushroom that grew in the sandy soil; they were quite small but absolutely delicious. If I was short of a carrot I'd nip down to Mr. Puntaen's garden – he was a solicitor, and had a gardener of course – and crawl under the wire, and pinch one – but only the one. Some villagers – Mrs. Beer was one – used to clear out their garages and hold whist drives for the Red Cross. I was no card player and always had the booby prize; it was always the best prize. Once I had a little hay box with small tomatoes ripening in it, and two slices of bacon; I appreciated that far more than an ornament.

We were encouraged to make Woolton's Pies; they were made of turnips and potatoes, and the pastry of dripping. If you could survive eating those, you could survive Hitler – that's for sure!" 'The ingredients of Woolton Pie could be adapted to fit what was available at the time. This was reflected in the name, which varied from the socialist sounding *Woolton Pie*, through *Lord Woolton Pie*, to the almost Messianic *The Lord Woolton Pie*. The original recipe was, in fact, created by the chef at the Savoy Hotel, who called it *Lord Woolton's Vegetable Pie*.'[7]

Alice discovered that despite war regulations, local farmers managed to provide an abundance of food at harvest-time. "After the corn was harvested, a threshing machine came round all the farms, and local farmhands who were available, helped. The farmer and his wife fed them all, and the table would be laden with food; it was the first time I saw potato salad.

Immediately after the war, my mother, my father's sister, and their friend went to Jersey to work. There they graded and packed tomatoes

---

7. Mike Brown & Carol Harris, *The Wartime House* (Phoenix Mill, Thrupp, Stroud, Gloucestershire, GL5 2BU, 2001) p. 78.

Alice celebrating Victory in Europe Day. Her dress was made from a cream and blue shangtung silk-type curtain material.

Alice in Trafalgar Square, London, 26 October 1947. The statue is still protected – a legacy of the war years.

in boxes; my mother considered it a holiday! The friend met a Breton gentleman there and married him. My mother didn't see them for years but they called unexpectedly on the evening of my father's funeral.

In October 1947, Charlie and I had our first holiday after the war; we went to London by train – it cost twelve shillings return – to see the film *Snow White and the Seven Dwarfs*. I had my photograph taken in Trafalgar Square with the pigeons. I look as if I am wearing a hat, but in fact it is a pigeon; the photographer put seed on my head to attract it. I had a shock of auburn hair then – loads of it – that my father said was my crowning glory. I was wearing a rust and cream tweed suit that I had made, and an Alexon rust coat. The barricades around the monument – a legacy of the war – can be seen in the background.

My husband and I had by now gone back to Fabian Street. I had started dressmaking at home again. I made the two bridesmaids' dresses for Harry and Myra (née Atherton) Secombe's wedding, which was on February 19th, 1948 – I was in school with Harry. However, I felt that dressmaking at home was not satisfactory in the circumstances: I was getting very little money; the back parlour would be piled high with parcels; I couldn't start work until six o'clock in the evening, and worked through until three in the morning. I was also fed up of being home with my mother-in-law, and applied for a job in Windsmoor, the clothes factory in Fforestfach; once they heard that I had worked in Struttons, I was employed straight away. I was on piecework again, and you had to be accurate, and you had to be quick; but I had no problem with that."

Ladies' fashion changed drastically in the years following the war. Women longed for feminine clothes – a reaction from the austerity of wartime styles with their necessary skimping of material. In 1947, Christian Dior founded his fashion house, near the Champs-Elysée in Paris, and presented a look that suited their needs perfectly: jackets were fitted, with nipped-in waists and fine shoulders; skirts were full and calf-length – and complemented by high stiletto heels. His lavish use of material – approximately ten yards was used for early styles – was found exciting, and eagerly adopted. *Life* magazine dubbed the line the New Look, and it became synonymous with the 1950s.

Windsmoor bought model garments from Paris fashion shows, which cost thousands of pounds; they were then copied in the factory. "I bought the one in the photograph," says Alice, "for my niece's wedding; it was made of heavy cream silk brocade with an umbrella cover to match. Windsmoor copied hundreds in the style, but not in that beautiful material.

Alice, on left, wearing model dress from Paris.

I was promoted to final passer, and the boss offered me a chance to work as a final passer in the Windsmoor Head Office, in Grovesnor Street, in London, where garments were received from other factories. Here the garments had their final inspection – checking that buttons were sewn on properly, seams not puckered, etc. – before going to catalogues and shops. Although all from the same pattern, the clothes for the catalogues were slightly inferior to those for the shops thus earning more money; the catalogues were called their bread and jam, and the shops, bread and butter for the cheese. I didn't go to London, however, as my husband was not happy about it."

In 1958, Windsmoor closed, and Alice left with the following reference from Messrs. Windsmoor, London, Ltd.:

'Fforestfach Trading Estate,
Swansea.
8th October 1958

Mrs. Alice Draper has been employed as a final passer on the staff of this firm for a period of four years. We have found her to be of sound character and would not hesitate to recommend her to any future employment. We would be pleased to act as referee on her behalf.'

Alice went to the labour exchange to sign on, where she was given a form to go to the old Swansea General and Eye Hospital. Alice was to be interviewed by the dreaded matron, but was not nervous at the prospect. "I was interviewed by the matron, Miss Davies – the battleaxe – in her flat in the tower of the building; I hadn't had any previous dealings with the hospital, so I wasn't particularly scared of her. She asked me, 'Can you start tomorrow?' I was given a job in the sewing room in one of the houses in St. Helens Road, opposite Billy Hole's newsagents. There were about four working in the sewing room: there were two old spinsters operating the machines; they hadn't spoken to each other for years.

The nurses' white aprons were washed and starched until they resembled paper. The matron instructed me to make a few aprons, giving me one to use as a pattern – a template; compared to my work in Struttons it was nothing: we worked in dozens there. The old staff made one complete apron at a time; I made them as I used to do my piecework in Struttons: all the belts, pockets, watch pockets, straps, etc. first, and then put all the bits together afterwards – the matron couldn't believe it and kept looking at me. She checked that the aprons were correct, which they were. My way was much quicker than the old way and she, and the existing staff, didn't like it: they didn't like change – although their way was like being back in the Victorian era.

When the nurses left, or were promoted, their uniforms were unpicked and each named, with size, and stored in the loft; there must have been hundreds up there. When the nurses needed a new uniform, their size would be found in the loft, and the pieces re-sewn; the new nurses wore checked uniforms and the second year, stripes.

I made nurses' caps; they were lovely big squares of gauze. I sewed quite a lot of their khaki capes with red flannel lining. I hemmed the capes using a special machine in the corner of the sewing room, which made hems with line stitch; the machine had never been used before. I also used the buttonhole-making machine that had never been touched. I was used to these machines, and they were child's play to me. We made things for the operating theatre: doctors' robes and caps, and bags for amputated arms and legs.

Once a week, everything was checked for repairs. We patched cotton sheets and pillowcases, and the curtains around the beds. When all was finished, we took them to matron in her office in the tower, to look at; she'd check them and remember exactly the condition of each garment before it was mended. She'd say to me, 'Well Alice, which ones did you do?' I'd say that I was not sure, but although she knew my work, which was good, she would not comment on it.

On the way up the staircase, sisters from the wards, dressed in immaculate uniforms, would be waiting for their weekly report, shaking. They'd ask me, 'What mood is she in? What is she like today?'

I'd tease them and say, 'Oh! She's terrible.'

I made the matron a dress: it was in navy blue material with covered buttons on the sleeve up to the elbow, and down the back of the dress. The assistant matron wore a maroon uniform.

In the early 1950s, when I was thirty-three and dressmaking at home, I was a patient in the hospital's Patti Ward over a Christmas; it was a fantastic Christmas – wonderful, although I was not in the best of health. On Christmas Eve, all the lights were switched off, and about twelve nurses, wearing their capes, came round the wards carrying lighted lanterns and singing carols, and at the same time, the bells of St. Paul's Church[8] rang – but I don't know if it was a recording. It put shivers up my spine, as it was so different from any other Christmas Eve I had known. On Christmas morning, one of the surgeons dressed up as Father

---

8. When the church closed, the building was initially used as a cinema, but is now an Indian restaurant called Miah's.

Christmas and gave all the patients a present; I had a pair of nylon stockings. The young interns were bad fairies dressed in tattered, green, frilly dresses with stars on their heads and wands, and when they came to my bed – I was the youngest in the ward – two of them jumped into bed with me! A big turkey was presented to the ward by The Townswomen's Guild – I think – and different business people in the town provided sweets and chocolates galore. The turkey was wheeled into the middle of the ward and a surgeon, wearing his theatre robes – white wellingtons and mask, etc. – stuck a huge syringe up the bird's backside and then performed the operation – the carving of the turkey. On Boxing Day we had a goose. I had been on a diet of jelly and blancmange before, and after eating the goose, I was as sick as a pig; I'll never forget it. A lady doctor gave me a drip, which immediately stopped the sickness: they were afraid my stitches would break. Later in the day we had an open evening, and as many visitors as we wished were invited to tea; my husband and my young sister came and Charlie led the conga around the wards and canteen.

We had a competition for the best decorated ward. Our sister was quite artistic and decided not to have the usual tinsel but lots and lots of daffodils. All the patients made paper daffodils – we had hundreds of them – and some of our visitors, at a great expense I expect, brought in fresh ones. The ward was bright and cheerful and the judges – the surgeons and consultants – awarded us the winners: they thought our theme was spring-like and hopeful.

A factory was opened in Morriston in the old billiard hall. Somebody had told the owner that I was a good machinist, and he came to my house and pestered me to work for him. It took him a fortnight to persuade me that I would be better off: I was to be manageress and have an increased salary. Miss Davies didn't want me to leave the hospital. "Don't go back to an old factory,' she said, but assured me that if I was unhappy there, my old job would be waiting for me.

I went to the factory and I'll never forget it. It was on New Year's Day and it had been snowing; there was slush everywhere. There were about ten school-leavers – tough girls they were – outside the factory. I said, 'Why haven't you gone in?'

'We can't,' they replied; 'the door's locked.'

'Well,' I thought, 'this is great.'

After waiting about an hour, a chap walking by told us that he thought the keys of the factory were in an Italian café opposite. I was informed in the café that the keys were in the police station. By now the kids were freezing cold and two of them wanted to go home. The police came up and opened the factory and helped me put on the heating and the power for the machines.

When I asked the girls, 'How many of you have used the machines?'

'Never Miss; we never had no lessons Miss,' was the reply.

The boss had gone to Birmingham to buy material. He had left no instructions but huge piles of children's dungarees in green, brown and blue – I can see them now – to be made up. I can remember thinking, 'If he thinks those are going to be made by the time he comes back, he's got a hope.'

I took all the needles out of the machines and sat each girl by a machine. I sat on the end machine, and told them to switch the power on by the green buttons. I spent most of the morning teaching them to stop and start the machines; they thought it a great game but eventually conquered it.

It was time for a break but there was no canteen; all I could find was a small teapot and a kettle. We all had a pasty and a drink in the Italian café, which I said the boss would have to pay for.

In the afternoon I found sheets of brown paper, which I pleated, pressed and unfolded. I replaced the needles in the machines and instructed the girls to sew on the creases of the paper. The sewing lines were crooked at first, but they succeeded eventually and so I then put the cotton in. It took me the best part of a week to train the girls. By the end of the week we had about half-a-dozen dungarees that we kept: the rest were only good for dusters.

The girls were fifteen years of age but were lucky: I was only fourteen when I started. They all turned up for work again on the Monday and so did the boss. After I had words with him – with my ginger temper – he begged me to stay. How we managed to complete the order I'll never know, but we did.

Bit by bit I eventually had sixty working for me and we made our own improvements – buying saucepans, etc. If one of the girls got the needle in her finger, I'd run to her, tell her to take her foot off the pedal, slowly pull the needle out, fill the hole with iodine, and the girl would continue working – hard to believe as it wasn't that long ago!

The heating system in the factory was very poor and the winters cold. Some materials were delivered wrapped in corrugated cardboard, which we used to wrap around our legs to keep warm; trousers and jeans were very rarely worn then.

We were asked by a firm – either Cow & Gate or Galaxy – if we would be guinea pigs for a new 'flu vaccine, and promised a small payment. We all volunteered, including the boss. A medical team arrived and set up a temporary clinic in the factory. One of the girls was a good worker, and a nice old girl, but an awful bully. When it was her turn to have the jab, she lost courage, ran out, and clung to a lamp-post. We were determined that she would not get away with it and it took six of us to get her into the clinic. It was a terrible injection and we were all ill after it for a day or two. It was my job to record the results: the vaccine worked and nobody contracted 'flu.

I made quite a few of the staff into good machinists and some are dressmakers now: they were young and very agile.

We turned up for work one day – payday, Friday – to find the factory locked and barred. The boss had been robbing Peter to pay Paul and the bank had closed him down; I'm not sure what happened exactly. At the time, the girls were paid for the week, and their holiday pay, but I got nothing, as I was staff.

I went back to Windsmoor; it had reopened. Mr. Speed, the floor manager, spotted me coming towards the entrance, tapped on the window and said, 'Come for your old job back, have you?' I just walked into his office, walked out of his office, and sat on a machine. I became supervisor, but I wasn't there very long before I left.

I'd seen an advert in the paper for first-class alteration hands, in David Evans. The store was built in 1954, replacing the old David Evans (built 1900) which was bombed in the war. I went along without an appointment and saw their personnel officer. We had a chat and she said, 'I think you'll do very nicely. When can you start?'

'Tomorrow,' I replied.

'That's fine,' she said, 'but you'll have to change your name.'

David Evans' policy was not to have more than one staff of the same name: it was to safeguard against a wrong member of staff being blamed for mistreating a customer. There were twins named Draper, and so I decided to be called Miss Drayton, and was Miss Drayton for almost ten years. They were lovely, wonderful people to work for – Edward Andrews and Mr. Ross. I did all the Windsmoor alterations as I had worked in their factory, and Weatherall clothes, which were very expensive; I was also involved in the fittings. I loved it there but we were overwhelmed with the workload. We were sixteen alteration hands in the workroom at the top of the building, overlooking Castle Gardens, and I had apprentices working for me – sometimes one, sometimes two. I nearly always took the worry of work home with me: 'Oh! That woman from Llanelli is coming in tomorrow and I haven't got it ready for fitting; Wednesday was Pembrokeshire day and they'd be flooding up.' If you were altering a garment that cost fifty pounds, which was a lot of money then, you had to worry about it.

One day we were working round this big table in the workroom, now in the front of the building, and it was thundering; some of the girls were terrified. I happened to look out and saw a red glowing ball hit the flagpole of the building and split it in two; it was a thunderbolt and you'd never heard such screaming in all your life.

We had wonderful days out. We would go to Llanwrtyd Wells – six or seven busloads of us – and have two wonderful meals, and games. In David Evans' early days it boasted a food hall situated on Princess Way. It was Swansea's first supermarket but closed in 1975 because of competition from other supermarkets. We had fancy dress competitions and one year we – 'the ladies of the workroom' as we were known – dressed up as parts of a salad; one girl was a lettuce, another a cucumber, etc.

The DVLC (Driving and Vehicle Licensing Centre) had opened in Morriston in the early 1970s, and one or two of the girls working in David Evans went to work there, changing over the log books to a faster style. They told me that I must be mad to stay in David Evans: they were getting twenty-two pounds for very little work then, and I was only earning nineteen pounds for all the amount of work and responsibility in David Evans. I bought myself a grey Windsmoor suit in the sale – it was lovely – and went to the DVLC, again with no appointment, and was lucky: I was employed as a messenger. I loved it there but when they opened in Orchard Street I moved. I got on with everyone and loved it there also; we were like one big happy family. I became friendly with Olive Hackford,[9] who had worked as an usherette in The Castle cinema. I retired on my sixty-fifth birthday and after the staff arranged a wonderful send-off in the office in the afternoon, and The Grand Hotel in the evening, I was literally dragged out screaming."

Alice says of the Rag Trade, "Today, machines are electronic and far more sophisticated; we had to make the machines do what we wanted, but now the operators have to do what the machines want. There are few factories in this country; they are mostly in the Far East – Korea, China, Hong Kong – where labour is cheap."

Age has not diminished Alice's artistic talents. She enjoys crocheting, tapestry work, and embroidering self-painted botanical canvases – inspired by her great love of gardening. She says of her trade, "I loved sewing – it came naturally to me – and I always enjoyed my work."

---

9. See Chapter 3, pp. 120-123.

Alice, back row on far right. David Evans' picnic and fancy dress competition. 'Ladies of the workroom' dressed as salad ingredients.

Felicity Davies, née Regan, wearing classic style wedding gown with cathedral train, sewn by her Aunt Alice.

The Way of Ways

Alfred R. Way opened his book and stationery shop, Ways, in Wind Street, Swansea in 1885. Many Swansea characters and celebrities patronized the shop and Alfred's son, Arthur Raymond, remembered one such occasion. 'One of my earliest memories is of hearing my father giving the result of the 1910 General Election to Madame Patti.'[10] Six years later Arthur, then sixteen, joined his father in the business.

1924 saw Arthur relocate Ways to the premises at the corner of Cradock Street and Northampton Lane, opposite The Music Hall – later The Albert Hall cinema. During the General Strike of 1926, Arthur volunteered for duty with the Special Constabulary in Swansea, but was not called on to serve. However, he joined the Specials in 1938, to be promoted to sergeant the following year. By 1940, he had been promoted to inspector's rank, and became chief inspector two years later. On the retirement of Bertram Charles, the Special's commandant, Arthur was appointed his successor. Retiring from the force in 1965, he was awarded the BEM (British Empire Medal) for his service in the Specials, and the long-service medal with two bars.

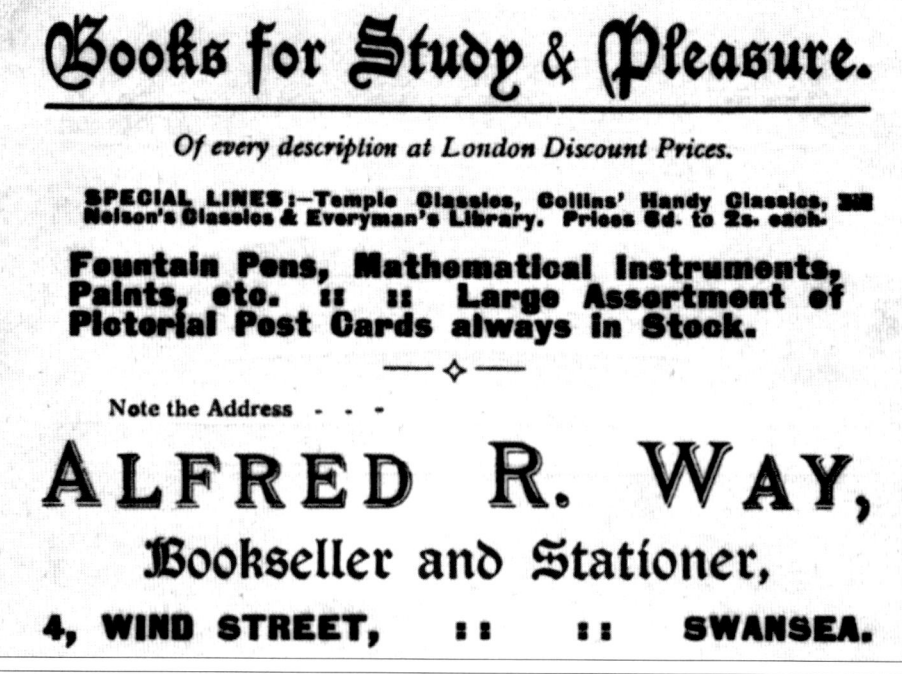

10. *South Wales Evening Post*, 13 December 1966.

*Ways Book Shop, Cradock Street, Swansea, c.1920.
Upstairs bay window advertising Watermans Ideal Fountain Pens
and Swan Pens (swan, with head lowered, on pedestal).*

A. R. Way, Ltd.
BOOKSELLERS AND STATIONERS

**8, CRADOCK STREET,
SWANSEA**

Splendid Assortment of Bibles, Prize Books
and Stationery.

Telephone—4755

William James (Jim) Treharne

His education completed in 1937, at the age of fourteen Jim Treharne was employed in a butcher's shop, Llewellyns in Frogmore Avenue, Sketty. "A teacher called Mr. Whittikar told my father, 'I have a better job for your boy, in a book shop'," remembers Jim, "and so I went to work in Ways as a messenger boy.

I started work in the morning at nine o'clock and finished at six; Friday I finished at seven o'clock and Saturday at eight o'clock; Thursday was half day. I spent my time in the ground floor of an outbuilding; the top floor was used by Mr. Way and the girls and was connected to the shop by a walkway. I was surrounded by old books, string and paper, and if not delivering was expected to sort them out. Any rubbish

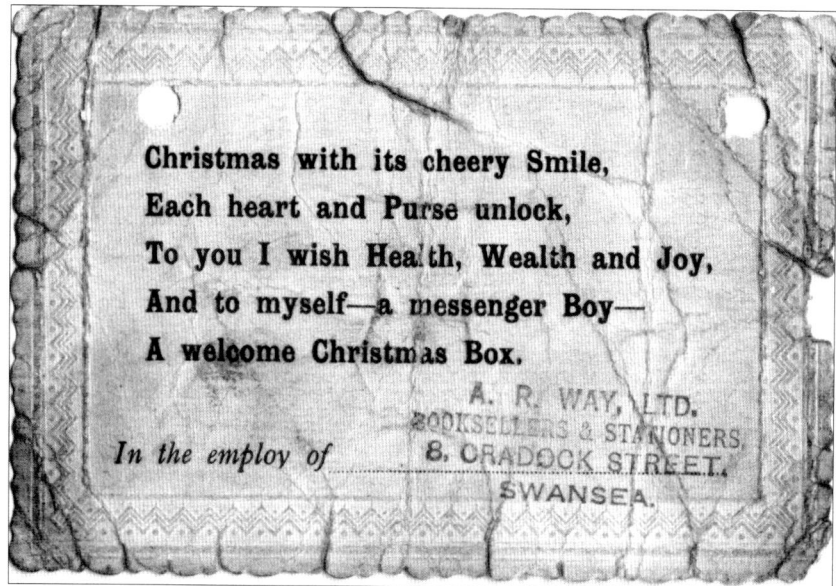

Presented to Jim Treharne by Arthur Way on Christmas Eve.

I took to Mr. Green's sweet factory in Northampton Lane, and as a reward he gave me a gob-stopper (dangerously large sweet). Greens made boiled sweets – unwrapped in those days – and had a stall in Swansea Market. Another of my tasks was to see if there was any grease on the windows of the shop from the Windsor Café – fish and chip shop – and if so, to clean them.

I used to go to the wholesalers Williams, in Mariners Street and Smiths, in Alexander Road, for periodicals. I had a sack truck – like a porter's – and delivered parcels to Glanmôr Grammar School, Llwyn-y-Bryn High School, The Technical College on Mount Pleasant, the Teachers' Training College on Townhill and Terrace Road Elementary School. I took periodicals to customers and business literature to businessmen – solicitors, etc. I then had my dinner at the back of the shop, which I took to work with me. The afternoon was spent delivering again.

I remember old Mr. Way (Alfred) at the cash desk and his wife coming in periodically. They lived in Calvert Terrace and the young Mr. Way lived in Mansel Street then.

The card was presented to me by Mr. Way on Christmas Eve with delivery tips that I had earned from customers over the Christmas period.

I did not work in Ways for very long before I left to work at Harold Field Engineers, in Bath Lane, on the North Dock. I earned about eight shillings with both employers."

Dorothy Evans

Dorothy Evans, née Ward, spent her formative years in Nicander Parade, Townhill, Swansea. "Our house overlooked the whole of Swansea. We had a fantastic view of the Blitz from our house; it was as if the whole of the town was burning. The Germans dropped incendiary bombs on Kilvey Hill – the other side of the River Tawe – setting it all alight.

I went to work in Ways straight from school at the age of fourteen, in 1941. Mr. Way sold all sorts of books. I was fascinated by the thousands and thousands of foreign stamps that he stocked; they were very pretty. Stamp collecting was very popular then and it was through selling them that I started to save them. I used to walk to the Uplands and Sketty Road delivering magazines and books to regular customers; it was a very personal service, and I thoroughly enjoyed it, particularly if the weather was fine.

I remember Mr. Way's mother in the shop; she was a stocky woman with white hair and lived in Calvert Terrace.

Everything was on ration and the staff of Lovells, the sweet shop across the road, used to let us know when they had a new stock of sweets.

I'd been working there for nine months when my friend, who was working in Woolworth, said, 'Why don't you come and work with me?' I left Ways to join her, but for no other reason; I got on well with Mr. Way."

Joan Lewis

Joan Fry was an employee of Ways for eleven happy years, from 1950 to 1961. "I had an interview with Mrs. Way and went to work in Ways when I left school at fifteen, earning one pound and five shillings a week.

I can remember Mr. Way telling me that George V, when on a visit to Swansea, came into his father's shop in Wind Street. In my early days, Dylan Thomas came into our shop in Cradock Street. He was friendly with Ralph who owned Ralph's book shop in Northampton Lane. Ralph also had a branch by the railway station in High Street, which was run by his sister. Vernon Watkins the poet, and a friend of Dylan Thomas, was a customer; he worked in Lloyds Bank. Stars of The Empire Theatre came in – Harry Secombe, David Hughes[11] the singer. Kingsley Amis was a lecturer at Swansea University and lived in the Uplands; he was a

---

11. David Hughes, tenor (1925-1975), a popular 50s singer who moved to opera in 1960, singing with the Welsh National Opera.

regular customer. Daphne Day of Day's Garage worked in the shop; she was a scream. On her days off she would come in with her little sausage dog under her arm and say to it, 'Say hello to Joan, say hello to Jean,' and wave its paw at us. She was very glamorous with dark, dark hair and beautifully dressed – like a film star. She married an American airman called Grayson Spurlock and went to live in Texas.

When I started work the staff were Barbara Thomas, Mary Powis, Marilyn Carlson, Jean Llewellyn, Pat Collins, Betty Lawrence, Joan Eynon and Jean Lawrence – the senior girl. They were a great bunch of girls and we all went on day trips together to Porthcawl and Barry.

Daphne Day.

I wore a cotton, button-through overall with buttons on the cuffs, and stockings – even in the summer. Later I wore a nylon overall, which was awful. We had an art section and sold books of every description. The students from the university came in for books, slide rules, etc. I hadn't been there that long when a student asked me for *Infinitesimal Calculus* by Gaunt. I was only fifteen and had never heard of it: I'd only had a

Front row, left to right: Jean Llewellyn, Jean Lawrence, Pat Collins, Betty Lawrence, Joan Eynon. Back row, left to right: Barbara Thomas, Joan Fry, Mary Powis, Marilyn Carlson.

basic education in Hafod School. Mr. Way was a Freemason and only he could serve customers with anything to do with the Masonic; we were never allowed, as it was very hush hush. Sometimes Mr. Way would say, 'Do you fancy a trip out?' and we'd take parcels to the university and different schools. Later, after Harry (Lewis) and I were married in 1959, Mr. Way would hire a van and Harry and I would do the delivering for Mr. Way. Harry was a fireman and did this in-between his shift work – unpaid labour of love! The sales assistants' pay was not brilliant, and I think that was one of the reasons why there was a big turnover of staff; but I had always been into books, and to me it was lovely. When a new novel was published Mr. and Mrs. Way often asked me, 'Would you like to take it home and read it, and tell us about it?'

In the mid-1950s, the front of the shop was altered to accommodate newspapers, magazines and cigarettes. It was separated from the back of the shop by double doors. Mr. Way received the newspapers and opened the shop early. Mr. Symons lived in the Uplands and was a lovely, lovely man. He was in his late seventies but very sharp. He was often the key holder, but one night I was in charge. The police had to come and get me. They arrived at my home saying, 'The alarm has gone off in the shop.' Someone had broken in through the fanlight in the roof, but mostly cigarettes were stolen.

I was the window dresser. At Christmas, I'd display all sorts of toys; at Easter the windows would be full of fluffy chicks and brides' white leather Bibles.

Mrs. Way's Christian name was Dorothy but her husband always referred to her as Dolly. Mr. and Mrs. Way's son Raymond was away at boarding school in Bromsgrove. Mrs. Way's sister, Mrs. Jones had two sons, Harold and Brynsley. Mrs. Jones came to live in Pennard from Bournemouth. They all used to serve at Christmas as well as extra girls taken on; it was a busy, busy shop.

Manleighs the men's shop was next door. Mr. Cohen owned it by then, but he kept the original name. My mother used to baby-sit for Mr. and Mrs. Cohen. We used to socialize with the girls in the nearby shops – Eynon's Café, Taylors the greengrocer's, Lovells; we had trips to Porthcawl and Barry; we went to dances in the church hall of Our Lady of Lourdes, in Townhill – Pat Collins was a member of the church. If we went to dances such as the Casino in Mumbles, there'd always be buses outside to take us home – to all areas of Swansea. If we went to the Embassy in Swansea we'd walk home singing all the way, and never feel threatened. We used to have such good times. At first, the tobaconist and newsagents' annual dinner and dance was held at the Mack-

*Tobacconist & Newsagents Dance at the Embassy, Swansea.
Left to right: Harry and Joan Lewis, Dorothy and Arthur Way.*

worth Hotel, and later at the Embassy. When I attended with Harry and Mr. and Mrs Way, I wore my wedding dress cut down, with a pink, can-can petticoat underneath.

The shop was opened at half-past eight every morning, closing at half-past five on Monday and Tuesday. Thursday was half-day and the shop closed at six on Friday and Saturday. When the shop was closed, we'd take it in turns to sprinkle wet sand on the wooden floors – not to raise the dust – and then sweep them. When I later went in at seven o'clock for the paper deliveries, I finished at four o'clock. By now the staff had changed. Sonia Barrett, Julie Charles, Pat Woollard, Dorothy Thomas and myself caught a bus to Langland on our half-day off. If Raymond was home from school, he used to come with us; we thought he was lovely, and a bit lonely, so we used to let him tag along. Julie had beautiful, long hair; when she decided to have it cut in Langleys Hair Salon, on the Kingsway, she sold it to them for wig making.

Two of my sisters worked with me for a while, Beryl and Pam. Pam, the youngest was only thirteen. She worked on Saturdays and Mr. Symons would always tease her and say, 'Here's a thruppenny piece for you to stand on so the customers can see you.'

I remember Mr. Way being awarded the BEM and everybody coming into the shop to congratulate him. He was a quietly spoken, thoughtful man. When Harry and I were married in March 1959, Pat Woollard, with whom I worked, was my chief bridesmaid. Mr. and Mrs. Way and Mrs. Jones were guests at our wedding. After the reception at the George Hotel in Mumbles, we arrived at High Street Station to find Mr. Way there with sandwiches for our journey to Bournemouth. He knew that there was no buffet car on the train and that we were not to arrive there until eleven o'clock that night.

Mr. and Mrs. Way gave Harry and myself a clock for Christmas with the enclosed message:

> 'As the clock ticks in the seconds of 1959, may each one prove silver to you and Harry until March. May they then turn to golden and outshine any that have gone before. Good health, good fortune and your dream home be yours in March 1959.' Dorothy and Arthur Way.'

That summer, Mr. and Mrs. Way went on holiday to Bournemouth. We received a pack of picture postcards from them with the words:

> 'This may enable you to see Bournemouth, which you failed to see earlier in the year owing to your star-gazing into each other's eyes.
>
> Dorothy and Arthur Way'.

I left in 1961, when I was expecting our first child."

Left to right: Sonia Barrett, her friend Elaine, Julie Charles, Dorothy Thomas.

Sonia Machell

When Sonia Machell, née Barrett, was interviewed by Mr. Way in 1957/58, mother came too. "It was conducted standing in the foyer of the shop," recalls Sonia. "'How old are you? When can you start?' is all I can remember, and then my mother and Mr. Way discussing my wages. It didn't seem strange to me at the time. Looking back, I was very shy then, and I don't know if I'd have gone into the shop if I'd been on my own.

Mr. Way was always at the door to wish us good morning and to lock the door in the evening and say goodnight. He was very much head of the family which included his wife and their son, Raymond, Mrs. Way's sister, Mrs. Jones and her son Harold. It was the era of employer and employee, us and them, and I was very much the shop girl. One day Harold asked me out. We went to The Castle cinema and saw *Jazz on a Hot Summer's Night*. The next morning when I came into work – I'll never forget it – Mr. and Mrs. Way, Mrs. Jones and Harold were in a line waiting for me at the end of the shop. It was the longest walk I ever did. I was told that under no circumstances was I to go out with Harold again. Harold just stood there and took it; but it was he who asked me and not me him. My colleague, Julie (Charles) said to me, 'I never thought you'd go out with anyone called Harold,' but I thought he was very nice. Because of all the fuss, everybody in the shop knew, and I didn't really want them to. I was always caught out. A very nice young man used to deliver the *Evening Post*, and asked me out. He was able to borrow the van and took me out in it. The first people I saw were Joan, who I worked with, and Harry. The next morning it was all over the shop.

I enjoyed working in Ways and we had some laughs. I worked with Pat and Cynthia; they were the same type, and both elegant. I also worked with Dorothy; Julie and I got on very well with her. I think it was she who loved the smell of TCP and used it as perfume; she reeked of it.

The front of the shop sold papers, postcards, paperbacks, etc. Through the double doors, on the left, was a counter displaying fountain pens – Watermans, Parkers – and on shelves behind, were Bibles. Students came in to buy the pens, and also parents of students. We enjoyed the students coming in, with fresh faces every new intake at the beginning of the school year; it was something to dress up for every day. I wore two-inch heels when working and three-inch heels in the evenings to go out, and my long auburn hair in a ponytail. We had a large roll of brown paper and string to wrap the books, etc., which we were taught to do. Eventually Mr. Way gave us permission to use Sellotape; I couldn't wait to get to work that day! We sold books to Clarke's and Greggs Colleges, which we wrapped and packed in boxes for Mr. Way to deliver. I took an interest in the greetings cards, which were on the ground floor at the back of the shop, and eventually helped Mr. Way to order them.

I lived in Penlan. When I started working, Mr. Way bought me a six-monthly season ticket and then a yearly one. It was a great help as it was not restricted to daytime and so I could use it outside working hours; I don't know if he thought, 'I'm determined to get them to work *by hook or by crook*. We had an hour and a quarter for lunch and so I had plenty of time to go home; my mother always had a meal ready for me. A few times a month she would come to Swansea, and we would have lunch together, either in Eynon's or the Restaurant in Woolworth, High Street.

I usually went out in the evenings with Julie and a friend who worked in Boots the Chemists. We could go to the Glanmôr Jazz Club – Modern on Tuesday and Trad. on Wednesday, the Casino dancehall in Mumbles on Thursday, Friday and Saturday, and the cinema on a weekday and Sunday. I can remember where I saw films for the first time. I saw *Singing in the Rain* in The Welfare, Fforestfach, *Some like it Hot* and *Rock around the Clock* in The Castle, *The King and I* in The Carlton, *Jailhouse Rock* in The Plaza, and my first Elvis Presley film in The Manor in Manselton. We saw the death of Buddy Holly, in a plane crash, on the newsreel in 1959; he was my hero and he was now gone and I never had a chance to marry him!

As well as the Harold incident, another of my abiding memories was when Julie was sacked by Mr. Way on Christmas Eve. We were leaving the shop when he called her back for some reason. I waited for her, and then we walked around the corner into Mansel Street to the bus stop outside the bridal shop. She suddenly burst into tears. I said, 'What's the matter?'

She said, 'I've been sacked.' It was that quick! That afternoon, Julie had been one end of the shop and a male customer the other. He clicked his fingers at her for attention. She was so appalled at his rudeness that she ignored him. He walked closer to her and clicked again and again and she still ignored him. He went right up to her and clicked his finger; she was so disgusted by his behaviour that she looked at him and walked away. He complained to Mr. Way that his shop girl had insulted him, and Julie got the sack.

Julie went to work in Lamas on the Fforestfach Industrial Estate earning twice the salary of Ways. She encouraged me to find another job. On one of my Thursday afternoons off – everywhere closed in Swansea on Thursdays then – I caught a bus to Fforestfach. I walked into Louie Marks, had a job there, and gave my two-week notice to Mr Way the following day. I had earned two pounds, seventeen shillings and six pence a week in the shop, and was to earn over four pounds in Louie Marks. It was easy to find employment then. You could come out of the job centre with a handful of interviews to go to."

Anne Karim

In the mid-1950s, while a pupil at Glanmôr Grammar School for Girls, in Swansea, Anne Karim, née Gilbert, worked on Saturdays and during the school holidays in Ways. "When I went to work on the first day I asked where I was to put my coat. They all looked a bit flummoxed. I was taken up to the next floor and through a secret door that looked like a cupboard door, and up again onto the roof outside. We walked along a catwalk to the roof of the next-door building and went into what looked like a little stock room on the roof. That was where we put our coats.

Ways was a tall narrow building with a newspaper counter housed in a separate unit on the ground floor in the front. I enjoyed working there as the newspapers were marked with their prices. After working for several hours my hands became black with the print. The rest of the shop on the ground floor, where stationery and maps were sold, was a complete nightmare. The sheets of card and paper were kept in drawers, in no order, and not priced. I had to pull out a drawer and hope that the required size of card would introduce itself to me. I often had to do a bit of detective work, or ask Mrs. Way, to find out the price.

Everything was very formal. Mrs. Way always referred to her husband as Mr. Way in our presence, and never by his Christian name, Arthur. If I asked her a question that she could not answer, which was quite often, she would call 'Mr. Way! Mr. Way!' and he would come and help. He was a quiet, unassuming man – a very, very nice man – with a wealth of knowledge of all the books held in stock. He was always looking over the top of his glasses; he had the status of a guru.

We had no instruction on how to serve customers, but we all understood that we really had to put ourselves out to please them. By the time they left, they had to be satisfied with their purchase. I can't remember working to any strict hours; it was a total dedication to work. Customers weren't as rude and demanding as they are today. I had trouble understanding some of the customers' accents especially those from the Swansea Valley. One day a man was pestering me for a runny decker. I had no idea what he meant, but Mrs. Way and I eventually worked out that he wanted a ready reckoner.

There were no perks to the job. We didn't even have our own kettle and each break we went to the café further up the street to have tea and a snack. The buildings in Cradock Street to the north of Ways had been destroyed in the Blitz and Nissen huts had been erected in their place. The café was in one of these huts – I think it was Eynon's. It was a bit of a surprise to me that I had to spend my own money during work breaks, but it was the first work I had done and so wasn't going to argue.

I enjoyed working in Ways. The first floor was like an Aladdin's cave with all those books. I don't remember any of the other staff apart from Mr. and Mrs. Way. It was a very busy shop and we were rushed off our feet, especially at Christmas-time, and so had no time for socializing."

Ann McDonnell

Ann McDonnell, née Burrington, left St. Helens Secondary Modern School for Girls in the Sandfields, Swansea, in 1959. She commenced work in Liberty's, a small branch of the London stores, situated in the front of YMCA buildings. The shop sold material, pictures, pottery and art and crafts. Ann had only worked for one month, when the shop closed. Armed with a reference from her employer, she went to the Job Centre in Wind Street and obtained an interview with Mr. Way, in his shop.

"I started working with Sonia Barrett, and Joan Lewis who was in charge," recounts Ann. "When they left I became senior, and worked with Josephine Ellis, Jean Smith and Ellen Ward.

The premises was very antiquated. We had no staff room, but put our coats in a storeroom that was situated on the roof of the building, which was reached by a bridge. The shop had a break-in and an alarm system was installed; it was very primitive by today's standards. I was upstairs and called downstairs to test it. I walked through the wire that had been placed across the bottom of the stairs, which activated the alarm. At the back of the shop was a little room that had an old fashioned telephone; it had dials and a mouthpiece on the wall with a connecting ear-piece. The premises had no central heating. There was a heater at the back of the shop by the cards and we used to stand near it to keep warm; the winters were very cold then.

Reps. used to come in selling books and stationery; Basildon Bond writing paper and envelopes were very popular. We supplied local schools and colleges. I remember delivering books to a local junior school with Mr. and Mrs. Way's son, Raymond, in his car. The children's books, film-star and Christmas annuals – *Schoolfriend, Girl, Eagle, Beano, Dandy* – were kept upstairs. I can remember *Lady Chatterley's Lover* and the *Karma Sutra* being published; we were not allowed to display them on the shelves and kept them under the counter – but we sold loads.

We had a lot of student customers. The boys from Dynevor Grammar School, whose main gate was across the road in Pell Street, often came in. Fountain pens were very popular – Parkers, Conway Stewarts. A young girl came in one day with her mother to buy a pen; we learned later it was Mary Hopkin, the up-and-coming Welsh singer. The staff – mostly men – of Calders, and Wildings, the men's outfitters in the Kingsway, bought their morning paper in Ways before going to work, and local office men and window cleaners bought papers, pens, pencils, and cigarettes, etc.

We had to be polite to customers. One day, we were very busy, and I had no idea what I had done wrong but a customer had complained about me, and I was told off. There were two windows either side of the front door and more – plus a side door – at the side of the building in Northampton Lane. Mrs. Way came in occasionally. She used to check the window dressing. On one occasion I had dressed the front window with little lead soldiers. She said, 'Who did that?' I thought, 'Oh, what have I done?' but she said that it was lovely. I had to keep the books tidy and dusted as Mrs. Way inspected them. Mr. Way or Mr. Symons opened the shop very early. I was asked to come in early one morning, at six o'clock, to receive the paper deliveries, and fair play, Mr. Way gave me a one pound premium bond as a thank you.

Our salaries were paid in cash, but Mr. Way didn't use wage packets; he pressed the folded notes into our hands – about three pounds I think.

Mr. and Mrs. Way lived in 25 Glanmor Park Road. He was a special constable and I remember him on duty in Singleton Park, but didn't dare to associate with him outside work. Mrs. Way had a sister, Mrs. Jones who used to pop into the shop; she lived in the Promenade, in Mount Pleasant. The shop was cleaned by Mrs. Parker; she was lovely and such a case.

I lived in Rhondda Street and walked up and down Mount Pleasant Hill to and from work every day; sometimes I caught the bus up to St. Jude's Church, for thruppence. Some scenes of the film, *Only Two Can Play* starring Peter Sellers, Mai Zetterling and Kenneth Griffith were filmed in Cromwell Street around the corner from where I lived, and on the Promenade, with its wonderful views over Swansea and Mumbles. Josephine and I used to watch the filming in our lunch hour always hoping that we would be chosen as extras; but of course, we couldn't hang around as we had to go back to work. I remember seeing Peter Sellers, Mai Zetterling and the big car they used.

I loved working in Ways. I don't think I would have left but Mr. Way kept threatening to retire and close the business. Josephine and I went for an interview in the Mackworth Hotel for a job in Wymans – it was later Menzies – situated at the corner of Oxford Street and Whitewalls in the new market block. I was successful and left Ways in 1962."

Josephine Budge

Josephine Budge, née Ellis, a native of Llansamlet, was employed by Mr. Way on her second attempt. "I left school at fifteen, in the early 1960s. My mother was working in Morriston and so my sister, Branwen, took charge of me. When you left school then, you weren't allowed to hang around the house; you had to get out and find a job. She saw an advert for a sales assistant in Ways and told me to go and get a job there. I was very nervous in those days; I used to have the shakes and my head used to nod; later my children used to call me Noddy. I went to Ways by bus. I got as far as the outside of the shop, but I was too nervous to go in. I went home and told my sister that the job had gone. She told me that I was fibbing, and to go back on the bus and not come home until I had the job. Again I hung around outside the shop, but Joan noticed me and asked if I was there for an interview. 'Come in,' she said, 'and don't be nervous. It's OK.' I went in and had the job straight away. It was a great relief: I could go home and tell my sister that I had the job.

It was a new experience for me working in the shop. It helped me to get to know people and to improve my self-confidence. The tills were so big you had to stretch your hands to reach all the numbers, and of course, had to add up the items on a piece of paper. I learned about things I hadn't known in school – protractors, etc. I delivered books such as Shakespeare's *Midsummer Night's Dream*, to the Teachers' Training College up the hill. I went up the winding staircase in its tower to the library, I think it was, at the top. When *Lady Chatterley's Lover* came out we could sell the book but were warned by Mr. Way not to read it; well, we couldn't resist it and used to have a quick look through the pages, tittering as we read. We had to sweep the shop floor and the pavement outside. The books had to be taken out and the shelves dusted. I hated stocktaking, which took place on a yearly basis; I'd do anything else rather than that.

My lunch was up in Ann's house with a pound of bananas bought in the corner shop. One Christmas, Mrs. Way bought us a box of Terry's Old Gold chocolates; they were dark chocolates and had only just come out. I hated dark chocolate and am afraid was not greatly appreciative of my present. I used to go out with the girls in the shop to dances, the cinema, and for a drink in the Park and Dolphin Hotels.

I enjoyed working in Ways, but after about eighteen months, I left and went to work in Dolcis shoe shop."

Christina (Tina) Tomkins

Tina attended Llwyn-y-Bryn High School for Girls, in Uplands, Swansea. When about sixteen, she felt she would like to have a Saturday/holiday job. "My mother, Anne Parton, was the manageress of Eynon's Café, in Cradock Street," says Tina, "and bought magazines and daily papers in Ways. She promised me that she would have a word with Mr. Way.

I started working on Saturdays and later in the school holidays – Christmas, Easter, summer – when the shop was particularly busy. The permanent staff took their holidays in July and August and so I worked in their place.

The shop sold good-quality writing paper, pens, geometry sets, etc. and the shelves were laden with books of every type – Bibles, religious books, children's books, etc. – but specializing in school/college books. School pupils were issued with textbooks but were advised by their teachers to buy extra books as aids to help them in exams. – as in Shakespearean plays for example.

I loved my job; it was so good working with all those books. Greetings cards – birthdays, religious, Easter, Christmas – were sold at the far end of the shop. I remember the beautiful collection of padded, boxed Christmas cards for fiancées, husbands, wives, etc. The one job I didn't like was adding up the price of the cards. The till was old fashioned and not an adding machine. Receipts were written by hand and sales were listed on paper and added up in your head. The cards usually had one farthing, a halfpenny or three farthings in their price. I wasn't very good at figures and found fractions difficult to add up, but I always got there in the end.

The floors were wooden and uncarpeted and creaked when walked on. When I was in charge of the first floor, I'd stay downstairs until a customer went up. I'd follow and wait quietly at the counter or dust some books. They might be there for an hour but I didn't bother them.

When asked, I'd attempt to find a requested book, but if unsuccessful, I'd ask Mr. Way; he would either find it or order it for the customer. I'd wrap the books in brown paper and seal with Sellotape from a dispenser – no bags then.

Mr. and Mrs. Way were a charming couple. Mr. Way was quite a tall man with grey/white hair. Mrs. Way was very refined – a real lady. For some reason she insisted on calling me Christine. They had one child; Raymond was the apple of his mother's eye. An elderly gentleman – Mr. Symons – used to serve in the shop occasionally; he was also charming and, I think, a friend of Mr. Way's. At Christmas, we were given a small present such as a Yardley product; I think Mrs. Way used to buy them in the chemist on the corner opposite in Cradock Street. It was such a nice, personal touch.

We had a fifteen-minute break in the morning and afternoon and one hour for lunch. As there was no staff room, we usually went to a local café. A few doors down was the Sweet Briar Café; it served coffee and toast in the morning and later cooked lunch; it was always very busy. The Windsor Café was also there.

Cohen's, the man's clothes shop was next door (to the south). My mother used to wind up Mr. Cohen – being Jewish – and ask him if he wanted a pork sandwich, but he'd take it in good part and say, 'Oh Anne!' Lovells was opposite, next to The Albert Hall; it was a high-class sweet shop.

I left the shop when I went to college in 1963; I had been working there about three years. Mrs. Way told me she would have loved me to stay and work full-time, and gave me the offer of full-time employment. When I declined she said, 'Are you sure you won't change your mind?'

I think Mr. Way became a court usher after he retired from the shop. My mother told me she thought he was a special constable."

On Christmas Eve, 1966, Arthur closed the doors of Ways for the last time. He explained, 'I think it's time my wife and myself had a rest. I am sixty-six now and have been in the business for fifty years. I joined my father in the business in 1916, and except for my service in the Royal Flying Corps during the First World War, when I served as wireless operator for two and a half years, I have been in this business all my working life.'[12] The *South Wales Evening Post* paper reported on 13 December, 'Their shop – the oldest booksellers in the town – is known to scholars and students scattered now in many lands, and when its doors finally close, one more remaining part of an older, and more leisured Swansea will be gone for ever.'

---

12. *South Wales Evening Post*, 13 December, 1966.

6.

Determined to Volunteer

It was realized in the years preceding the Second World War that, unlike in the First World War, the civilian population of Britain would be directly threatened by the German Luftwaffe. In 1937, the Air Raid Precaution Act (ARP) was passed to make preparations against German attacks. The department appealed for one million volunteers. The response decided the home secretary, Sir Samuel Hoare to set up a women's organization to help with the task. On 16 May 1938, the Women's Voluntary Service for Air Raid Precaution was founded. The Dowager Marchioness, Lady Reading was appointed chairman, and the Queen, and Queen Mary the Queen Mother, became joint patrons. On the outbreak of war, the work quickly diversified and the organization soon changed its name to the WVS for Civil Defence.

By September 1939, buildings had been sandbagged, gas masks issued, air-raid shelters constructed, and blackout imposed at nights. Air Raid Wardens – both male and female – were appointed to supervise specified areas during an attack. This was part of the organization of Civil Defence, which played a vital part during the Blitz.

The government had learned from the First World War that mobilization of the nation was essential in a total war. The Emergency Powers Acts (1939 and 1940) provided the government with complete authority to direct the lives of people in the interest of the war effort.

Conscription (compulsory military service) was introduced for men aged eighteen to forty during the summer of 1939. By May 1940, German forces were moving rapidly across France and the Low Countries, and an invasion of Britain seemed imminent. Anthony Eden, Secretary of State for War, called upon all able-bodied men between seventeen and sixty-five years, not in the services, to join the Local Defence Volunteers – later to be renamed the Home Guard. Their official duties were to observe and defend strategic points in the local areas – such as roads and factories – to sabotage enemy movements in the event of invasion, and to attack small enemy detachments.

After the declaration of the Second World War on 3 September 1939, thousands of women joined the three highly organized military services

– the WRNS (Womens Royal Naval Service), ATS (Auxiliary Territorial Service) and WAAF (Womens Auxiliary Air Force). Others performed important work in industry and on the land. Never before had women undertaken so many varied tasks in the country's defence. As thousands joined the organizations, there was no shortage of volunteers, but in December 1941, the Ministry of Labour introduced measures to further help the existing conscripted male force and to release them to active service: single women between the ages of nineteen and thirty were called up.

The Royal Family did not exclude itself from the war effort. On 28 February 1922, Princess Victoria Alexandra Alice Mary – known as Princess Mary – married Henry Charles George, Viscount Lascelles, later in 1929 to become the 6th Earl of Harewood. On 1 January 1932, King George V declared that his only daughter should bear the title the Princess Royal, following the death of her aunt, Princess Louise. Keenly interested in women's movements, at the outbreak of war she became chief controller and later controller commandant of the ATS (renamed the Women's Royal Army Corps in 1949). In that capacity, she travelled Britain visiting its units, as well as wartime canteens and other welfare organizations.

In April 1942, at the age of sixteen, King George VI's elder daughter, Princess Elizabeth, registered for war service. Despite opposition from her family and the War Cabinet, in March 1945 she joined the ATS where she learned to drive and maintain army motor vehicles, and was to hold the rank of a second lieutenant. Morwyn Elliott, a native of Penclawdd, joined the ATS and trained at Queen's Camp, Guildford, Surrey, where Princess Elizabeth had been stationed. "She was there the April before I joined in the May. She did not sleep at the camp," says Morwyn, "but returned to Windsor Castle each evening."

The majority of women who had not volunteered for, or were not conscripted into the forces, or were not involved in essential war work, gave their time voluntarily to organizations on the Home Front.

Ann Beck – ATS

Annie Mayville – known as Ann – daughter of Lewis and Mary Elizabeth Rees, of Penclawdd, was anxious to serve her country during the war years, and was also hungry for adventure. Before women were conscripted, at the age of twenty-two she volunteered for the ATS and was one of the twenty thousand who worked in camp cookhouses.

"My Aunt Kate lived in Burley, near the New Forest. She had tearooms in her garden where she served Hovis teas. She was a wonderful cook and made lovely fairy cakes with a cherry on the top. She charged fivepence for brown bread and butter, cakes and a pot of tea. I spent many holidays there, helping her in her business. I often walked in the forest and watched the beautiful deer. I loved it there: it was so peaceful. I was at my aunt's when I heard girls were joining the ATS. I would never have worked in a factory; I'd sooner have gone on a farm. I said to my aunt, 'I think I'll volunteer for the ATS.'

When I returned home, I went to the YMCA in Swansea, and joined the ATS; I was the first in the village to do so.

When I went to Talavera Camp in Northamptonshire for my training, my mother came to see me off at Swansea High Street Station; my father was too upset to come but he was always there to meet me when I came home. There was no sign of any other ATS girls at the station. I changed at Cardiff, and got out at Northampton. There I found lots of army trucks waiting, and by Jove, I was surprised how many got off the train – all in civvies then. We got in the trucks, and palled up immediately.

We slept in double bunks. At the training school were two sisters – Marjory and Dorothy – who very religious and every night knelt at their bunks to pray. Some of the girls used to make fun of them, which used to annoy me intensely. I prayed also, but silently in my bunk. The sisters were extremely quiet and not used to going out on their own. I used to look after them and say, 'Come on. Let's go to Kettering.' They presented me with a little Testament before I left.

I was hoping to work on the guns, but at the end of my course failed the eyesight test. I was very disappointed, but thought, 'Well the next best thing will be to work in the cookhouse: at least I'll have plenty of food.' I was on the staff at Talavera Camp for about eighteen months, and then I was posted to Alton Towers in Staffordshire – the only one from Talavera.

We ATS girls were in Nissen huts in the woods, and the soldiers were in the mansion – The Towers. Our salary was eleven shilling a week with free uniforms and food. We were issued with clothing coupons, which weren't much use to us as we nearly always wore our uniforms. They consisted of khaki skirts and jackets, green shirts and ties, brown stockings and black shoes. We were provided with working hats, and off-duty hats – small hats that we wore at the side of our heads. We wore blue and white striped pyjamas and looked like convicts; but we used to laugh at ourselves, as we all looked the same.

Ann Rees.

We wore all white uniforms for kitchen duty. Some girls worked as waitresses in the canteen. Eight of us worked in the cookhouse with a chef in charge; he was spotlessly clean, and there was no messing about, with him. We were split into two, working two shifts per day – morning and afternoon. We were up at six thirty in the morning, and reported for duty by eight o'clock. The morning shift finished at two o'clock when the evening shift took over, finishing after dinner in the evening. We cooked on four big ranges fired by coal, which were fed by large pipes underneath the tiled floor. We wore clogs to protect our feet from the fierce heat. On the morning shift, I served porridge from a large bowl; the hotplate was so high that I had to stand on a box to serve. The cooked breakfast was horrible: eggs, stringy tinned bacon and awful sausages. The soldiers would say to me, 'What's for breakfast today Taff?'

I'd say, 'Sausages.'

They'd reply, 'Deliver us from heaven!'

However, there was no shortage of food with plenty of large joints of meat and an abundance of fresh vegetables.

We catered for the officer cadets and the privates. They ate in the same room, but the ranks were separated by a wall. Gertie Evans (née Guy) of Penclawdd had told my mother that her elder son, Kenneth, was an officer cadet at Alton Towers. I thought I'd never meet him amongst the six hundred stationed there, and also he was an officer cadet and we privates were not allowed to talk to them. However, one day, as I was running to fetch a paper, we met at the doorway. I said, 'Well blow me Kenneth,' and we had a nice chat, but that was the only contact we had.

HRH The Princess Royal.

I remember being issued with a new white uniform for a very important occasion: a visit from the Princess Royal – Princess Mary. She came into the cookhouse, declined coffee, and asked us how we were getting on, did we like it there, and this and that. She wore her ATS uniform and no make-up. She was quite ordinary really and refused lunch at the officers' mess, insisting on eating at the canteen.

I met my first husband, Donald Jones – a Northwalian from Conway – at the camp. We went out together for two years before marrying in Conway Church. Previous to our having met, Don, who was a sergeant major in the Royal Welsh Fusiliers, had applied to train the natives in Africa. We were married by special licence as Don was going abroad. Six months after our marriage, he was posted to the Gold Coast in Africa. One afternoon, my sergeant called me saying, 'Will you come to my office please?' Off I went with curlers in my hair as I had been working morning shift. All the girls teased me, shouting, 'What have you been up to now?' My sergeant told me that Don had died of pneumonia and heart failure; I found that hard to believe as he had passed his medical A1 – my father said he had been killed by the natives. I was not allowed to go out there – it was called white man's grave – and I do not know where he is buried. I had compassionate leave, went home, and then visited his mother to tell her. Don was her elder son. She immediately guessed something was wrong and said, 'It's Don isn't it?'

I said, 'Sit down Mam,' put my arms around her, and told her the awful news. She died in my arms from shock.

I returned to work and got over it in time. I enjoyed myself at Alton Towers and we had lots of fun. The soldiers used to travel to Manchester and Hanley in big army trucks to buy food. On our afternoons off they'd shout to us, 'Anybody for Manchester/Hanley? Come on!', leg us up into the trucks and off we'd go. We'd walk around the shops and have tea and coffee; we couldn't do much else as we had very little money. We'd then return to barracks in the truck. The men were very good to us.

I shall never forget one terrible tragedy we experienced. Four or five of the Canadian soldiers stationed there had been confined to barracks for some misconduct – I don't know what. That night, they drew the blackout shutters and stoked the stove in their Nissen hut. As they slept, the stove became red-hot, burnt some electric wires, and they all perished in the ensuing fire. Some parents had travelled all the way from Canada to see their sons, and one of them was among the fatalities of the accident. We couldn't get over it, and were upset for months and months.

At one time we were told that we were going to be transferred to Germany, and had our vaccinations. I naturally wrote and told my mother, and my father said, 'We will never see Ann again.' It was a false alarm and nothing came of it; but I must admit, I was disappointed as I was looking forward to it, and would have gone anywhere: I was young and adventurous.

All the soldiers were lovely lads. When they were leaving we shook their hands and wished them all the best. Some went to Dunkirk and were killed. It was so sad as we had come to know them so well. A little boy from Scotland always asked for a second helping of porridge; *Duw* (God) help, he was one of the many killed in Dunkirk.

I had been a widow for four years when I met Cecil Thomas Beck, from Grantham in Lincolnshire, at the camp.

I was sorry when the day came for me to be demobbed. I came home to Penclawdd, but could not settle: I'd made my own life and I missed the camaraderie of the girls, and of course Cecil, so much. I went to Grantham and married Cecil in a registry office. We bought a house and settled there, but he loved visiting Penclawdd and my family. I was lucky in that both my husbands were lovely people; they were so kind and respectful."

Jenny – Wren

It was through her work for the war effort that a young girl from Purley, Surrey, came to know and love Mumbles. The war over, she married a native of Swansea, and has remained in the village to this day.

The then twenty-two year old tells her story. "At the beginning of the war, I was working in the civil service and was evacuated to Southport. Nothing much happened during the first year of the war. At the end of the year, a colleague of mine told me that her sister, who was working in the War Office in London, wanted to come to Southport, and would I be interested in a transfer. I said that I would, and went back to London on the first night of the Blitz.

I thought, 'What have I done?' This lasted for three months, and it was no life at all travelling back and forth between Purley and London during the bombing. It was dreadful, and I got a bit fed up with it. I had a brother who had joined the Navy before the war, and had worked his way up from a naval cadet. He was, by then, a naval officer – and later a commander – stationed at Dover Castle, and was telling me of the good time he was having. This tempted me to try and join the Wrens. My job at the War Office was a reserved occupation, and so it was a heck of a job to get out. At the time one had to have a relative in the Navy, and so I was helped by my brother's position. My friend and I applied and said we wanted to do visual signalling.

We were told, 'As it happens, there is a course coming up next week in Lancashire. We'll send for you.'

The training school was in-between Manchester and Liverpool. There were five hundred Wrens, five hundred sailors, and the band of the Royal Marines there at the time. We had divisions every morning – the padre was there – after which the Royal Marines played the national anthem of each of the allies. As each anthem was played, their flag was hoisted. Once, I had to hoist the White Ensign; timing was essential, as it had to unfurl at the top of the pole just as the anthem was finishing. It was a terribly difficult three months. We were divided into classes, each named after different ships; mine was the *Victoria*. We learned Morse code, telegraphy, and semaphore. It was freezing cold there. I don't think we had any leave, but we used to hitch at weekends to Manchester and Liverpool. Blackpool was out of bounds, but we went there once and had ice-cream; fortunately, we were never found out. We had to pass the exams. otherwise we would have been turfed out. My friend and I came out top. The rest were having a knees-up while we were working hard.

Jenny – Wren.

We were older than the other girls – some were only seventeen-and-a-half – and so felt it essential that we do well.

At the end of my training I had a short leave at home, and then went to my drafting at the Port War Signal Station on the Tut,[1] in Mumbles. I was a mobile Wren and could be posted to any other station in the country at any time. Living in Purley, Surrey, it was not possible for me to be an immobile Wren – living at home and travelling to a station everyday – as, needless to say, there were none near Purley.

I shall never forget my feelings on entering Swansea by train. The valley was black with industry. This sight was so unfamiliar to me and I thought, 'Gosh! Where have I been sent?' I travelled through Swansea to the Wrens' Headquarters at Coed Saeson, in Parc Wern Road, Sketty. It was 1942 and the town was a pile of rubble after the Blitz the previous year. However, the next day I walked down Brynmill Lane to catch the Mumbles Train to my station, and there was the sea. What a relief it was to see the beautiful Swansea Bay.

But that first day I was terribly sick: I must have eaten something that upset me. Oh! It was terrible, but I was alright afterwards. Coed Saeson was a very large house with wide staircases and beautiful spacious grounds. I was only at Headquarters for a week, travelling from our station every day, to learn the job. There were many Wrens billeted in

---

1. Tut Head – the Coastguard Station Hill.

the offices at Coed Saeson, but I didn't want to be in an office, and thought our job was much more interesting.

Our station was previously the Coastguard Station: the coastguards had been taken over by the Navy and we, in turn, relieved the Navy for other duties. We were ten signallers and two wireless telegraphers. As Wrens, our main job was to receive signals from, and send messages and instruction to, ships sailing into the bay – convoy ships, examination vessels and mine sweepers. We received their request orders for food, etc. and reported the information to the signal office at the naval base – the *HMS Lucifer* – on the docks in Swansea. For this we used ten-inch projectors and Aldis Lamps – portable signalling lamps.[2] We were also in charge of the foghorn. We worked naval watch-keeping hours: four hours on and four hours off, night and day.

We lived in quarters where the restaurant, Castellamare, is now situated. It was only a shack; the winters were cold and the snow used to come through. There was only one boiler in the middle of the room and it was freezing cold. The quarters were surrounded by barbed wire and very eerie. There was a narrow lane leading from them to the station. Climbing up there in the middle of the night wasn't very pleasant. We were often there on our own in the night for half an hour, as we changed watches.

We had a petty officer cook – a Wren – and a signal bosun in charge of us, who lived at the quarters. The bosun didn't like us as he thought women couldn't do anything, but we were lucky in our cook as she used to cook us cheese dreams – a sort of fried cheese sandwich, – which were gorgeous. We were always hungry as we worked hard, and our work was very exacting.

We were paid about one pound and five shillings a week. When at work, we wore navy trousers of rough serge with a flap up the front, which we called matelots, so named because sailors – matelots – wore the same sort of trousers. We had a navy jacket and a white shirt with a collar and tie. When we went out we wore a navy skirt, black stockings and black lace-up shoes. We were allowed to wear makeup but it wasn't very heavy then. Our hair had to be short, above the collar, but mine was a little longer in the photograph. We could wear a watch, but no jewellery. It wasn't so bad in Mumbles as nobody inspected us, and we were a bit freer than in other stations.

Nissen huts were suddenly erected where the car park now stands. It was rumoured that an American regiment was to be stationed there; the rumour proved to be right. We had no trouble from the soldiers, and in

---

2. Named after its inventor, A. C. W. Aldis.

fact, they were extremely kind to us. When we came off watch they'd give us a shout, and present us with dishes of peaches, etc. I became friendly with one of them. They had ships – Y boats – in Swansea Docks.

Although we worked hard, I enjoyed the camaraderie of my colleagues. The signal bosun was so miserable, and wouldn't let us have any men in the station. But when he went on holiday, we sent invitations around and had the biggest parties imaginable. Apparently, he complained about us to the Admiralty and said that he couldn't control us; but I think we were very good really. We did sometimes slip out through the barbed wire and go to the Pier; it was our local, and very nice. We played darts and all the marines were there; it was good fun. We had to sign in at ten o'clock in the evening and weren't allowed out if we were going on duty at midnight. The Admiralty sent down another bosun, but he was young, and would join us saying, 'Come on girls. Let's have a party.'

Although a mobile Wren, I remained in Mumbles throughout my service, and was there on 6th June 1944 for Operation Overlord – D-Day. On the eve of the invasion, all the Americans were suddenly gone. The bay was filled with about fifty ships and landing craft, ours and the Americans. All our ships were sending us non-stop requests. It was a very hectic time. We had to mark the ships' positions with a cross on a sort of chart. They sailed out into the bay but returned because of a storm. They anchored in different positions and so we had to redo the chart. At the time, we didn't know what was happening and were not told that it was the invasion. The ships sailed again the next day; it was an incredible sight. The ships from up the channel – Avonmouth, Bristol, Cardiff, etc. – sailed past Mumbles and the ships from the bay joined them; there were hundreds and hundreds of them. All those ships, and then suddenly, nothing. We waited a while. I can remember the first one coming back; it had been shot and was towed into the bay. We heard later that the Americans had gone to France and all had been killed."

'The invasion of Normandy was the initiation of the last phase of war, leading to the liberation of France and the Benelux countries. It was the largest military operation in the history of warfare.'[3]

Jenny concludes, "Our work over, we were sent to Blundell Sands Hotel – a naval establishment – in Lancashire. They didn't know what to do with us then, so we were told, 'If you want to get out you can.'

So we thought, 'Well, we might as well.'

The station was abandoned, and after VE Day in 1945, the coastguards returned.

---

3. Stephen Badsey, *D-Day, The Illustrated History*, Godalming (Surrey, 1993) p. 11.

Although my colleagues were from all over the country – Scotland, etc. – not one of us wanted to leave Swansea. I went home for about two weeks, and my friend went to work as receptionist in the Caswell Bay Hotel. She encouraged me to return, which I did, and worked in the Mermaid Hotel, and later in the Osborne Hotel.

I met and married a South Wales Sea Pilot, and am still living in Mumbles sixty years later."

Gwilym Davies – Nursing and Blood Transfusion Orderly

While Jenny, stationed in Mumbles, was involved in the organization of the D-Day landings, Gwilym Davies was also involved – in active service. It was government policy to keep service men and women in the dark of their plans, and so, while both contributed so much to the operation, neither knew their true objective.

Gwilym, a Penclawdd inhabitant for nearly fifty years, relates his story, which started in Swansea eighty years ago. "I was born in 1924. My mother died in childbirth having my sister, when I was three, and my paternal grandmother, Catherine Davies, brought me up. She was a wonderful woman. When I was fourteen, she got me a job in the Co-op Warehouse in Brynhyfryd, Swansea. The job entailed packing and delivering orders. The different butters were kept in casks, and customers were invited to taste before they bought. It was usually a quarter of a pound: they couldn't afford more. Sides of bacon were delivered wrapped in sacking. They were boned and cut into smaller pieces and then sliced on the machine into various sizes, one, two, three, etc. – the larger the number, the thicker the slice or rasher. Customers usually bought by the rasher, as opposed to the pound, then. I worked with a sixteen-year-old chappie who was my senior. One day he had opened the sacking, and was on his knees cutting the bacon on the floor, and I was leaning over him. The knife slid off the bone towards my face. I instinctively jerked backwards but not before the knife went into my right eye. I covered it thinking it was going to run out. My father had always warned me, 'Watch your eyes!' and I was more afraid of telling him, than worrying about my fate. I was rushed to the old Swansea Hospital and had a few operations. The saltpetre on the knife had gone into my eye. The surgeons tried to scrape it off, but it was spreading to my other one. My father was advised that I should have my eye out, which is what happened.

Morgan Davies, Parkhouse Camp, Salisbury Plain, 1914.

Gwilym Davies, with his father.

Morgan Davies, back row on right, on active service with the 9th Battalion Welsh Regiment, five miles behind the firing line, Merville, 1915.

I had started to play the piano and organ and had an excellent teacher, Eurfryn John, who was later the organist of Tabernacle Chapel in Morriston. The blackout regulations were in force by now, and I found it very difficult to read music with one eye, and in gaslight.

At the time, Ruth and her mother, Ruth Brenton, from Penclawdd, were selling cockles in Treboeth. Ruth's mother told her, 'Have you heard about that poor boy who had his eye out working in the Co-op?'

Ruth replied, 'Oh dear, dear,' and was quite cut up about it. We didn't know each other at the time, but I learned about it later.

My father, Morgan Davies, had been in the First World War and had come through the trenches and survived – otherwise I wouldn't be here now! After the war, he went to work in Tawe Lodge – Swansea Workhouse – in Mount Pleasant. He was the vagrant superintendent – looking after tramps who came in for food and shelter. He made sure they had a shower, and provided them with bread and dripping, and a mug of cocoa. He'd then put them to work in the garden; they grew their own vegetables. The next day they'd leave and probably tramp as far as Neath or Port Talbot. My father, by now widowed, met and married the assistant matron of Tawe Lodge, Hannah Maria Lewis.

He was one of the first to join the Home Guard in Swansea. He was stationed in the infantry department in Treboeth Hall. One of his duties – armed with a Lee Enfield rifle – was to check people's identity cards at Llangyfelach Cross to safeguard against German spies in the area. I decided to volunteer, and joined my father, and later was transferred to the anti-aircraft battery in Raven Hill – we were Home Guards, soldiers in the regular Army, and ATS girls all working together. My father and I had our own rifles, fifty rounds of ammunition and two bombs each.

I had a lucky escape one night. One of our Spitfires was chasing a German bomber, and the bomber jettisoned his bombs: he was probably offloading to make a quick getaway. The first bomb went through the viaduct in Landore, went into the road, and although didn't explode, killed two people; the second landed in Pwll Street behind my house in Cwmlan Terrace; the third had a direct hit on a shelter in Penfilia Road, and killed all in there. My grandmother and I were hiding under the table in our house. The bomber had flown from Cherbourg. After the Germans occupied France, they could fly directly to Swansea where Atlantic convoys were docking to feed the people of Britain. The Bristol Channel became known as the Western Approaches.

I left the Co-op and went to work in Duffryn Steelworks in Morriston in a reserved occupation: I was controlling the ingots of shell steel going through onto the rolls to be rolled into billet steel – used in the making of bombshells. In early 1943, I was called into the office and told that because of the loss of my eye, I could not be insured.

I was forced to leave and so *went on the buses* as a conductor for South Wales Transport Co. I wanted to be a driver, but it was not possible because of the loss of my eye. I attended a conducting course at Brunswick Street in Swansea, which was the headquarters and garage of the SWT (South Wales Transport). I passed the PSVC (Public Service Vehicle Conductor) course; most of us passed. Its main object was to teach us to make out a waybill, which recorded our bus trips. Our bus had to keep to the scheduled time – not early and not late – and this was checked by recorders who waited at certain bus stops, unknown to us. Inspectors came on the bus to spot-check that all passengers had bought tickets. So many people travelled by bus then – often having to stand in the gangway – that it was not always possible to sell tickets to all the passengers during their journey. I issued tickets from a TIM machine and wore a dark navy uniform with a peaked cap. I worked on the Mumbles Train – owned by SWT – for a while, and then on the No. 71-77 which was from the Guild Hall to Cwmrhydyceirw. I transferred to the No. 10, which was from Swansea through Dunvant terminating at Gowerton, and later the No. 16, which was from Swansea through Gowerton and Penclawdd, terminating at Llanrhidian, or continuing through Llanmadoc and terminating at Llangennith. I worked on the buses until the June of that year, and for the Home Guard as well, after working hours.

I was nineteen in the May, and found my call-up papers in the post the following month. I was stationed with the Welsh Regiment in Derring Lines, a barracks about a mile outside Brecon. We were D. Company in Hut 56. I trained in the infantry. We did route marches. We marched up Cwmgwili – eight miles there and eight miles back – in full kit of forty to fifty pounds in weight. When I came back to barracks, my feet were like pumpkins. I had a couple of days off and soon got hardened to the training. One day, when I was in the firing range, the sergeant noticed that I was using my left eye. He said, '14635650 Davies, what are you doing firing with your left eye?'

I explained, 'I only have one eye sergeant.'

'What are you doing here then?' he said, and disappeared into the office.

For some unknown reason I had been passed A1. My condition was reported and I was transferred to the RAMC (Regiment Army Medical Company) stationed in Farnham, Surrey. We were later to be involved in

Gwilym Davies, centre, with two mates, on blood transfusion course in Southfield Hospital, Bristol.

Ruth, on left, with sister Mary.

the 21st Army Group, formed before the Second Front, and commanded by Montgomery. We were trained in stretcher bearing, bandaging, etc. – light work. After a while, I was called into the office and the sergeant said, 'Davies, would you like to go on a course? I think you'll be good enough for it. I'd like you to go to Southmead Hospital in Clifton, Bristol, for a course on blood transfusion.' It proved to be quite a stiff course – practising putting needles in intravenously, cross matching and finding out blood types.

One day we were in a lecture room – part of the university. There were ATS girls on the course. One of them came over to me and said, 'You're from Wales aren't you?'

'Yes,' I said, 'I'm from Brynhyfryd.'

'I'm from Wales too – Penclawdd. My mother and sister used to go up there selling cockles.'

She told me that her name was Mary, and I decided to ask her for a date. I was a very shy person then and chatting up a girl was a new thing for me. However, I asked her if she'd like to see a film in Westbury-on-Trym, and we agreed to meet at the famous landmark, the white tree, in Bristol. I waited, but there was no sign of her coming. 'Well,' I thought, 'I've had the brush-off.' I waited about half an hour and then went back to my billet; it didn't affect me much.

My billet was a civilian one with a Mrs. Batty – she was batty too. I was later moved to another civilian billet near the hospital. They were private houses, and it was like being in lodgings: I ate with the family and the Army paid for my keep.

We were working in a huge workshop learning to blow glass, make our own blood sets, take and give blood; it was quite complicated. Blood has quite a short life span. Sometimes it would have solidified by the time we received it, so the glasses would have to be cleaned; it was quite dirty work. We learned how to take out the blood cells from the plasma – a yellowish liquid in which the cells of blood are suspended – dry it until it looked like sawdust, and reconstitute it by adding sterile water. At the end of the course I qualified as a nursing and blood transfusion orderly.

There was another Welsh girl on the course; she had been a plotter stationed at Leamington Spa. We were all having a chat one day, when I said to her, 'You're Welsh. Where are you from?'

'Penclawdd,' she answered.

'But I have been talking to a girl – Mary – from Penclawdd recently.'

'She's my sister.'

'What's your name?'

'Ruth Myfanwy.'

When I told her that I was from Brynhyfryd, she said that she used to sell cockles there with her mother. I made a date, and we went to the cinema in Westbury-on-Trym to see *A Watch on the Rhine*. I held her hand during the film but there was no kissing or snogging – nothing like that! We continued going out together while I was in Clifton.

Gwilym Davies in Scarborough, 1 June 1944.

Our unit moved to Scarborough – it was coming up to the Second Front (Operation Overlord). We were practising climbing up and down the cliffs, preparing for the beaches of Normandy – we learned later. At the time, we knew very little; it was all cloak-and-dagger stuff. We knew that there was going to be an invasion, but we had no idea where, or when. While there, I was made batman to my doctor, Major Sam Gordon.

We were then moved to Worthing. We sailed from Southampton in LCTs – Landing Craft (Troops), which were flat-bottomed boats with fronts that came down – to the beaches of Arromanches. There, we discovered that the infantry, paratroops, etc. had previously landed, and the beaches were strewn with wounded

The D-Day landings – 6 June 1944.

and dead soldiers. The beachhead had been formed, and so there was no room for a hospital – just field dressing stations. Those with slight injuries we bandaged, and they returned to their units. Soldiers that were more seriously injured, we prepared to take back to Southampton. We dressed their wounds, and gave them plasma – four pints only: it was impossible to give them whole blood, as we had no way of knowing their blood group. The administration of plasma was often very difficult, as when injured, the soldiers' blood pressure would automatically have dropped, making the veins deep-seated. Some never got off the boats, or were drowned, and many thousand had been killed, so they had to be identified and taken back to Southampton. While we were working, the planes were flying over, and we were near enough to the action to guess what was going on. The beach was small, and we could easily have been pushed back into the sea by the Germans."

Between 6 June and 15 September 1944, about two million Allied personnel arrived in France; forty thousand were killed, and about one hundred and sixty thousand wounded. In earlier wars, many of the latter would have died or become permanently disabled. In every major conflict in history up to 1914, more men died of *battlefield diseases* like dysentery, malaria, and typhus than died of wounds. In World War One, about fifty-four percent of men with chest wounds died, while in World War Two, only six percent died. The number of deaths of wounded decreased drastically during the Second World War. Major reasons include the introduction of antibiotics like penicillin; the discovery of plasma and the establishment of blood banks; increased provision of surgical field hospitals; and speedy air evacuation of badly wounded men to base hospitals.

"When I came back to Southampton for the second time," recalls Gwilym," Ruth kept writing to me, 'We've got to get married. We've got to get married. If something happens to you, I'll be left with nothing.'

I wrote back, 'We can't get married: we're in the middle of the Second Front.' But I eventually relented, went to see the major, and told him, 'I've got to get married,' and not, 'I want to get married' – a big difference in those days, but I said it in all innocence.

'Davies,' he said, 'what are you talking about? We're in the middle of the Second Front.' However, he told me to see the padre who was more sympathetic, and gave me permission. The rules of the King's Regiment stated that you could have three days off to get married whatever the circumstance.

I went home and borrowed my father's suit: I didn't have one of my own. Ruth and I were married on 19th August 1944, in Bethel Chapel, in Penclawdd, by the Reverend W. E. Williams of Tabernacle Chapel: the Reverend Henry Hughes – minister of Bethel – was away at the time. We spent the first night of our marriage in my father's house in Brynhyfryd, very conscious of the fact that he was in the next bedroom. I arrived back a day late to discover that my unit wasn't there, and so I phoned the RTO (Railway Transport Officer), stationed at the railway in Worthing, and said, 'I've just got married and my unit has returned to France permanently.'

He said, 'Stay where you are until further orders.'

I found lodgings, and Ruth and I honeymooned in Worthing. I was then stationed at an RHU (Reinforcement Holding Unit) in Oxford, and so Ruth and I had a week in Oxford. We had a fortnight's honeymoon on the Army, in the middle of the Second Front!

I had a posting to Bayeux. We sailed in a Liberty boat and got off by climbing down the side netting. The swell of the tide was about twenty inches, and we had to drop down about twenty feet with full kit – blankets and ground sheets, etc.; it was very difficult and your stomach came up to your throat. Fortunately, being medics, we didn't have any firearms, so that lessened the burden to a certain extent. We marched inland from the beach, and met German prisoners coming towards us to board ships for Britain; they were looking a bit doggish.

We took over a civilian hospital – the 121 British General Hospital in Amiens. The Americans were defending the Ardennes. While we were there, the Germans came roaring through the American lines with about two hundred tanks and advanced sixty miles causing a huge bulge in the front line – known as the Battle of the Bulge (December 1944); they cut through the Americans like a knife through butter. Fortunately, the German tanks ran out of oil, otherwise we would have been cut off from the channel ports and taken prisoner – we only learned of this years afterwards.

We stayed there a while until suddenly, we had orders to load up the whole hospital into about forty big wagons – to become mobile. We travelled a long distance, and eventually were stationed at Hasselt, in Belgium, near the German border. The Germans had bombed the bridge at Nijmegen, in Holland, so we crossed the River Rhine over the Bailey bridge,[4] and into Kleve in Germany. We travelled on motorways; we had never seen motorways before. We travelled through the night piled up

---

4. A bridge of lattice steel designed for rapid assembly from prefabricated parts, used especially in military operations, designed by English engineer, Sir D. Coleman Bailey.

in the back of lorries; some of us were on hospital beds, and the rest hanging onto whatever we could. We had no idea where we were going. We stayed in Neustadt for about two hours, where we had something to eat and a cup of tea in the army kitchens, and the German civilians were looking at us a bit askance – British troops in Germany! We continued right across Germany saying to ourselves, 'Well, where is the German Army? Why are they falling back to allow us to come in?' However, unknown to us, the Russians were attacking East Germany – advancing towards Berlin. We went to Celle and then took over a hospital in Braunschweig. The Russians were on the opposite side of the River Elbe, and they used to come across with big bottles of vodka. Comradeship was good: there was no Iron Curtain then.

My eye became sore – it was a glass eye – and needed attention. I hitch-hiked across Germany to the 109 British General Hospital in Brussels where I was given a new eye, and then hitch-hiked back.

I was asked to work in the operating theatre of the maxo facial department in Braunschweig Hospital; my job was to keep the blood pressure up of patients having operations. They had suffered shrapnel wounds to their heads; some of their facial injuries were horrible. I was called into the office and told that I had a posting back to U.K. It was September 1945 and I thought, 'The end of the war is coming. I'm going to be demobbed,' – but no such luck.

I sailed from Dieppe to Newhaven, and to my posting at the medical centre in Farnham. I immediately had a month's leave, and Ruth and I went home. The time passed far too quickly, and Ruth insisted on returning with me, although I told her that it was hardly worth it seeing that I was soon to be posted abroad again. I found a civilian billet with Mr. and Mrs. Ecott in Fleet, and Ruth and I stayed there: there were no married quarters in those days.

I waited for my next posting having no idea where. The boys were going all over the place – Belize, South Africa, Burma, Cyprus, the Middle East. I was told, 'No. RH00Z (a draft number), you are going to Egypt.' We sailed to Dieppe where we caught a train to Toulon. We sailed to the toe of Italy, and then on to Cairo, calling in Malta and Port Said. We arrived at a one thousand-bedded hospital in Helmieh in Cairo, but I was based outside the city at an RAMC (Royal Army Medical Company) base. We were still in our thick khaki uniform, but were then issued with lightweight khaki uniforms with shorts, and also Australian uniforms, which were made of green lightweight serge. I was not involved in medical work there but worked in a sports centre in charge of kit for football, snooker and billiards equipment, etc. I had a place of my own and a little dog called Fritz; I gave a German prisoner of war chocolates and cigarettes – I didn't smoke – and in return he gave me Fritz. While there, I contracted sandfly fever, and was in hospital for about a fortnight. I then had leave, and a few of us went to Aswan.

Gwilym Davies, in front on right. Lake Timsa, Suez Canal.

Gwilym Davies, back row on right, on trip to Aswan in Egypt with the boys of the 109 British Hospital.

Gwilym Davies, centre, with German POWs – Peter and Paul.

The Army was bringing men back to Cairo from Tobruk and Benghazi. The railway only ran as far as Tobruk, and so motor convoy was used to Benghazi. I was instructed to replace a man on leave. We loaded the train with food – we were a corporal, three men and a cook – and travelled to Tobruk, via El Alamein. The harbour was full of sunken Italian warships: the British had blocked them in and bombed them to prevent the Germans using them. We used to go skinny-dipping in the harbour: there were no women around. The water was beautifully clear; it was forty to sixty feet deep, and we could see the bottom. The sand was white, and so hot that it burnt our feet. We then continued to Benghazi.

I did many of these runs, and was then posted to the 109 British General Hospital in Suez. We were waiting to go to Burma where medical staff was needed. I was now back on my own work that I had done in Bristol: testing for the blood group of the patients and registering it in their pay books for future reference; cross matching blood units; making my own blood sets; sterilizing dressings. I worked on my own, but was helped by two German prisoners of war – Peter and Paul; they were wonderfully co-operative and did the heavy work. When taken prisoner, the Germans had a different attitude to ours. If we were captured we'd try our best to escape. The Germans couldn't understand this and said, 'The war is over for you. Take it easy. You'll be a prisoner of war until the end of the war, and then you can go home.' We had the usual army food: everything was mashed into potato – Bully beef, cauliflower, cheese; we also had sausages and bacon; breakfast was always porridge – and if you didn't get up in time, you went without. The rock cakes were like a piece of rock; but they were nice, fair play. We were living in Nissen huts. One day, the sergeant announced, 'The war is over – the Japanese War – and we've dropped two bombs on Japan and they've surrendered.'

'Thank goodness,' we thought. We were saved going to Burma; we had not been looking forward to that.

I was given a month's LIAP leave to the U.K. It was the winter of 1947. We sailed from Port Said across the Med. to Toulon to find it covered in a thick layer of snow. Our blood had thinned while being in the Middle East, and we found the cold weather extreme. Everything was on stop, and we had to wait a fortnight for a train for Dieppe and home.

My wife was now living in my grandmother's house in Swansea. I saw my son, Peter for the first time. He was ten months old. Few recognized me on my return, as the temperature in Suez had been about 130/140 degrees F in the shade, and I was very sun-tanned. At the end of my leave I had to return to my unit, and was very cut up about it. I had just got off the gangplank and boarded the ship when the tannoy announced, 'Anybody in Group 50 report to the RTO' – my group. We were told, 'You are not going back to the Middle East; you are to stay here.' It was fantastic news! My wife was overjoyed.

I was posted to a hospital in Chester. I had left all my kit in Suez, including a marvellous pair of boots that the Germans had made for me. I thought that they would miss me in the unit but I didn't worry: I was home. Ruth contracted 'flu, and I asked for compassionate leave to look after her, but I was told that it had been stopped. I didn't ask why: you didn't question a sergeant. However, I managed to get a posting in Withybush Hospital in Haverfordwest, from where I was able to come home every weekend. I was given the option of working in the operating theatre or the cookhouse, and I chose the latter. Everything was on the black market. On Fridays, the cook gave me anything that was leftover in the kitchen to take home – butter, tinned cheese, which were on ration.

I had orders to return to Chester, and from there went to the demob centre in York. I caught a train to Paddington, and then to Swansea. I was provided with a civilian suit and a trilby; I looked like an American gangster. It was strange to be wearing civilian clothes: I was twenty-three and had had been in uniform from the age of fourteen.

I was awarded the Defence Medal through my work in the Home Guard, the 1939-1945 Star, the France and Germany Star, and the Victory Medal."

Gwilym Davies, on right, Gurnos Road, Gowerton.

Gwilym returned to his work as a bus conductor: it was government policy that employers re-employ their pre-war employees who had served in the forces.

Later, Gwilym was involved in the building of prefabricated houses (in Cwmfelin). 'By June 1945, it was estimated that four and a half million houses would be needed over the next ten years – an average of four hundred and fifty thousand to be built each year. . . . The huge demand for new houses, and the dearth of skilled building labour, made many minds turn to the factory system; if aircraft could be built in pieces in factories, the argument ran, why not houses. They were cheap, easily and quickly assembled, and required little in the way of skills at a time when craftsmen were at a premium. These prefabs, as they were soon generally known, began to be put up in 1944, the earliest being built in London where the raiding had been heaviest. The very first to be erected was completed on 30 April; it was built in three days and cost five hundred and fifty pounds.'[5]

Through his war work, Gwilym had qualified as a SEAN (State Enrolled Assistant Nurse). On enquiring as to whether he could enrol on a course to obtain an SRN (State Registered Nurse) he discovered that the salary was inadequate, and so became an assistant to the anaesthetist in Mount Pleasant Hospital. He later worked in the boiler house there.

His son, Hywel Morgan was born seven years after Peter, and Kathryn four years later. The family moved from Swansea to Penclawdd in 1957.

In 1962, Gwilym was employed in the boiler house of Gorseinon Hospital. Before his retirement in 1984, he found himself in the unique position of working in the boiler house, and also in the operating theatre as assistant to the anaesthetist. "There were two of us working in the boiler house," he says. "The first time theatre was short staffed, I scrubbed up, and said to my mate, 'I'm going to work in the theatre now.' He was quite astounded."

Vincent Rees – Wireless Operator, RAF

More then one hundred and twenty-five thousand men laid their lives on the line for the service of Bomber Command's desperate campaign – mainly targeting German factories and oil terminals. It is said that they were the fittest, cleverest, and most technologically skilled men, and probably the most highly trained front-line fighters, in the history of war. Over fifty-five thousand lost their lives in the skies over Germany, and many more were injured or mentally broken by their ordeal. "Everyone played their part in the war," says Vincent, "but Bomber Command broke the will of the Germans.

My father was a miner, and I was one of six children. I was born in 1915, and the Miners' Strike of 1926 caused problems for our family. Then came the American Wall Street Crash in October 1929, and I left school that Christmas; there was no hope of continuing my education.

One of my first jobs was in the old tin-plate works in Gorseinon, but I didn't stay there long: the pay was poor, and the bus fare about four shillings, so I had little to take home. I did various jobs before I volun-

---

5. Mike Brown & Carol Harris, *The Wartime House, Home Life in Wartime Britain, 1939-1945* (Phoenix Mill, Thrupp, Stroud, Gloucestershire, GL5 2BU) pp. 170 & 172.

teered. I was working for a builder – T. & G. Spragg – in Cockett, but building materials were hard to come by in the war years, and so I was forced to leave. As I had worked in the tin-plate works, I easily obtained a job in part of Cwmfelin Steelworks – making shell equipment.

My youngest brother, John Leyton, was the first of us to be called up. He was in the Welsh Guards and one of the first prisoners of war – captured at Dunkirk. I was partly in a reserved occupation, but all the men at that time felt it was the thing to do to join the services, so I volunteered for the RAF. I was now twenty-five. Six months later, I was asked to report to the YMCA in Swansea. I saw an Army major there; he was a very nice chap indeed. He said, 'You're just the chap for the Royal Engineers.' I was disappointed and told him that I'd rather go to the RAF. He could tell that I was determined and he said, 'All I can do is to pass your papers to the wing commander.' I was asked a few questions on general knowledge and what I knew about flying; to the latter I had to reply, 'Nothing.'

'We will get in touch with you,' he said, and I went back to work.

I thought they'd forgotten about me, but three months later, I received a letter asking me to report to the RAF station in Padgate, Cheshire; I knew then that I was definitely in the RAF. I was given a thorough medical examination and it was discovered that my hearing was not one hundred percent. However, I had my ears syringed and found that dust had got into my ears while working in the steelworks. My hearing was then excellent; and still is so today. I passed my medical A1.

In July 1941, I was posted to a receiving station for aircrew, which was situated in the Winter Gardens in Blackpool. I had no hope of being a pilot as I didn't have the senior education required. I decided to train as a wireless operator and attended a ten-week course. I passed my Morse code exam. – ten words a minute – in ten weeks; it was pretty tough going as I hadn't even heard of Morse code before. Only thirteen out of thirty of us passed. The next day Norman Jack Crisp and I were the only two to pass the twelve words a minute exam. I had leave, and went to my home in Sketty, Swansea.

I received a letter asking me to report to a more advanced signal school in Yatesbury, Wiltshire. I learned to send Morse code at sixteen words a minute, and semaphore. I managed to get through, and went home on leave.

After Christmas, I reported to my next station in Andover, Hampshire where I stayed until the July. It was now 1942. There I learned to charge batteries for aircraft, radio maintenance, repair telephones, guard duty, etc.

I received my first call for flying in the August and reported to a training school in Madley, Herefordshire. Three of us went with an instructor in a plane where I had about an hour on the Marconi transmitter equipment, sending and receiving messages to various RAF stations including the Isle of Man and Scotland. By 30th September, I was a fully qualified wireless operator for aircrew, and was issued with a logbook. Wages were very small: about four shillings a day. I had the opportunity to go on an air-gunner course at Stormy Down, which would give me another one shilling and six pence a day. I was planning to get married in the November, and felt that five shillings and six pence a day would just do. I passed the course, and during my day's leave, Ann (Stevens) and I were married at St. Teilo's Church, Bishopston, on 3rd November.

My next posting was a further RAF station in Millom, Cumberland. I was flying now – still with an instructor, mostly over the North Sea – passed the course, and was made a sergeant.

I had the usual ten days leave, and was posted to an OTU (Operation Training Unit) in Leighton Buzzard, Bedfordshire. That course was tough. Two Welsh boys – Johnny Phipps from up the valleys, and I – were top of the course. Johnny went out to North Africa to fly, but I stayed, as I had been booked for Bomber Command.

There were eighty of us on the course. At the time, we were using twin-engine Wellingtons and were five to a crew – pilot, navigator, wireless operator, bomb aimer, rear-gunner. The officer in charge said, 'I want you to form into crews.' We were all in a large aircraft hangar, and many had never spoken, or seen, each other before. I approached a navigator – I could tell his qualification by his badge – and asked him if he was crewed up. He wasn't, and so after about half an hour we found a gunner, a bomb aimer and a pilot. The officer in charge asked the pilots the names of their crew. Our pilot was a Scottish chap called Bill Jolly; a nice chap he was and aptly named. We had to take part in a sport, and football seemed the most appropriate in January, so my crew and three others formed two football teams – ten against ten. Bill Jolly was our goalkeeper and bless my soul, a chap came to score a goal, kicked Bill on his wrist, and broke it. We were now without a pilot.

While the other crews were dispersed, we four were posted to Little Horwood, near Aylesbury, where we met an officer pilot who was an accountant named Sam Smart. He joined us to complete our crew, but at first we were not happy with the situation: we were all sergeants in the

Left to right: Dees (bomb aimer), Alan Davies (navigator) Vincent Rees (wireless operator), Bob Taylor (engineer), Sam Smart (officer pilot), Bert Hislop (rear-upper gunner), Tom Davies (mid-upper gunner).

Stirling plane.

sergeants' mess and he was in the officers' mess. However, when we got to know him, we discovered that he was a nice chap. Our crew did a number of cross-country trips locally – Mumbles, Worms Head – getting to know each other and getting used to working together: it was important for us to learn to work as a team, trusting and relying on each other. Leave followed with us thinking that it wouldn't be long before we would be posted to a squadron.

We were sent to Waterbeach, Cambridgeshire to learn to fly Stirlings – four-engine planes. The change didn't affect me as the radio equipment was the same, but of course, it did affect the pilot – it would be like a driver today changing from a Robin Reliant – a Del Boy car – to a Rolls. We had to have two extra crew: a mid-upper gunner, and a flight engineer. Tom Davies, a Canadian farmer became our mid-upper gunner; I still hear from him. So we were now a crew of seven: pilot, navigator, wireless operator, flight engineer, bomb aimer, mid-upper gunner, rear-upper gunner.

Lakenhead in Suffolk was our next posting. We were attached to 149 Squadron, which had a very good record. The squadron had three flights, A B and C and about six crews per flight. There were about fifteen airfields in Suffolk; they were almost touching each other. We became familiar with our airfield, and squadron life, and at last had our first op. (operation)."

Vincent's logbook, in which he recorded every flight, during his training, and the operations he undertook is still in his possession. The night flights were written in red, and the day flights in black. It was checked and initialled by the OF/C (officer in charge). Vincent refers to his logbook while recounting his operations.

> "*5 June 1943*
>
> It was a short flight. The Germans controlled the coast from Norway to Spain, and were shipping out food from Norway. Our job was to try to obstruct them by dropping mines about ten miles off the coast off the Friesian Islands. We were very apprehensive during this first operation, as the Germans were only twenty-five miles across the water with fighter planes.
>
> *14 June*
>
> It was June, and so little night-flying hours. We left at 22.15 p.m. and were back about five the next morning. We were again dropping mines – in the Bay of Biscay.

Vincent Rees, RAF Lakenheath, 1944.

21-25 June
Five nights of bomb dropping over the Ruhr Valley, in Germany. We bombed Krefeld on 21st, Mülheim on 22nd, Elverfeld on 24th, and Gelsenkirchen on 25th. Everywhere was defended with hundreds of searchlights. It was sarcastically nicknamed Happy Valley.

On one occasion, Ewan Paton – who had been a bomb aimer on our crew – and I were wearing each other's helmets by mistake. I noticed mine was slack, and so we exchanged them. He later took off for a bomb-

JUNE 1949 SQUADRON

Time carried forward :— | 118.10 | 104.25

Date	Hour	Aircraft Type and No.	Pilot	Duty	Remarks (including results of bombing, gunnery, exercises, etc.)	Flying Times Day	Night
14·6·43	15·45	STIRLING EF 412	F/O SMART	W/OP	N.F.T.	1·05	
14·6·43	22·15	STIRLING EF 412	F/O SMART	W/OP	OPS. MINELAYING. BAY-OF-BISCAY.		6·40
18·6·43	11·40	STIRLING BF 512	F/O SMART	W/OP	N.F.T. NIGHT FLYING TEST	1·10	
19·6·43	13·45	STIRLING BF 512	F/O SMART	W/OP	N.F.T	00·15	
19·6·43	15·55	STIRLING BF 512	F/O SMART	W/OP	N.F.T	00·20	
20·6·43	15·25	STIRLING BF 512	F/O SMART	W/OP	N.F.T	1·15	
21·6·43	10·15	STIRLING EH 883	F/O SMART	W/OP	BOMBING - AIR FIRING - N.F.T.	1·45	
21·6·43	00·15	STIRLING BF 512	F/O SMART	W/OP	OPERATIONAL TRIP. KREFELD		3·35
22·6·43	23·55	STIRLING BF 512	F/O SMART	W/OP	OPERATIONAL TRIP. MULHEIM		3·30
24·6·43	10·55	STIRLING EF 412	F/C SMART	W/OP	FIGHTER AFFILIATION. N.F.T.	1·15	
24·6·43	25·43	STIRLING BF 483	F/O SMART	W/OP	OPERATIONAL TRIP. ELBERFELD		4·25
25·6·43	23·31	STIRLING BF 412	F/O SMART	W/OP	OPERATIONAL TRIP. GELSENKIRCHEN		4·35

Total Time ... | 125·15 | 127·00

Excerpt from Vincent Rees' logbook.

ing raid, and was shot down; he never came back. I know it wouldn't have made any difference what helmet he wore, but it played on my mind, and my nerves – and I was flying that night.

I had been on many courses with George Riley, from Lancashire. One night, he and his crew were to be on the same op. as us. As usual, they tested their plane that morning. They were coming in to land with the carriage down, it just touched the tops of the trees, the plane turned over, and the seven were burned to a cinder. Before the op., George had said to me, 'If we're not flying tomorrow, Taff – all Welshmen were Taff – we'll all go out for a pint.'

We'd be twenty-one sleeping in a hut, and the following day we'd only be seven. New chaps would come straight from training to fill the empty beds. We'd tell them that the beds were unlucky; they'd accuse us of being superstitious!

I had, by now, realized how dangerous life had become, and was so pleased when my wife had the chance of coming to see me. Our rear-gunner, Bert Hislop was expecting a weekend visit from his wife. He asked if Ann would like to keep her company. Ann had been working on ammunitions at the ICI in Landore, but by then was in Cardiff working as a supervisor on naval ordinance. Her sister had been a maid in Sketty, but was sent to an aircraft factory in Bristol: girls were sent all over the place then. There was a little local newspaper shop nearby. The owner had two children, and her husband was in the Army in Africa. Ann managed to have time off work, and I found a room for us there, but I wasn't allowed to sleep out at the time.

We were losing a lot of planes when bombing over the centre of Germany. Air Chief Marshal Harris, of Bomber Command, suggested that the attacks on Germany be increased. It was decided to carry out a saturated attack on a major German city; Hamburg – a big seaport and Germany's second city – was chosen. The radar specialists devised a plan to confuse the Germans; it was called *Window*.

24 July
Certain planes carried a considerable quantity of metallic strips, approximately twelve inches long by one inch wide, black on one side, and silver on the other. When dropped, they would give the similar effect of planes, on the German radar screens. I started dropping the paper through the release chute, about fifty miles off Hamburg, at about sixteen to eighteen thousand feet. I understand that one of our chaps listening in to a German commentary heard them say, 'There are thousands of the swines.' It was a great success: out of eight hundred and forty aircraft, we only lost eight.

25 July
We went to the Krupp armament works in Essen – a very dangerous place. We had to return to base early as one of the engines was overheating.

27 July
Went back to Hamburg again.

29 July
We flew to Hamburg for the third time. The plan was to bomb the city all in one go – hence the intensive raids. The flight took five hours and five minutes.

30 July
Another visit to the Ruhr – Remscheid. The weather was favourable, but we had to wait until after 10.45 p.m. to take off.

2 August
One more raid on Hamburg. We were approaching the city from the sea and suddenly found ourselves in the middle of an electric storm: we were losing height; ice was forming on the wings; lightning was playing around the propellers – they looked like spiders' webs. Luckily, we weren't earthed up there in the sky: we would have been blown to bits. The pilot was concerned because we dared not go in at a low height: we would have been shot down. The engines were by now affected, and so we had no alternative but to return to base. I contacted control as usual, and we were instructed to drop our bombs in The Wash: we never dropped them indiscriminately.

10 August
That was a long, tough one, taking seven hours and thirty minutes. Our mission was to bomb the German headquarters in Nürnberg. By now, the Germans had got wind of *Window* – they'd discovered the metallic strips on the ground – and so it was no longer of use to us.

16 August
Substitute raid on Turin, in Italy. We set off at 20.10 p.m. The trip took eight hours and twenty-five minutes. I tuned into Bomber Command for any urgent messages, which I always did every half

an hour. Instructions were received to land at Boscombe Down, with no reason given. I passed the message to the pilot, who in turn informed the navigator, who then worked out a course to Boscombe Down. We were flying over the Alps – a beautiful sight. It was a moonlight night, and the frozen water was shimmering like lakes, in the peaks. Thankfully, we landed safely. They weren't expecting us, and we weren't even offered a cup of tea. We slept somewhere – I think it was the sergeants' mess – in chairs, or whatever we could find. However, we were very lucky, as the next day we discovered that we had very little petrol in the tanks and would never have made it to Lakenheath.

30 August
To Mönchengladbach in the Ruhr Valley.

31 August
The big one – to Berlin itself. The city was very heavily defended with night-fighters. Oh my golly, that was some trip! We were about seven hundred planes over the target, which was extremely dangerous. We went in at about five-minute intervals; we were at eighteen thousand feet and the Lancasters – a bit lighter – at twenty-two thousand feet. The damn German fighters were above us at twenty-five thousand feet, and could see our planes in the searchlights. It is purely through luck that I'm here today; there is no question about that. Out of over one hundred thousand airmen in Bomber Command – British, Australian, New Zealanders, Canadian – only fifty-three thousand survived; one in two was killed. However, when flying, we had no time to worry about our safety: there was always something to do. We survived Berlin and were glad to see that over.

22 September
To Hanover in Germany.

18 November
To Mülheim in the Ruhr Valley.

In early November, I heard that my eldest brother, Desmond had been killed in action, and I was anxious to be with my mother. I could have applied for compassionate leave, but if my crew undertook ops. while I was away, I'd have to have made the number up at a later date with a strange crew. I explained this to Sam our pilot, not thinking he could help, but he asked me, 'Is there an airfield near your home?'

'Yes, Fairwood,' I replied, 'but it's not a very big airfield.'

He said, 'Get hold of Alan (navigator) and Bob (engineer).'

At 3.55 p.m. on the seventh, they flew me down to Fairwood. How Sam obtained permission to land the Stirling there, I'll never know. He dropped me at the end of the airfield without bothering to contact flying control, turned the plane, and flew off. I walked to Killay and caught a bus home; I took longer to get from the airfield to home, than I did from Suffolk to Fairwood. My mother was delighted to see me. 'Mam,' I said, 'don't worry. John is a POW but he's alright, and will be home one of these days. I pacified her the best I could about Desmond, and was on the eight o'clock train back the next morning, without missing a flight. It was a mystery for many years afterwards why a very large, unidentified plane landed at Fairwood that November afternoon.

28 January 1944

A very dangerous one. The Germans were using a lot of shipping in the Kiel Canal, in the Baltic. They were our target. I honestly think that one of our chaps saved our lives on that operation. A Messerchmitt 110, a German twin-engine night-fighter got amongst our bombers. About a hundred yards from us he started following one, and shot it down. It was impossible for the crew to bail out at that speed. Just as the plane was about to hit the water, the gunner – within the last minutes of his life – managed to shoot the German plane, and the two went down together, one on top of the other. If he had been unsuccessful, I feel sure that we would have been the German's next target.

10 February 1944

The Second Front was starting. The French Resistance – the Maquis – were working with the bombers – blowing up factories, etc. We were told in the briefing room that we had a special target – and that was all. We flew, on a moonlight night, under five thousand feet to avoid radar, down the coast of France. We turned inland at Bordeaux, and followed the River Loire. We flew over a train with an anti-aircraft gun, and it hit us right through the starboard of our engine and damaged it. We continued until we saw the flashing of an Aldis lamp in the corner of a field, and I identified that it was the correct signal. We dropped our containers – they were like tea chests – as fast as we could. There was smoke coming out of the engine and the pilot gave instructions to stand by to bail out. The flight engineer and I had opened the escape hatch and, with our parachutes by our sides, were ready to jump, when the pilot cancelled the instruction: he probably realized that at only four thousand feet, it would have been extremely dangerous. Our immediate problem was to get out of that area. The pilot and engineer discussed the problem and I returned to my wireless set to commence emergency procedures. The pilot was brilliant in controlling the situation. He thankfully landed at base very well, running into a pile of sand at the end of the runway – there for that purpose. Airsea rescue was standing by, and we were sprayed with foam even before we were out of the aircraft. It was a tough, heavy plane, and it got us back, but it was written off and never used again.

15 February
We were back on the very same trip, but this time, we steered clear of trains!

7 March
Another special target.

23 March
To Laon.

18 April
To the Kiel Canal in the Baltic.

27 & 28 April
Two more droppings for the Maquis. We were used to finding them by now.

We had completed twenty-six ops. – one over our quota. Aircraft crew had to do twenty-five ops. followed by a break as an instructor for six months and then twenty more ops. to complete tour of operations. It transpired that the two trips, when we nearly lost our lives, were discounted – our trip to Hamburg in the electric storm, and the French trip when our plane was damaged by gunfire – and so we did another special target op. to France on 1st May.

Before I left the squadron, the squadron signal officer recommended that I should be awarded a commission – to become an officer.

Vincent Rees, eighth from left. Instructors at Silverstone.

Vincent and Ann Rees shortly after Vincent was commissioned.

I was classed as a staff instructor and posted to Upper Heyford, in Oxfordshire. I was involved in flying training, but never flew on an op. again.

Credenhill, Herefordshire, was my next posting. It was an AOCS (Aircrew Officers' Commando School).

When I was an instructor at the training school in Silverstone, we had an open day every so often, for the local inhabitants, as a compensation for disrupting their lives with our day and night flying. They were taken around our prefabricated quarters – where we lived and worked – and on aircraft. Sometimes they were even allowed to sit in the pilot's seat. They greatly appreciated these visits.

There were German and Italian POWs waiting to be posted home. They used to clean my office and I got to know them well. One day, one of the Italians said to me, 'What planes did you fly?'

'Stirlings, I replied, 'in 149 Squadron.'

'Oh yes, Stirlings. They're big planes.'

About a week later, he presented me with a beautiful painting of a Stirling plane – a replica of the one I flew in – framed in polished wood, which he'd probably made from the broken tables that were lying around. I so appreciated the kind gesture, and treasure it to this day. When my wife saw the painting, with the P on the side, she said, 'If we have a boy, we'll call him Peter.' When our son was born in February 1947, we christened him Peter. My wife and I were from large families and didn't want Peter to be the only child; in 1953, our daughter, Elaine was born.

I was posted to an RAF station at Digby on a junior commando course. My next posting was to Swinderby, Lincoln as a senior signal officer with the rank of flight lieutenant. I was demobbed from there in October 1947.

Our pilot, Sam Smart was awarded the Distinguished Flying Cross and the Distinguished Service Order – the highest award that can be given for service and I think he fully deserved it.

When my brother, John, was first taken prisoner in Belgium, he somehow managed to escape and found shelter with a farmer and his family. The farmer had a daughter named Julie Rondo and it seems she and John became fond of each other. After being there for about six to eight weeks, he realized that if he were caught, the family would be shot, so he gave himself up. He was imprisoned in Stalag Luft B in Germany for the rest of the war. John and Julie corresponded, and after the war, he returned to the farm. I don't know the circumstances but he came home and remained a bachelor for the rest of his life.

I was awarded four medals: the 1939-45 Star, the Aircrew Europe Star, the Defence Medal, the 1939-45 Service Medal. I thought of making the RAF my career, but when my wife and I discussed it, we decided we had travelled enough and said, 'Let's go back to civvy street; there's no place like home.'"

Gwyneth Ellis MBE – WRVS

Gwyneth was born in 1914, the only child of George Llewellyn and Harriet Jones, 6 Station Road, Penclawdd. When she was ten years of age, the family moved to Glan-yr-Afon, in Hendy Road. In 1936, Gwyneth married Gwilym Ellis, a native of Gowerton.

Gwyneth has led an extremely active life, demonstrating not only relentless mental and physical energy, but also great kindness. She was awarded the MBE in the New Year's Honours List of 2003, for her sixty-two years service in the WRVS, from 1940 to 2002.

She reminisces, "Few people had cars in the village then. Before the doctor owned his own car, he used to hire Tom Booley's (confectioner and cycle shop proprietor). I was very friendly with Stella Booley, and as children, we used to play in the car. Johnny the Blue (John Rees, owner of the Blue Anchor pub) was another car-owner. When my grandmother died, her sister Ann came to live with us. Every August, she organized Johnny to take us to our relation's farm in Nicholston. We stayed there the day, having dinner and tea; it was our treat. Lord and Lady Blythswood were living in Penrice Castle then; I can remember them coming to church; Lord Blythswood was huge and she was like a little doll. Mr. E. M. Rees, owner of the Emporium shop in Penclawdd, was a guardian at Penmaen Workhouse. When he went to the Board of Guardians meetings once a month, he used to take us to the farm, which was near the workhouse. Travelling by car was not a smooth ride then, as it is today; often when we were going up Penmaen Hill, something would happen to the engine and we would all be thrown violently."

Gwyneth's first public work was from 1934 to 1939, when she organized the house to house sale of poppies in Penclawdd for Armistice Day: "It proved to be hard work as I didn't always have helpers, and sometimes did it myself.

Nurse Harris, of Mill Street, was our village midwife. Babies were born at home in those days and only in emergencies were expectant mothers admitted to hospital. We always knew there was a baby on the way if we saw her walking in Penclawdd with her bag under her cloak. She worked extremely hard, and was always spotlessly clean in her uniform of blue twill with a starched white collar. However, one day, Doctor David Jones Hughes, our village doctor, had instructions from the Health Authority that a qualified district nurse was to be appointed. This was, of course, before the National Health Service, and so the new appointment had to be paid out of private funds. I was asked to organize a house to house collection in the village, of one penny per household, per week. Two residents of Penlan, Rhoda Eaton and Margaret – wife of Alderman Henry Davies – were two of the helpers.

The first baby clinic in Penclawdd was held in the church hall, and later in Tabernacle vestry.

The WVS was founded in 1938, but did not come to Wales until 1940. I officially joined the WVS at Penclawdd on 20th March 1940, having previously been a member of Air Raid Precaution and Civil Defence; my first badge was WVS/Civil Defence. We had emergency training in first aid and home nursing. The classes were given by Doctor Hughes at his home in Burry House, Station Corner. Our district organizer was Carys Hughes, one of his three daughters. Doctor Hughes ran two classes a week, Wednesdays and Fridays, and his teaching was excellent: I really enjoyed them and went to both classes. One evening, a bomb dropped in Loughor. Although we had our helmets on, Doctor Hughes shouted, 'All under the table!' He was such good fun. He was lucky to have Miriam Guy as his housekeeper; she was always rushing; it was a big house to look after."

After the declaration of war, the government organized the production of munition – an essential commodity. Some raw materials were imported but many were provided by *salvage*. The WVS organized house to house collections of metal – tin baths, saucepans, tin cans – as well as scrap rubber, rags, waste paper and old animal bones.

Gwyneth continues, "During the early part of the war, we were asked to collect all the scrap iron we could find. Everybody rallied together during the war, and there was always a lorry and driver at our disposal, but what a mess we got into. One day, Vida, Doctor Hughes' oldest daughter, came on the collections wearing a lovely big white coat – what a mess her coat was in by the end of the collection. Even worse was collecting bones from the local butchers – George Francis, Harry Howells and Hughes of Llanmorlais. The butchers were killing their own animals then and put the bones in hessian sacks for us; but by the time we collected them, the sacks were crawling with maggots and the smell was horrible.

We were so small a group that we had to be on duty for twelve hours every other night – even longer during the Three-Night Blitz of Swansea. We had an urgent call to the surgery one night. A man from the village was on the outskirts of Swansea when the siren went and they started bombing Swansea. He had contacted the doctor, begging someone to come and meet him, so three of us went in the doctor's car over Fairwood Common to the outskirts of Killay, picked him up, and raced home. The following morning we heard that there had been a number of unexploded bombs on the common!

We had a *do* with the WVS and wanted a tea urn. The rugby club told us that we could borrow theirs from the pavilion at the Rec. as long as we collected it ourselves, and were warned that it was very heavy. Carys and I struggled with it up the bank behind the pavilion to the stile, but when we went over the stile, a drop of water came out of the urn. We realized that we had been carrying it full of water. We collapsed laughing saying, 'How dull can you get?'

I had been driving a motor bike for many years. This proved quite useful when I was on duty – unofficial despatch rider!

I belonged to the Social Service Women's Club held in John Willie's shed behind his shop in Sea View. It was excellent, supplying teachers for cookery and handcraft classes once a week.

An experimental station was opened on Salthouse Point in Crofty under the Ministry of Supply, run by the military. Members of the Royal Artillery were stationed there. They tested all guns, bombs, fuses, etc. for the arsenal at Bridgend. During this time, we had a request from the colonel in charge for a canteen, or something, for the troops to go to in the evenings. Within days, we were offered a shop premises in the centre of the village, in-between Robert John Davies' fruit and confectionery shop and the Emporium. It was in a dreadful state, so first we had to clean it. We scrubbed and painted it inside and out. We were given a coal-cooking stove, chairs, tables and china and we opened our canteen. We provided tea, coffee, beans on toast, etc. for all the soldiers stationed at Crofty and at the camps in the west-end of Penclawdd. They were all so grateful for what we did for them. Our most famous customer was the late Frankie Howerd.[6] I remember he thrived on our baked beans on toast. For years afterwards, he often spoke on the radio of his stay at Penclawdd, and how well the WVS looked after him.

---

6. Born Howard, he changed his name from *a* to *e* for his professional career, thinking it would attract a little more attention on a billboard.

Many civilians worked at the station. I started there as a telephonist earning a meagre three pounds a week. After ammunition was tested, I telephoned the information to the arsenal in Bridgend and arranged for its transport. They would say, 'How are you? When you send us the stuff, put a bag of cockles in it for us.' I didn't like the job as the rest of the staff finished at half-past four and I at half-past five, so after a while, I moved to a different department. I got to know Frankie Howerd very well. He was no good as a soldier. He was in charge of the catering and was hopeless. He was a very shy person and the girls whom he dated said that they couldn't get a word out of him. However, he thrived on entertainment – being centre stage. He was a real comedian – a natural. He used to come into the office and say, 'Oh, I can't do a thing with my hair.' He organized wonderful concerts in the village and was the star comedian. However, he was also interested in serious drama and organized plays within the office.

We fed and entertained soldiers from Gorseinon Hospital. A coach was provided for transporting them to Penclawdd free of charge. We served tea in Tabernacle vestry. Everything was home made such as the apple tarts cooked in large oval meat dishes. They enjoyed the Penclawdd cockles, which many of them hadn't tasted before. We held a concert party in the evenings with all local talent. It was such a pleasure to see the soldiers enjoying themselves. Harry Roberts, of the Railway pub in Penclawdd, then living in Gorseinon, was married to my Aunty Addie. He was a great worker for Friends of Gorseinon Hospital and really should have had an award for all his good work in the field."

Penclawdd hosted evacuees from the Germans' target areas – London and the south eastern counties of England. Pupils from the Sir Roger Manwood Grammar School in Deal, Kent stayed in Penclawdd for about three weeks in May 1940. Gwyneth recalls, "The WVS helped with the reception at the Elementary School and the distribution of the evacuees to various homes in the village. Three boys of about six years of age stayed with us at Glan-yr-Afon. We were given five shillings per boy for their keep. They loved going to gather cockles and riding on the donkeys. Gowerton County School was unable to accommodate them for a longer period and so they were forced to leave. They were found homes in Carmarthen and attended the local Grammar School.

After the war, I still continued my voluntary work in Penclawdd, helping anyone in need and being a member of most of the organizations in the village. I continued training in first aid and home nursing.

Some of us reached the Gold Medal standard for the St. John's Ambulance, but as we had to pay for the medals and the gold was so expensive, we bought the silver ones because they were cheaper.

An elderly uncle of mine, living in Penmaen, buried his wife and not having any children, was left on his own. He was so lonely that I used to visit him every Thursday, cook him a dinner, clean his little cottage and fill his cake tin with his favourite cakes. He looked forward so much to my visits. We had long talks in the afternoons and, if it was fine, I used to take him for a ride in the car. I did this for nine years, even travelling from Port Talbot after I moved there in 1949. It was not possible for me to visit him one Thursday. As he was not on the telephone, I was unable to let him know, so I went on the Friday morning instead. He was delighted to see me but kept asking me where had I been the day before as I had never missed a Thursday. As I was preparing his dinner, I turned around to speak to him. He just collapsed on the floor and died. He was eighty-nine. I just felt I was meant to go down that Friday morning. I missed him so much.

Having moved to Port Talbot, I was transferred to the WVS there and continued training in emergency feeding, rest centres, etc. Having now passed my driving test on a motorbike and car, I was immediately given the job of driving the WVS van and was appointed transport officer, a post I held for many years.

In 1956, the King George VI Memorial Hall was opened in Port Talbot by Princess Margaret. The following Easter, our organizer asked for suggestions for raising money for the hall at the Easter Fair held there. I suggested we buy undecorated chocolate Easter eggs and pipe individual children's names on them on request. They thought it an excellent idea, and gave me the job! I was hoping for short names, because the eggs were not very big. Imagine my face when my first customer was a little girl called Felicity.

I drove the van every week with Meals on Wheels. We used to leave the hall at 11.45 a.m., deliver about forty meals, return to wash our containers, and then help with about sixty to seventy meals served to the over sixties at the hall. One day we were taking Meals on Wheels to a pensioner when *Workers Playtime* was on the radio and Ossie Morris the Port Talbot comedian was on. The lady kept going on about not knowing what people saw in him, and that she didn't find him funny at all. My mate, Megan, began serving the potatoes with a very heavy hand: the carrots crashed to the plate; the gravy flicked over the tablecloth; and she said, 'That's my brother!' By this time I was silently helpless with laughter.

The old lady said, 'Oh love. I wouldn't have said it if I'd known.' We were all the best of friends by the time we left.

Every Christmas, we were given gift parcels by the local gas showroom for every recipient of our Meals on Wheels. I drove the van for many years collecting the gifts. We were always served a glass of wine and a mince pie each at the showroom.

Meals on Wheels continued for eleven years. Eventually the demand for meals became so great that we were unable to cope with the numbers, so we very reluctantly handed over to the local authority. We helped them for six months to get organized, which they were very grateful for. Later, the Medical Officer of Health told us it was the saddest day for the town when WVS had to give up Meals on Wheels. We had that interest and personal contact with the pensioners, and they looked forward to us coming every week, some not seeing anyone until we came again. We also saved many lives by reporting to Doctor Williams, the MOH anyone whom we thought needed medical attention.

The older part of Aberavon flooded when the river overflowed its banks during a storm. We were called out at 5 o'clock in the morning. Many of the houses were flooded but we had difficulty trying to persuade the older people to leave their homes. We provided hot meals for them, which we delivered in our hot containers.

I attended a Police Driving Course at Bridgend organized by the WVS. It was an excellent course in spite of half our members disappearing when we were told we had to go on the skid pad in the afternoon.

From 1955 to 1957, my husband and I built our own four-bedroom semi-detached house in Port Talbot. We used sub-contractors when necessary, but did most of the work ourselves. I was clerk of the works!

From the early 1960s, as transport officer, I was a member of centre staff.

In July 1966, I was appointed district organizer of Port Talbot. Her Majesty Queen Elizabeth honoured the WVS by adding Royal to its title and since that date the service has been known as the Women's Royal Voluntary Service. The first letter I received after the announcement was 'To the Royal Women of the WVS.'

The same year we attended an excellent week's course for district organizers from all over the country at the Civil Defence College at Sunningdale. We had lectures every day from 9 a.m. until 5.30 p.m. but when Lady Reading paid us a visit, we finished at 9 p.m. Lady Reading was the founder of the WVS. Her husband was in the Home Office. The heads of the Army, Navy and Air Force – all the big noises – were there. At the end of the week, we had to sit an examination. The county organizer, Mrs. Cox, who accompanied me, stayed up all night swotting. She was so afraid she would fail, but we all passed and were presented with our *Wings* – a lovely silver brooch. I wear mine with pride.

I remember Lady Reading telling us an amusing story. In 1938, when the nation was becoming aware of the dangers of impending war, the Home Secretary, Sir Samuel Hoare, invited Lady Reading to his office and asked if she would recruit two thousand women for a nucleus for the Air Raid Precaution Service. When she went home, she told her very faithful servant – who had been with her for many, many years, and was unmarried – of her conversation with the Home Secretary. The servant replied. 'You are looking for two thousand women and all I am looking for is one man.'

I was approached by Mrs. Howe (mother of Sir Geoffrey Howe), the first WRVS organizer for Port Talbot, to become a caseworker for the Soldiers, Sailors and Air Force Family Association (SSAFA). I was duly appointed and went on various courses. I found the work so very worthwhile. I don't know how I found the time, but I managed it. I was able to help so many ex-service people in the town. I had to interview and give a report on every case. The applicants' success depended so much on my report and I was so pleased that they had such a high rate of success. I had so many lovely letters of thanks.

We had an urgent call to go to Aberfan a few days after the terrible disaster of October 21st 1966 when children and teachers were killed after the mountain behind the Junior School slid and engulfed the whole school. I took a team of our WRVS there late at night. We left at 11 p.m. and spent the night at the bottom of the mountain serving hot soup to the miners who had come from all over the country to help. We had a telephone nearby to warn of any danger of another landslide, which was likely to happen anytime. I was standing on the school playground as dawn was breaking; the children's clothes and books were strewn in the mud; there was a car that no one had claimed; on a hill nearby, they were digging the graves for the children.

According to the constitution, from 1956 to '67, the centre organizer of WRVS was also chairman of the King George VI Management Committee. When it came to my turn as centre organizer, after chairing the committee for twelve months, I asked Miss Vatchell from the Wales office, and Miss Fletcher, county organizer, if I could stand down owing to pressure of work. I suggested that Mrs. Mainwaring, a member of WRVS, the Management Committee, and local councillor be appointed in my place. They agreed, and I became vice-chairman. However, when I retired as centre organizer in January 1969, I was asked to continue as a member of the Management Committee, which I did until 1994.

I was involved in the War Widows Welfare. In 1970, one of my widows was to celebrate her hundredth birthday. I had a phone call from London the day before her birthday inquiring as to whether she was still alive and well. I was asked to forewarn the warden of the Sheltered Home, where she lived, that there would be three letters arriving early the following morning: from the Queen, the Social Services and one other. I was invited to her birthday and had my photograph taken with her. She introduced me to her boyfriend who was her new neighbour. He was in his eighties and extremely smart!

1974 saw my appointment as deputy organizer to Mrs. Stafford (district organizer) who was teaching full time and couldn't drive. The same year I was made president of the British Steel Ladies Hockey Club, having made tea for all their home games for twenty-five years.

I represented WRVS on the Neath/Afan Community Health Council for eight years between 1974 and 1982. We had to visit all the hospitals and health centres in our area. This was particularly interesting for me, having been involved over the years with local hospitals through WRVS work in the canteens and trolley shops. Although I was nominated to be vice-chairman, I reluctantly had to retire from the council owing to the age limit.

Mrs. Stafford retired as district organizer in 1978, Mrs Wilkinson was appointed in her stead, and I was re-appointed as deputy. In April of that year, I attended a Thanksgiving Service at St. Paul's Cathedral, London, commemorating forty years of WRVS service.

Two years later, I became relief hostess at King George VI Club and went on a course to London Headquarters.

I attended a Service of Thanksgiving – a rededication to mark the Golden Jubilee of the WRVS – at Westminster Abbey on 26th May, 1988. On 2nd June, a garden party was held at the Royal Welsh Agricultural Society site at Builth Wells to commemorate the Jubilee. I was one of four representing West Glamorgan.

The next year I was again one of four of our members representing WRVS when at the Festival of Remembrance, at St David's Hall, Cardiff, which was televised to the nation.

My work in SSAFA was rewarded in 1990 with my being made a life member. Sir Michael Llewellyn presented me with a framed certificate, which read, 'In grateful recognition of twenty-six years devoted work amongst service families'. I was also presented to His Royal Highness, Prince Michael of Kent, who is the President of the Council of SSAFA, at the annual meeting of the association in City Hall, Cardiff."

Gwyneth Ellis, centre, attending Garden Party at Milton Hill House.

Gwyneth Ellis at WRVS shop in Port Talbot Cottage Hospital shortly before it closed.

It is hard to believe, but true, that Gwyneth is involved in other activities, outside her WRVS work.

"I am the founder and oldest member of the Aberavon Townswomen's Guild which was started in 1958, and held the offices of chairman and treasurer for many years. I am also a founder member of the Aberavon Gardening Club, which is still very successful and has a record number of members.

In June 1998, I was honoured to be given the WRVS award for the Swansea, Neath and Port Talbot areas – Diamond Volunteer of the Year. The award was introduced to mark the sixtieth anniversary of the founding of the WRVS. I was delighted to be asked to attend the garden party to mark the service's Diamond Anniversary held in the grounds of Milton Hill House. The highlight of the day was when the Queen approached our group and spoke to me as she mingled with the Welsh contingent. It was such a special celebration for my husband and me that week, as we were also celebrating our Diamond Wedding Anniversary.

Over the years, my work in the WVRS involved assisting the Blood Transfusion Service, and anywhere help was needed. Sadly, our cottage hospital at Port Talbot closed at the end of 2002 as did Penrhiewtyn Hospital, in Neath. In their stead, we now have a new general hospital, the Neath/Port Talbot Hospital. There are three shops at its entrance, run by the WRVS, which are doing well.

Selected by Lady Reading, the Spray of Remembrance, of rosemary and ivy, has a special significance for the WRVS: ivy as a symbol of steadfastness and rosemary typifying remembrance and friendship. The ideal is *Service Beyond Self*, which embodies the aim of true voluntary service and carries a message and a reminder for us all. I am very proud to have been a part of such a wonderful organization. I was awarded the MBE in the 2003 New Year's Honours List for service to the WRVS.

I am now eighty-nine years young, with two children, five grandchildren and one great-grandchild. I look back on my sixty years with the voluntary services with a great deal of enjoyment: with happy memories of the many people I have met, the friends I have made, and the fun we have had. I have received many letters from people over the years thanking me for having the time to sit down and listen to their problems. I could not have done all this without the help of my dear husband, who has supported me throughout our sixty years together."

INVESTITURE

AT

BUCKINGHAM PALACE

HELD BY

THE PRINCE OF WALES

ON

Friday,
23rd May 2003

at 11.00 am

OFFICERS ON DUTY

Lord in Waiting
The Viscount Brookeborough

Master of the Household
Vice Admiral Tom Blackburn, CB., LVO.

Equerry in Waiting
Lieutenant Commander Alistair Graham, RN.

Secretary of the Central Chancery of the Orders of Knighthood
Lieutenant Colonel Robert Cartwright

Mr. Stephen Johnson	For services to the Highway Network in West Sussex.
Mr. John Mason	For services to the Sea Cadets in Cheshire.
Mr. Stanley Matchett	For services to Photo Journalism.
Mr. Peter Menhennet	For services to the Leukaemia Research Fund in Nottingham.
Mr. Manzoor Moghal	For services to Racial Equality and to the community in Leicester.
Mr. Gordhandas Patel	For services to the community in Brent.
Mr. John Phillips	For public service in Northern Ireland.
Mr. Paul Shenton	For services to Podiatry.
Mr. Samuel Steele	For services to Transport and to the community in Northern Ireland.
Mr. Alan Thompson	For services to the Lord Chancellor's Department.
Mr. Richard Tickell	For services to Family Mediation and to the community in Wiltshire.
Mr. Victor Verrier	For services to Horticulture and to the community in Somerset.
Mr. Adrian Walsh	For services to the Department for Education and Skills.
Mr. David Waters	For services to the Electricity Industry.
Shirley, Mrs. Morgan	To receive the insignia conferred on her late mother, Gwyneth, Mrs. Ellis, for her services to the Women's Royal Voluntary Service in Wales.

THE ROYAL VICTORIAN MEDAL (SILVER)

To be Decorated:-

Gladys, Mrs. Bushell	For services to the Royal Household.
Mr. Bernard Flannery	For service to His Royal Highness The Prince of Wales.

Gwyneth's daughter Shirley reminisces, "When my mother attended the Diamond Anniversary of the WRVS in June 1998 in their headquarters in Berkshire, Queen Elizabeth was present. There were three thousand guests there from all over the country. The Queen did her walk-around while the members stood behind ropes. The Queen made a beeline for my mother for no particular reason. She asked her, 'How long have you been in the WRVS?'

'Forty-five years,' answered the member standing next to my mother.

'Isn't she marvellous?' replied the Queen.

My mother was absolutely thrilled that the Queen had spoken to her. You never know how things are going to turn out. Perhaps she was meant to meet the Queen then. She was to receive her MBE in Buckingham Palace on Friday 23rd May, 2003, but passed away on the previous 19th March. My husband, Gary Morgan and I, my brother Wynne and his wife Kathleen were invited to Buckingham Palace: my father would have found it too difficult emotionally to attend. I was presented with my mother's MBE posthumously by Prince Charles. It was a very emotional experience, and I thought Prince Charles very kind and understanding of our situation – a real gentleman. He also praised the organization highly."

Kathleen Ellis, Wynne Ellis, Shirley Morgan, Gary Morgan at Buckingham Palace.

Bibliography

The Express, Thursday, 25 March 1999, pp. 40-41.
The Sunday Express, 14 September 1958.
Joanna Martin, *Wives and Daughters* (102 Gloucester Avenue, London NW1 8HX).
Isabella Beeton, *Mrs Beeton's Book of Household Management* (London and Melbourne).
Robert Lucas, 'John Collins of Oxwich', *Gower Journal*, Vol. 38.
The Express, 25 March 1999.
J. Mansel Thomas, *Yesterday's Gower* (Llandysul, Dyfed, 1982).
The Express, 25 March 1999.
Midge Frayne, *The Gower Stripper* (The Forge, Fairy Hill, Reynoldston, Swansea, SA3 1BS, 1996).
Annual Report of the County Archivist 1997-1998, West Glamorgan Archive Service.
David Berry, *Wales & Cinema. The First Hundred Years* (6 Gwennyth Street, Cardiff, CF2 4YD).
The Book of Knowledge, Vol. 596-97 (Farringdon Street, London EC4).
Halliwell's Film & Video Guide 2001 (77-85 Fulham Palace Road, Hammersmith, London W6 8JB).
Jill Forward, 'The Way We Were', *South Wales Evening Post*, 6 March 1991.
Gerald Gabb, *Jubilee Swansea. A Town in the 1890s* (Llandybie, SA18 3YD, 1995).
Our Memories of Llanrhidian, compiled by Pat Williams for Llanrhidian Local History Group (Rawlings Road, Llandybie, Carmarthenshire, SA18 3YD, 2004).
South Wales Evening Post, Thursday, 18 February, 1999, p. 22.
Cambrian newspaper, December 1898.
Jill Forward, 'Looking Back', *Evening Post*, 15 March 2004, p. 2.
Everyman's Encyclopaedia, Vol. 8 (Milan, Italy, 1967).
Shall We Join The Ladies, edited by Jilly Cooper & Tom Hartman (Oxford, England, 1988) .
South Wales Evening Post, 13 December 1966.
Stephen Badsey, *D-Day, The Illustrated History* (Godalming, Surrey, 1993).